The United Stories of America

COSTERUS NEW SERIES 122

Series Editors:
C.C. Barfoot, Hans Bertens, Theo D'haen
and Erik Kooper

The United Stories
of America

Studies in
the Short Story Composite

Rolf Lundén

 Amsterdam-Atlanta, GA 1999

ISBN 90-420-0692-7

Cover design: Hendrik van Delft

Excerpt from "The Wanderers" in THE GOLDEN APPLES, copyright 1949, and renewed 1977 by Eudora Welty, reprinted by permission of Harcourt Brace & Company

© Editions Rodopi B.V.
   Amsterdam - Atlanta, GA 1999

Printed in The Netherlands

Contents

Introduction

It would seem that the first long prose forms in the history of mankind were short story composites. The Turkmenistan epic of Köroglu, the Turkish *Dede Korkut*, the Japanese *Heike*, the African *Mwindo* and *Lianja* epics, the Finnish *Kalevala*, and most of the Icelandic sagas existed in their oral versions as independent, yet interrelated stories, episodes, or *þættir*, and the collection of them into written, edited, and therefore more unified prose forms, could not conceal the episodic, fragmented structure of their origins.[1] These age-old sagas and epics may then be said to constitute the first expressions of a mode of writing that has since continuously been in existence. During the more than century-long period from the 1830s to the 1960s, when the hegemony of the traditional novel and critical organicism marginalized almost all other prose forms except the novel and the short story, the loosely constructed mode of connected narratives managed to survive and, after the turn of the century, to regain strength. In this century this ancient mode of fiction manifests itself in what has variously been called the short story composite, the short story cycle, the short story sequence, or the composite novel.

In *Theory of Prose*, Viktor Shklovsky points to the circumstance that the modern novel was preceded by the collection in which stories "were ordinarily put together in such a way that the individual stories bore some relationship, however formal, to each other." Many of these early collections — *Panchatantra*, *Kalilah and Dimnah*, *Hitopadesa*, *Tales of a Parrot*, *The Seven Viziers*, *A Thousand and One Nights*, *The Book of Wisdom and Lies*, *The Decameron*, and *The Canterbury Tales*, to name a few — were held together, according to Shklovsky, by means of a framing story. Another early unifying narrative feature, apart from framing, was what Shklovsky calls "threading"; the continuous presence of a protagonist or of the device of the journey — or a combination of the two — unified the individual episodes. A mixture of framing and threading often characterized the early novel, such as the picaresque and the adventure novel. But such unifying strategies could not hide the discontinuous structure of these texts: "In the concluding parts of works composed along the threading

---

[1] See Carol J. Clover, "The Long Prose Form," *Arkiv för nordisk filologi* 101 (1986): 10-39.

principle, we frequently have the feeling that these constituent parts once had an independent existence all their own."[2]

The post-Kantian, Coleridgean ideal of esthetic organicism, so dominant in the nineteenth and the first half of this century, contributed both to the privileging of totalized prose forms such as the social-realistic novel and to the marginalization of previous, more openly constructed forms of narrative.[3] Even though early forms of the short story composite continued to appear, written by, for instance, George Eliot, E. T. A. Hoffmann, Turgenev, Poe, and Melville, this mode of writing was more or less subsumed into the traditional novel. And until very recently the short story composite was refused critical acknowledgment, in spite of the fact that during this century more and more writers have started to exploit this mode of fiction. With very few exceptions, scholars have tried to make sense of the short story composite by applying to it the critical values and the apparatus of organicism, developed in their study of the poem or the novel; unity, coherence, and closure have been privileged at the expense of discontinuity, fragmentation, and openness.

The present study is determined by four objectives: to contribute to a wider acknowledgment of an age-old, long suppressed form of writing and help bring into the light a genre still dwelling in the shadow of the novel; to counteract the still all too common organicist readings of the short story composite; to continue the discussion started by others concerning the composite's generic specificity; and to focus especially on the American short story composite and, to some extent, on the Americanness of the genre. In an attempt to recreate the structure of the short story composite, the chapters/sections of the study were written as independent, yet interdependent studies; this approach has resulted in a degree of repetition and overlapping but hopefully not tediousness. While the book is informed by the theories of narratology, I have avoided too rigid a taxonomy in my discussion of generic features since it is my conviction that absolute boundaries between genres cannot be drawn and that, therefore, only generic tendencies can be outlined.

My discussion is based on numerous composites by authors like Sherwood Anderson, Hemingway, Faulkner, Steinbeck, Welty, Swados, Selby, Erdrich, Naylor, Otto, and Jayne Anne Phillips. Chapter One, "On the Definition of a Genre," focuses on the critical confusion as to the short story

---

[2] Shklovsky, *Theory of Prose* (Elmwood Park, Il.: Dalhey Archive Press, 1990) 65-71. See also pp. 72-100, "The Making of Don Quixote."

[3] See, for instance, Graham Good, "Notes on the Novella," in Charles E. May, ed., *The New Short Story Theories* (Athens, Ohio: Ohio UP, 1994) 151-54. For a historical survey of the short story composite and its predecessors, see Susan Garland Mann, *The Short Story Cycle: A Genre Companion and Reference Guide* (New York: Greenwood Press, 1989) 1-7.

composite, as it lists and analyzes the proliferation of terms used to define the genre, and also discusses the general critical tendency towards a totalization of this mode of fiction as well as a few, recent alternative approaches. The second chapter, "Sketching the Generic Boundaries," attempts to outline basic generic features of the short story composite by suggesting four major subgenres—the cycle, the sequence, the cluster, and the novella—and by situating the short story composite in a continuum ranging from the short story collection to the novel. The chapter also addresses borderline cases and discusses criteria for including or excluding individual texts into or from the genre.

Chapters Three and Four contain a structural analysis of the short story composite from the point of view of closural and anti-closural narrative strategies. Chapter Three, "Coherence and Closure in the Short Story Composite," is devoted to a discussion of such unifying patterns and devices as end-orientation, retrospective patterning, intratextuality, narrativity, and framing, while Chapter Four, "Indeterminacy and Open Form in the Short Story Composite," is concerned with such narrative strategies as anti-teleology, discontinuity, family resemblance, multiplicity, and potentiality.

The fifth chapter, "*E Pluribus Unum*: The Americanness of the Short Story Composite," asks whether the short story composite is a particularly American mode of writing and whether it is part of a larger construction of an American identity.[4] Taking as its object of study what I call the "fringe story," a story only tangentially connected to the whole, Chapter Six, "The Fringe Story, Or, How to Integrate the Resisting Text," argues in favor of its being regarded as a generic feature rather than an aberration; the chapter also outlines the numerous, often ingenious, critical strategies used to integrate such fringe texts into the whole of the composite. Finally, Chapters Seven and Eight both consist of readings of Eudora Welty's *The Golden Apples,* readings informed by my discussion in the preceding chapters.

In the protracted time I have devoted to the writing of this book, I have been fortunate to meet genuine encouragement, inspiring suggestions, and constructive criticism from a number of institutions and individuals; without grants from the Fulbright Commission, the J. F. Kennedy Institute at the Free University, Berlin, and Uppsala University, my project would have foundered at an early stage. At Uppsala I am privileged to work in a stimulating environment, and I am grateful to colleagues and friends who have taken the time to read and comment on sections of my book: Arne Axelsson, Erik Löfroth, Danuta Fjellestad, Alan Shima, Øyunn Hestetun,

---

[4] This chapter has been published previously, in slightly different form, as "The United Stories of America: Fusion and Fragmentation in the American Short Story Cycle," in Kristiaan Versluys, ed., *The Insular Dream:Obsession and Resistance* (Amsterdam: VU UP, 1995) 285-302.

and Bo G. Ekelund. Elisabeth Herion-Sarafidis has read the entire manuscript and saved me from many errors and instances of less felicitous wording, for which I am greatly indebted to her. Large parts of the manuscript were read also by professors Seymour Chatman, University of California, Berkeley, Ann Charters, University of Connecticut, and Carl Malmgren, University of New Orleans; in their invaluable comments they pointed out dead ends and suggested new approaches. I have also benefitted greatly from discussions with Robert Kellogg and David Levin of the University of Virginia, and Carol J. Clover, Hertha D. Wong, Dorothy Hale, Richard Hutson, and Charles Altieri of the University of California, Berkeley. My gratitude to all these scholars is deep; while they have contributed to whatever worth this study has, they should of course not be blamed for the inadequacies that still remain. Therefore, I would like to repeat, from the introduction to *Magnalia Christi Americana*, Cotton Mather's rewriting of *The Æneid*, ix, 427: "Me, me sum qui scripsi; in me convertite Ferrum."

One:
On the Definition of a Genre

Until very recently one form of narrative fiction was relegated to an existence in the shadowland: the book consisting of autonomous short stories which interconnect and join into a larger whole, the mode of writing that has gradually come to be known as the short story composite, the short story cycle or the short story sequence. Located in a "fictional no-man's land"[1] between the novel and the short story collection, it has not been acknowledged as a separate genre, and, as a consequence, until twenty years ago it was absent from critical works on genre and narrative. Even today most literary scholars and critics fail to immediately identify the concept of the short story composite/cycle/sequence.

During the twentieth century, the critics who did see it as a distinct genre were frustrated by its evasive nature and by the subsequent difficulty of defining it. The critical uncertainty about this kind of fiction was expressed again and again. Like the prose poem, it was often looked upon as a hybrid form, and was as such often denied legitimacy.[2] Malcolm Cowley, for instance, in reviewing Faulkner's *Go Down, Moses*, revealingly called it "a hybrid: a loosely jointed but ambitious novel masquerading as a collection of short stories."[3] Evoking the same miscegenated connotations more than thirty years later, Burhans designated Hemingway's *In Our Time* "a literary hybrid, with something of the variety of the anthology combined with something of the unity of the novel."[4] Even critics like Lohafer, Luscher, and Kennedy—who argue in

---

[1] Charles Shapiro describing Harvey Swados' *On the Line*, "Harvey Swados: Private Stories and Public Fiction," in Harry T. Moore, ed., *Contemporary American Novelists* (Carbondale: Southern Illinois UP, 1964) 188.

[2] See Ron Silliman, "From the New Sentence" in Ron Silliman, ed., *In the American Tree* (Orono, Maine: National Poetry Foundation, 1986) 564-65.

[3] Cowley, "Go Down to Faulkner's Land," *The New Republic* 106 (June 29, 1942): 90.

[4] Clinton S. Burhans, Jr., "The Complex Unity of *In Our Time*" in Jackson J. Benson, ed., *The Short Stories of Ernest Hemingway: Critical Essays* (Durham, N.C.: Duke UP, 1975) 29.

favor of the independent generic status of the short story composite—on occasion characterize this form of writing as a "hybrid."[5]

Seeking to establish some sort of legitimacy for the hybrid genre, many critics have felt obliged to emphasize its unity and coherence in order to make it resemble the novel, which still enjoys privileged status. In this legitimization process much of the genre specificity of the short story composite has been lost. The tension between variety and unity, separateness and interconnectedness, fragmentation and continuity, openness and closure has been, if not ignored, at least given less attention than it deserves.

A Plethora of Terms

The "spuriousness" of this form of writing, and its considerable variety, have made critics pronouncedly insecure in their labeling attempts. Numerous terms have been suggested, all of them problematic, except one. For a while, in the 1980s, it seemed as if the term *short story cycle* had won the battle and gained general acceptance, but in the 1990s several scholars have advocated the labels *short story sequence* and *composite novel*. In my view neither of these terms is satisfactory for reasons that will be given below. I prefer the term *short story composite*, even if the re-introduction of this term will add to the proliferation, because it is the only term, it seems to me, that is broad and neutral enough to function as a generic one.

Some attempts at labeling what I will, then, from now on refer to as the short story composite have taken the novel as their starting point. The composite has thus been termed *story-novel*,[6] *storied novel*,[7] com-

---

[5] Susan Lohafer and Jo Ellyn Clarey, eds., *Short Story Theory at a Crossroads* (Baton Rouge: Louisiana State UP, 1989) 113, 150; J. Gerald Kennedy, "Toward a Poetics of the Short Story Cycle," *Journal of the Short Story in English* 11 (Autumn 1988): 14.

[6] Olga Vickery's term for Faulkner's *The Unvanquished, Go Down, Moses, Knight's Gambit*, and *The Hamlet* in *The Novels of William Faulkner: A Critical Interpretation* (Baton Rouge: Louisiana State UP, 1964) 306. The equivalent German term *"Kurzgeschichtenroman"* has been used about *The Pastures of Heaven* by Hildegard Schumann in *Zum Problem des kritischen Realismus bei John Steinbeck* (Halle: Max Niemeyer Verlag, 1958) 26, and by Klaus Lubbers in *Typologie der Short Story* (Darmstadt: Wissenschaftliche Buchgesellschaft, 1977) 143-62.

[7] See Ronald Schleifer, "Faulkner's Storied Novel: *Go Down, Moses* and the Translation of Time," *Modern Fiction Studies* 28:1 (Spring 1982): 109-27.

posite novel,[8] *fragmentary novel,*[9] *episodic novel,*[10] *anthology novel,*[11] *collective novel,*[12] *para-novel,*[13] and *rovelle.*[14] Associating the short story composite primarily with the novel invites unfortunate connotations of unified story, coherent narration, and closure, neither of which is necessarily a characteristic of the composite. "Composite" novel is a questionable term since all novels in a sense are composite, and since it usually denotes a novel co-authored by several writers; "short story composite," discussed below, distinguishes in my view the genre much better. The difference between the two terms is obvious: "composite novel" makes the genre a variant of the novel, whereas "short story composite" denotes a composite made up of discrete short stories. While Howe's term "episodic" novel does not distinguish it from other forms of episodic novels such as the picaresque, the epithet "anthology" gives the impression of a work of collected stories written by more than one writer. And while the multiple meanings of "para-" may lead to misunderstandings, the term "rovelle" is too much of a strained construction; non-descriptive in nature, it confuses more than it clarifies.

Equally unsatisfactory are those attempts at categorization which use the short story collection as a basis of identification, since such terms put an undue emphasis on the separateness of the stories in the composite.

---

[8] Maggie Dunn and Ann Morris, *The Composite Novel: The Short Story Cycle in Transition* (New York: Twayne, 1995).

[9] D.H. Lawrence's term for Hemingway's *In Our Time* in *Phoenix: The Posthumous Papers of D. H. Lawrence*, ed. Edward D. McDonald (London: Heinemann, 1936) 365.

[10] Irving Howe's term in "Sherwood Anderson's *Winesburg, Ohio*" in Wallace Stegner, ed., *The American Novel from James Fenimore Cooper to William Faulkner* (New York: Basic Books, 1965) 154-65. The same term is used by Michael Millgate in *William Faulkner* (London: Oliver and Boyd, 1961) 61.

[11] Michael Grimwood, "Pastoral and Parody: The Making of Faulkner's Anthology Novels," Diss Princeton University 1976 *DAI* 37 (1977): 5828 A.

[12] Michael Toolan, "'Pantaloon in Black' in *Go Down, Moses*: The Function of the 'Breathing' Motif," *Journal of the Short Story in English* 2 (January 1984): 155-65.

[13] Used by Richard Cary in *Sarah Orne Jewett* (New Haven: Twayne Publishers, 1962) 149, about *The Country of the Pointed Firs*.

[14] Dallas Marion Lemmon, Jr., "The Rovelle, or the Novel of Interrelated Stories: M. Lermontov, G. Keller, S. Anderson," Diss Indiana University 1970, *DAI* 31 (1971): 3510-A. Lemmon writes: "This study defines the rovelle as a near-novel composed of short tales or stories—a series of stories so interrelated that their cumulative effects are novelistic. The word is coined from *roman*, or novel, and from the Italian *novelle*, the plural of *novella* or short story or tale."

Epithets like *unified short story collection*[15] and *integrated short-story collection*[16] fail to capture the uniqueness of the composite, the features of unity distinguishing it from the collection. In a misdirected attempt to invent an all-inclusive generic term for the short story composite Kennedy even suggests *short story collection*,[17] explaining that "this rubric would contain all aggregates of three or more stories by a given author, without regard to the history of composition or the presumed intention of the writer. It would encompass both tightly organized story sequences and more loosely bound or problematic works (such as Faulkner's *Go Down, Moses*)." Kennedy's term, however, is less than helpful since it coincides with an already existing term, generally designating a constellation of narratives distinct from the composite. Kennedy has later abandoned this term in favor of Luscher's "short story sequence" which will be discussed below.[18]

To avoid identification with either of the accepted genres of novel and short story collection, terms pointing up the fusion of the two have been suggested. *Blend*, or *blended work*,[19] is too imprecise even to indicate that it concerns fiction. As I have indicated, the term *short story composite* is much to be preferred. It points to a work of art that combines several separate pictures; it manages to characterize the whole variegated spectrum of the genre. It is certainly a term superior to *short story cycle*, with its undue stress on a cyclicality that is often absent from this form of narrative, and it is also superior to *short story sequence*, as it has been defined (see below). Silverman defines the short story composite as "a group of stories written by one author, arranged in a definite order, and intended to produce a specific effect. Though every story of a composite can be understood in isolation, the stories have an added dimension when seen as co-ordinate parts of the larger whole."[20] Creighton describes the composite as a work "made up of detachable

---

[15] Term used by Susan Garland Mann, *The Short Story Cycle: A Genre Companion and Reference Guide* (New York: Greenwood Press, 1989) x, xii.

[16] See Pleasant Larus Reed, III, "The Integrated Short-Story Collection: Studies of a Form of Nineteenth- and Twentieth-Century Fiction," Diss Indiana University 1974, *DAI* 35:10 (1975): 6730-A.

[17] Kennedy, "Toward a Poetics of the Short Story Cycle," 13.

[18] J. Gerald Kennedy, ed., *Modern American Short Story Sequences: Composite Fictions and Fictive Communities* (New York: Cambridge UP, 1995) xv.

[19] Term suggested by Stanley Tick for Faulkner's short story composites in "The Unity of *Go Down, Moses*," *Twentieth Century Literature* 8:2 (1962): 68.

[20] Raymond Joel Silverman, "The Short Story Composite: Forms, Functions, and Applications," Diss University of Michigan 1970, *DAI* 31:12 (1970): 6633-A.

but interrelated short stories" and suggests Joyce's *Dubliners* and Faulkner's *Go Down, Moses* as representative examples.[21] A similar term is *short story compound* which also expresses the composition of distinct individual items connected to form a united whole, but this term is less felicitous in that it implies a more or less complete merging of the parts into an organic whole.[22] In science fiction, the accepted term for the short story composite is *fixup*, a book most often made up of previously published stories fitted together, but on occasion composed as a composite without prior magazine publication.[23] Yet another term indicating fusion is *short story ensemble*, suggested in passing by Kennedy.[24]

Another attempt at finding a suitable term, referred to above, is *short story sequence*, defined by Luscher as "a volume of stories, collected and organized by their author, in which the reader successively realizes underlying patterns of coherence by continual modifications of his perceptions of pattern and theme."[25] Luscher's preference for this term is thus based on the fact that the reader's experience of negotiating the text and assembling its patterns is "sequential." However, this progressive development of meaning is not exclusive to the short story composite; a similar sequential experience of reading takes place in the reading of the chapters of a novel.[26] Had *sequence* been used to describe the *structure* of certain composites—i.e. a series of stories not forming a cyclical pattern—it would have been more convincing to me.[27] In a later analysis, of

---

[21] Joanne Vanish Creighton, "*Dubliners* and *Go Down, Moses*: The Short Story Composite," Diss University of Michigan 1969, *DAI* 31:4 (1970): 1792-93-A. Creighton employs this term also in *William Faulkner's Craft of Revision* (Detroit: Wayne State UP, 1977) 85-87.

[22] Joseph W. Reed, Jr., *Faulkner's Narrative* (New Haven: Yale UP, 1973) 176.

[23] See John Clute and Peter Nicholls, eds., *The Encyclopedia of Science Fiction* (London: Orbit, 1993) 432.

[24] Kennedy, "Toward a Poetics of the Short Story Cycle," 11.

[25] Robert M. Luscher, "The Short Story Sequence: An Open Book," in Lohafer and Clarey, eds., *Short Story Theory at a Crossroads*, 148-49; also used in passing by Kennedy, "Toward a Poetics", 12. This term in German, "Kurzgeschichtensequenz," is suggested by Klaus Lubbers in *Typologie der Short Story*, 145-47.

[26] This fact has also been pointed out by Hertha D. Wong in her "Louise Erdrich's *Love Medicine*: Narrative Communities and the Short Story Sequence" in Kennedy, ed., *Modern American Short Story Sequences*, 172.

[27] John Barth calls the stories of *Lost in the Funhouse* a "series." The series of fourteen pieces will, according to Barth, "be seen to have been meant to be received all at

Updike's *Olinger Stories*, however, Luscher uses the phrase "sequential arrangement" to describe, not the reader's gradual modification of the stories, but their chronological, linear sequencing.[28] The sequence, in this latter meaning, well defines one variant, or subgenre, of the short story composite, a characterization I will return to in the next chapter.

Another term that has been suggested as an inclusive generic one is *story-cluster*.[29] In my opinion, *short story cluster* rather captures, like "cycle" and "sequence," the nature of one subcategory of the composite. It suggests, as in a cluster of grapes, contiguity in an irregular form; it does not connote a cyclical, well-rounded form, but rather a loosely structured wholeness. The term thus combines the separateness and unity of the narrative. But at the same time it less well characterizes composites with a sequential or cyclical structure. Wong's suggestion "*web* ... of stories" for the structure of particular Native American short story composites falls, it seems to me, in the same category; as she puts it, "the spider's web is a common image to convey the interconnectedness of all aspects of life."[30]

Though having the advantage of emphasizing the discontinuous nature of the composite, Bredahl's *divided narrative* is, like both "blend" and "short story collection," too vague and too inclusive a term. Bredahl chooses this term on account of the physical divisions within each work which are the "most visually characteristic element"[31] of this mode of writing and because these divisions "simultaneously create breaks between stories and establish gaps which the activation of the stories (the moving force within them) seeks to cross."

The study which succeeded in launching the term *short story cycle* was Forrest L. Ingram's *Representative Short Story Cycles of the Twen-*

---

once and as here arranged." "Author's Note," *Lost in the Funhouse* (New York: Doubleday, 1968) ix.

[28] Robert M. Luscher, "John Updike's *Olinger Stories*: New Light Among the Shadows" in Kennedy, ed., *Modern American Short Story Sequences*, 160-61.

[29] Ian Reid, *The Short Story* (London: Methuen, 1977) 46; also used in passing by Wong, "Louise Erdrich's *Love Medicine*" in Kennedy, ed., *Modern American Short Story Sequences*, 185.

[30] Wong, "Louise Erdrich's *Love Medicine*" in Kennedy, ed., *Modern American Short Story Sequences*, 172.

[31] A. Carl Bredahl, "'The Young Thing Within': Divided Narrative and Sherwood Anderson's *Winesburg, Ohio*," *The Midwest Quarterly: A Journal of Contemporary Thought* 27:4 (Summer 1986): 423.

tieth Century (1971).[32] In spite of the fact that several scholars have not been too happy about this label, it has until recently been the one most commonly used. Ingram defines the "cycle" in the following manner:

> a set of stories linked to each other in such a way as to maintain a balance between the individuality of each of the stories and the necessities of the larger unit (15).

> a book of short stories so linked to each other by their author that the reader's successive experience on various levels of the pattern of the whole significantly modifies his experience of each of its component parts (19).

Ingram here well defines the problematics of the short story composite, the tension between separateness and unity and the accumulative and transcendent qualities of the individual stories.

Susan Garland Mann, in her *The Short Story Cycle* (1989), states that there is only one essential characteristic of this form of narrative:

> The stories are both self-sufficient and interrelated. On the one hand, the stories work independently of one another: the reader is capable of understanding each of them without going beyond the limits of the individual story. On the other hand, however, the stories work together, creating something that could not be achieved in a single story (15).

Again I find this a fair description of the short story composite. However, neither Ingram nor Mann makes clear why they have chosen the term "cycle" as central to their definitions, with so many other terms at their disposal. The cyclicality of the composite is thus never addressed.

It is true that the term "cycle" has lost much of its original meaning of completed circle, but the word still connotes, if not complete round-

---

[32] Ingram, *Representative Short Story Cycles of the Twentieth Century: Studies in a Literary Genre* (The Hague: Mouton, 1971). Friedrich Weltz used a similar term almost twenty years prior to Ingram in his *Vier amerikanische Erzählungszyklen* (Dissertation, University of Munich, 1953). In his 1960 "Introduction" to Anderson's *Winesburg, Ohio* (New York: Viking Press, 1960), Malcolm Cowley describes the genre as "a cycle of stories," 14. A variant of Ingram's term is Merrill Maguire Skaggs' *cycle tale* in Peggy Whitman Prenshaw, ed., *Eudora Welty. Critical Essays* (Jackson, Miss.: UP of Mississippi, 1979) 220. In *Typologie der Short Story* (1977), Lubbers discusses the term "Kurzgeschichtenzyklus," 147-50.

ness, at least a sense of coherence, finality, and closure.[33] The "representative" short story composite—if one can at all speak of "representative" in this form of writing—is not characterized by the roundness evoked by "cycle." Very often the short story composite ends not with closure but with a story or sketch that takes off in a new direction, a fact that Mann has noted about composites like *Dubliners, The Golden Apples*, and *In Our Time*. Speaking of Faulkner's *The Unvanquished,* she writes that "the final story in *The Unvanquished* forces the reader to reconsider the entire book. While this is not always the case, many cycles end with final stories that dramatically change the direction of the work."[34] As I will argue in the next chapter, "cycle" is a term better reserved for only one kind of short story composites.

Cyclicality also suggests a continuity of sorts, something which the short story composite betrays in a number of ways, for example by chronological disruption. In addition, many composites include texts— what I call "fringe stories"—which are not easily integrated into any cyclical pattern. One may just mention "Pantaloon in Black" in Faulkner's *Go Down, Moses*, "My Old Man" in Hemingway's *In Our Time*, and "Music from Spain" in·Welty's *The Golden Apples*, stories that have been troubling precisely because they disfigure any neat critical designs.

As must be clear from the discussion above, I find it unfortunate that both the terms "short story cycle" and "short story sequence" have become such established ones. With their books, Ingram and Mann did much to draw attention to and create respect for this narrative form, but the establishment of "cycle" as a label for this narrative was a less propitious result. Similarly, while the recent book edited by Kennedy is an important revisioning of the genre, I find the choice of "sequence" as a generic term infelicitous. Each of these two terms is descriptive in character, emphasizing a structural pattern limited to only one variant of the genre, thereby defining it too narrowly. The short story composite, on the other hand, is a neutral one in that it suggests few associations to a particular structure or paradigm.

---

[33] Kennedy rejects the term "cycle" on the basis that it "carries implications of an overdetermined, even circular, arrangement that defines the genre rather narrowly." See "Introduction," *Modern American Short Story Sequences*, xv.

[34] Mann, *The Short Story Cycle*, 38, 82, 114.

The Compulsion to Create Coherence
As the references above reveal, there have thus far appeared four books devoted to the short story composite as a separate genre[35] together with a few articles[36] and doctoral dissertations.[37] In addition, numerous articles and chapters in books have analyzed individual short story composites, often in relation to an author's complete *oeuvre*. With few exceptions, these studies have attempted to bring coherence and unity to the disconnected and fractured nature of the short story composite. In their desire to establish order, most critics have ignored the disruptive aspects of the genre, thereby in my view misrepresenting it. The criticism that Bakhtin leveled against many critics of Dostoevsky—that they reduced the views of Dostoevsky's heroes "to a systematically mono-logical whole, thus ignoring the fundamental plurality of unmerged consciousnesses, which is part and parcel of the artist's design"[38]—

---

[35] Ingram, *Representative Short Story Cycles of the Twentieth Century: Studies in a Literary Genre*; Susan Garland Mann, *The Short Story Cycle: A Genre Companion and Reference Guide*; J. Gerald Kennedy, ed., *Modern American Short Story Sequences;* Maggie Dunn and Ann Morris, *The Composite Novel: The Short Story Cycle in Transition (*New York: Twayne Publishers, 1995). See also Richard P. Cage, *Order and Design: Henry James' Titled Story Sequences* (New York: Peter Lang, 1988).

[36] Kennedy, "Toward a Poetics of the Short Story Cycle," and Luscher, "The Short Story Sequence: An Open Book."

[37] See, for instance, Joanne Vanish Creighton, "*Dubliners* and *Go Down, Moses:* The Short Story Composite" (University of Michigan, 1969, *DAI* 31:4, 1792-93A), Raymond Joel Silverman, "The Short Story Composite: Forms, Functions, and Applications" (University of Michigan, 1970, *DAI* 31:12, 6633A), Pleasant Larus Reed III, "The Integrated Short-Story Collection: Studies of a Form of Nineteenth- and Twentieth-Century Fiction" (Indiana University, 1974, *DAI* 35:10, 6730A), Harlan Harbour Winn III, "Short Story Cycles of Hemingway, Steinbeck, Faulkner, and O'Connor" (University of Oregon, 1975, *DAI* 36:7, 4500A), John Russell Struthers, "Intersecting Orbits: A Study of Selected Story Cycles by Hugh Hood, Jack Hodgins, Clark Blaise, and Alice Munro, in their Literary Contexts" (University of Western Ontario, 1982), Robert M. Luscher, "American Regional Short Story Sequences" (Duke University, 1984, *DAI* 45:11, 3350A), Stephen Lee Sniderman, "The 'Composite' in Twentieth-Century American Literature," (University of Washington 1970 DAI 31: 403A), and Michael Grimwood, "Pastoral and Parody: The Making of Faulkner's Anthology Novels" (Princeton 1976, *DAI* 37: 5828A).

[38] Mikhail Bakhtin, *Problems of Dostoevsky's Poetics*, ed. and transl. by Caryl Emerson (Minneapolis: U of Minnesota P, 1984) 9.

could also be leveled against numerous critics of the short story composite. The compulsion that we often feel as critics to create a unified whole out of the most fragmented text, to regard the well-rounded, totalized work of art as superior to the open-ended one, has had the unfortunate effect of turning many short story composites into almost traditional novels. The power of this organicist desire is well summarized by Krieger:

> Even today, in the midst of flourishing theories that would celebrate all that resists such unifying claims—theories that would celebrate margins rather than centers, the aporia rather than the filled gap, the arbitrary or even the random rather than the necessary—even today, most of our essays that seek to interpret texts usually do so by trying to account for why any particular textual element became the way it is and why it found its way into the text where it did.[39]

Forrest L. Ingram's *Representative Short Story Cycles of the Twentieth Century* (1971), the first comprehensive study of the genre, maps much of the territory, making distinctions and establishing definitions to which all subsequent scholarship has been indebted. He points to many subtle links and interrelationships in the composites. Initially, Ingram sees, as I have indicated, the short story composite as expressing the "tension between the one and the many" and as displaying "a double tendency of asserting the individuality of its components on the one hand and of highlighting, on the other, the bonds of unity which make the many into a single whole"(19). But the sound starting-point, emphasizing the tension and the doubleness of the genre, is unfortunately lost as he proceeds to analyze individual texts.

Ingram's growing concern is with establishing a pattern linking the stories into a unified whole. He admits that the fundamental assumptions informing his study correspond to those expressed by Cleanth Brooks:

> That the primary concern is with the problem of unity—the kind of whole which the literary work forms or fails to form, and the relation of the various parts to each other in building up this whole. (43)

This primary concern of the critic makes Ingram pay more attention to the unifying elements of the short story composite than to the disruptive ones. Rather than pointing to the *tension* between "the one and the

---

[39] Murray Krieger, *A Reopening of Closure: Organicism Against Itself* (New York: Columbia UP, 1989) 3.

many," he makes it his concern to defuse that tension in order to establish, if possible, the literary work as a seamless whole. The urge for order also takes the expression, early in the study, of a dissatisfaction with Faulkner's *Go Down, Moses*; there, Ingram claims, "the individuality of most of the stories almost demolishes the cohesion of the larger unit" (19).

Ingram devotes most of his analysis to three short story composites: Kafka's *Ein Hungerkünstler*, Faulkner's *The Unvanquished*, and Anderson's *Winesburg, Ohio*. Striving to create in the texts an impression of coherence, his often perceptive readings of these books are primarily thematic. Little or no attention is paid to the short story composite's structure of disjointure with its gaps, voids, contradictions, and silences.

Towards the end of his introductory section, Ingram asks the reader, while reading, to keep in mind a series of forty questions. Gradually, it is explained, the reader will understand "which of the above questions are relevant and what other questions must be asked if the work of art he is examining is to be grasped *as an artistic whole*" (45, emphasis added). But none of the forty questions is devoted to the disjunctive or contradictory elements of the short story composite. Not once does Ingram stop to ask himself or his readers the most elementary question—why the author employs this particular form of writing, instead of the form of the traditional novel, to express the central theme of the book.

At the beginning of his reading of Kafka's book, Ingram states that "one may and *must* ask: is the collection as a whole an aesthetic unit? Are the stories which Kafka bound together in this volume also structurally unified by a *single* aesthetic pattern?" (46-47, italics added). Only if one assumes, as Ingram does, that a work of art by definition should be an organic whole, does one feel an obligation to ask such questions, thereby running the risk of misrepresenting the very specific form of the short story composite.

Ingram holds that the "common thematic denominator embodied imaginatively in Kafka's four stories is the unstable balance precariously maintained between sets of opposites and antinomies: in other words, the fundamental ambivalence of human living" (63). Kafka's "essential ambiguity" results from "his refusal to opt unconditionally for one side of any of these sets of antinomies. He trenchantly refuses to simplify life in his stories" (63). Ingram analyzes the themes of angst, isolation, lack of communication, and fear of separation and argues that these themes serve to unify the book. While he is perceptive in his thematic analysis, he fails to realize that the *form* which Kafka has chosen for his book actually parallels and reinforces this theme of ambiguity and antinomy. The narrative structure of the text is as disjunct as the world of separation and lack of communication that Kafka depicts, and the voids and silences between the stories adumbrate Kafka's message of man's inability to communicate.

The analytic method employed for the study of Faulkner's *The Unvanquished* and Anderson's *Winesburg, Ohio* is the same; Ingram privileges, and overemphasizes, such unifying factors as narrator, tone, and theme without paying attention to the disconnecting elements, thus again failing to see the function of the form in relation to the theme. According to Ingram, the theme of Faulkner's short story composite is the following:

> The exigencies of war introduce serious disorder into human living on several levels: on the physical level—the ravaging of land and property; on the moral level—habits of lying, stealing, cheating, killing; on the psychological level—depersonalization, limiting the variety of human responses to a single kind of response, distortion of character; on the political level—gun rule, justice through vengeance, disregard for law; on the sociological level—the breaking down of family life, and the disruption of Negro-white relations. (121)

In the discontinuous structure of the short story composite Faulkner has found a form which convincingly expresses this theme of a society coming apart. But again Ingram does not seem to realize that *one* reason (there may have been other reasons) for Faulkner to write a short story composite is that he sought to express in theme *as well as* form this tension between order and disorder.

In Ingram's reading, *Winesburg, Ohio* depicts a "land of fragmented personalities and ruined dreams" (147), where loneliness and the inability to communicate are prominent characteristics (178, 193). In addition to this theme of disconnectedness, there exist in Anderson's book, according to Ingram, several inconsistencies at which the author seems to shrug his shoulders (167-68). Ingram sees, however, neither the contradictions nor the themes of fragmentation as part of a larger order that makes room for both unity and disruption.

In *The Short Story Cycle: A Genre Companion and Reference Guide*, Susan Garland Mann surveys the history of the genre, its distinctive generic features, and the content of some 120, mostly American, composites.[40] She pays special attention to nine "representative" short story

---

[40] Mann's presentation of short story composites is in no way exhaustive, something of which she is well aware. One might easily add to her list of composites. The following American short story composites, to name a few, have not been included in her list: Randall Jarrell, *Pictures from an Institution*; William Goyen, *The House of*

composites by Joyce, Anderson, Hemingway, Steinbeck, Faulkner, Welty, O'Connor, and Updike. In these analyses, apart from presenting her own readings, she surveys the previous scholarship devoted to the individual composites. The basis for her readings is the concept of unity; she presents various forms of unifying factors such as theme, setting, imagery, and character.

What becomes strikingly clear from Mann's overviews is the extent to which scholars have felt almost a compulsion to make short story composites unified. The overwhelming majority of critics have focused their readings to such an extent on unifying devices and patterns that the specificity of the short story composite has not been given fair treatment. In order to make Joyce's book more homogeneous, abortive attempts have been made to find a single external model for *Dubliners*, such as *Inferno* or *The Odyssey*. Reading *Winesburg, Ohio*, for example, critics have tried to classify the recurring characters on the basis of archetypal figures, or on the character's attitude toward sex. And the theme of the hunt or journey has been suggested as the unifying factor of *Go Down, Moses*. Quite rightly Mann expresses skepticism about the most extreme attempts at forced ordering, and she issues a warning that "one should not over-emphasize the importance of any single unifying pattern" (30).

At least initially, Mann herself demonstrates a more open attitude than most critics toward the short story composite as a genre. She points out in the introductory chapter that "because cycles consist of discrete, self-sufficient stories, they are especially well suited to handle certain subjects, including the sense of isolation or fragmentation or indeterminacy that many twentieth-century characters experience" (11). She also points to the fact that some literary characters are separated from one another by the boundaries of the short story, used by authors of short story composites to point to their "solipsistic and isolated lives" (11). The interplay between theme and form is also underlined when Mann says that "the lack of continuity (or the gaps that exist between the stories in cycles) is used by some writers to emphasize the fragmentary nature of life, especially in the twentieth century" (12).

With the exception of a few instances when she points in passing to links between theme and form (61, 130), in the rest of the book Mann unfortunately falls into the same trap as so many other critics by devoting her time to discussing and establishing the unity of these com-

---

Breath; Elizabeth Spencer, *Marilee*; Louise Erdrich, *Love Medicine;* Lee Smith, *Oral History;* Gail Godwin, *Mr. Bedford and the Muses*; Gloria Naylor, *The Women of Brewster Place*; Jayne Anne Phillips, *Machine Dreams;* Susan Minot, *Monkeys*.

posites. Thus she fails to emphasize the *tension* between separateness and unity, which her introduction promises. In pursuing wholeness, while she brings out many subtle connections between the stories in theme, plot, myth, imagery, and character, she does not seem particularly aware of the silences, gaps, lacunae, and contradictions that characterize these composites. She fails to see how many themes find expression in the narrative strategies of disruption.

Let me mention one example of Mann's "blindness." She identifies the unifying theme in Hemingway's *In Our Time* as "the movement from innocence to initiation to disillusionment to an attempt to reestablish values or a code of behavior" and argues that the "vignettes, the stories, and the book as a whole are unified by this theme" (79). Since the central theme of the book involves man's need to establish order out of the chaos of fear, violence, war, and lack of communication, it would have been interesting if Mann had analyzed the form of *In Our Time* to see how it supports this theme. But she fails to do so. Besides, it is obvious to every reader of Hemingway's composite that it includes many stories and vignettes that will never lend themselves to complete integration into an orderly design. Instead of ignoring these disruptive elements, we should account for them as "normal" parts of the short story composite's structure.

In conclusion, then, one can say that while Mann appears theoretically aware of the co-existence of the disconnected and connected elements of the short story composite, her analyses tend to give comparatively little attention to the discontinuous and the fragmentary. Symptomatically, Mann hopes that future research in this genre will be devoted, as she says of *Winesburg, Ohio,* to how the "different parts of the book work together" (61).

Maggie Dunn's and Ann Morris' *The Composite Novel: The Short Story Cycle in Transition* continues the critical project of attempting to establish organic unity in the short story composite. Their choice of term, "composite novel," is determined by their desire to emphasize "the integrity of the whole" (5) and the affinity of these texts to the novel proper. The focus of the Dunn/Morris study is on such unifying devices and patterns as setting, single protagonist, collective protagonist, "pattern" (another word for theme, it seems), and story-telling, narrative elements which combine to create "novelistic coherence" (37) and an "integrated whole text" (48). The narrative elements highlighted by Dunn and Morris are such that make for coherence and unity also in the novel and fail to characterize the specificity of the short story composite; this critical strategy is only in line with the authors' desire to integrate these works into a loosely defined novel genre.

While it would be an utterly impossible task to survey the numerous short critical attempts at unifying individual short story composites, reference to a few of these studies may illustrate the general attitude within them. Frustrated by such a loosely constructed book as Faulkner's *Go Down, Moses*, critics have tried to impose an order on it that simply is not there. Some, like Warren Beck, go so far as to claim that it is "the most subtly integrated and hauntingly attuned of all Faulkner's novels."[41] But even though he himself used that term, Faulkner's book cannot be regarded as a novel; *Go Down, Moses* is not characterized by the wholeness Beck invests it with. Secondly, Beck assumes that integration and attunement are by nature superior to a structure that also includes disruption. In an article, devoted to the unity of Faulkner's book, Tick also repeatedly labels it a "novel"[42] and finds "Pantaloon in Black" to be "largely irrelevant to the novel," and thus simply dismisses it from further discussion. The rest of the study then deals with the "six sections" (there *are* actually seven sections) and their unifying theme of "the fate of McCaslin blood, the fortunes of the McCaslin lineage." Tick holds that the "architecture of this six-part novel is so compelling that no single section is fully explicable out of its context" (68). Cleman's comment on Tick's reading seems appropriate: "It seems rather facile to discover unity by simply discarding what does not fit."[43] Although few critics are as radical in their effort to create order as to throw out a whole story, the tendency to ignore the elements that do not fit is not uncommon.

Dirk Kuyk suggests, for instance, an intricate pattern of unification for *Go Down, Moses*. The book is held together, he argues, by a structure of "juxtaposition" and "condensation," manifesting itself in a *pattern of voices* which we hear as a "chorus": 3rd person narrator, society, the McCaslin family, the voices of Ike and Cass; in a *pattern of action*, such as rituals, plot, fabula, and history; and in a *pattern of meaning*, in motifs and themes such as family relations, race, sex, possession. In conclusion Kuyk writes that

> [t]he fundamental pattern of *Go Down, Moses* is thus the paradox. The narrative affirms the static and dynamic patterns of juxtaposition and conden-

---

41 Beck, "Short Stories into Novels," in *Faulkner* (Madison: U of Wisconsin P, 1976) 333.

42 Stanley Tick, "The Unity of *Go Down, Moses,*" *Twentieth Century Literature* 8:2 (1962): 68-73.

43 John L. Cleman, "'Pantaloon in Black': Its Place in *Go Down, Moses,*" *Tennessee Studies in Literature* 22 (1977): 171.

sation. It demonstrates that while possession, which destroys what it tries to keep, can preserve the wilderness it relinquishes and the tamed land it shares, the mythic communal holding, lost forever when men first claimed the power of ownership, is nevertheless being restored through relinquishment and sharing. The mythic brotherhood, likewise irrevocably lost, is being replaced through the progressive interpenetration of family and society. Through these processes, according to *Go Down, Moses*, both myth and history are working toward the freeing of mankind; and both God and man are saying with one voice, "Let my people go." These paradoxical patterns are the threads cable-strong that bind *Go Down, Moses* together.[44]

Another short story composite that has often suffered from overly totalizing readings is Hemingway's *In Our Time*. Two kinds of order-inducing studies have been common: one that establishes coherence by means of excluding part of the text and one that applies too rigid a formula or paradigm to make the stories conform. An example of the first kind is Philip Young's reading,[45] which, while tracing Nick Adams' initiation into pain and his coming to terms with his war wound, ignores all the non-Nick stories as if they were not part of the book. His rationale for dismissing these stories is that since they are "unrelated to the main interest of the book" (30), they may therefore be "put aside" (31). The rest of the stories, however, those about Nick, constitute "nearly a novel" (32), describing a continuous development in "closely related" stories; "Big Two-Hearted River," for instance, cannot be comprehended unless one understands the earlier stories (30-31).

To show that Young's totalization of *In Our Time* is in no way an isolated phenomenon, let me refer to a few, more recent interpretations. *In Our Time*, writes Larry Grimes, is a novel, not a composite, unified basically by means of the concepts "looking at" and "living in." And he summarizes his argument in the following manner:

> An overview of *In Our Time* lends support to Hemingway's suggestion that the basic movement of the work is from looking at to living in the times. Looking at and living in not only describe the rhythmic movement of the work, but help to explain and establish its three basic chronological divisions: prewar, war, and postwar. These sections are bounded on one end by an introduction and on the other by an epilogue. The principle of double per-

---

[44] Dirk Kuyk, Jr., *Threads Cable-strong: William Faulkner's* Go Down, Moses (Lewisburg: Bucknell UP, 1983) 190.

[45] Young, *Ernest Hemingway: A Reconsideration* (New York: Harcourt, Brace and World, 1966) 29-48.

ception, the looking at and the living in, determine whether a chapter or a story belongs to the prewar section or the war section. As long as the central character or the reader is only looking at the world at war, the story or chapter belongs to the prewar section.[46]

The act of seeing is, to Jackson J. Benson as well, the "central unifying force" in *In Our Time*. He suggests a reading of the work based on two kinds of seeing, the act of seeing as overview and the act of seeing as person. In addition, Benson presents other unifying forces such as the chronology of the Nick Adams stories, recurring, fragmentary motifs such as screams, death, water, and knives, and the associative links between the interchapters and stories.[47]

A rather extreme case, in my view, of this tendency at overly ambitious unification is Debra A. Moddelmog's "The Unifying Consciousness of a Divided Conscience: Nick Adams as Author of *In Our Time*,"[48] which employs the nine pages that Hemingway excised from the end of "Big Two-Hearted River" plus two Nick Adams stories not included in *In Our Time* to convince her readers that Nick is the author of the book. She deplores the fact that Hemingway cut out the nine pages on Nick as writer, because the inclusion of them would have "reduced the story's tension." Maybe, just maybe, Hemingway followed Gertrude Stein's advice and refused to let the nine pages stand because he did *not* want to create the unity, the absence of which Moddelmog regrets. With her questionable strategy of reading the book through a text that is not part of the book, Moddelmog sets out to put together, from the stories Nick has "written," the range of his "psyche" and the characteristics of "his basic outlook on life" (596). All the stories not about Nick, she argues, are really more about Nick than the others:

> In a classic psychoanalytic paradox, the closer the matter is to Nick the writer, the further away Nick the character is likely to be. The non-Nick stories can thus hold the key to Nick's innermost secrets and fears (602).

As a consequence of this argument, Moddelmog concludes that Nick, in "Big Two-Hearted River," is a married man, uncertain of his marital

---

[46] Grimes, "*In Our Time*: An Experiment in the Novel," in *The Religious Design of Hemingway's Early Fiction* (Ann Arbor: UMI Research Press, 1985) 41.

[47] Benson, "Patterns of Connection and Their Development in Hemingway's *In Our Time*," in Michael S. Reynolds, ed., *Critical Essays on Ernest Hemingway's* In Our Time (Boston: G. K. Hall & Co, 1983) 103-19.

[48] *American Literature* 60:4 (December 1988): 591-610.

happiness, and fearful about the fact that he is about to become a father. Her reconstruction of Nick's life runs as follows:

> [U]pon Nick's return from Europe to America, he jumped into marriage, viewing it (at least in part) as a salve for his mental war wounds. However, he has since discovered that, far from healing anything, marriage has actually aggravated his pain. Nick's feelings about Helen thus make up the darker depths of the swamp he must one day fish. (605)

> [H]is impending or actual fatherhood is the most recent need that urged Nick's trip to the Michigan woods, even the one that may have directly motivated it. (606)

While it is true that I quote Moddelmog's speculations out of context, the fact is that the text proper of "Big Two-Hearted River" lends little support to this seemingly well-construed pattern. The danger is obviously that the desire for coherence might lead the critic further and further away from the actual text towards an "ideal text." This, I think, is what happens in Moddelmog's case: her conclusion presents a totalization that little resembles the actual book that Hemingway published:

> *In Our Time* is not at all fragmentary. It is a complete work, unified by the consciousness of Nick Adams as he attempts to come to terms through his fiction with his involvement in World War I and, more recently, with the problems of marriage and his fear of fatherhood ... the stories are ordered precisely to reflect the actual history and the psychological state of Nick Adams. (608)

It is evident to most readers, and also on occasion to Moddelmog, that the themes of *In Our Time* concern war, violence, strife, disintegrating marital relations (not necessarily Nick's own), and the lack of communication between human beings—all pointing to the fragmentation of the world of modern man. Would it not then be more honest to let also the form of the book remain at least in part fragmentary? There is a certain unity in the structure of *In Our Time*—I would be the last to deny that— but there are parts, I would argue, that defy being integrated into a neat, homogeneous design. The greatness of *In Our Time* and other short story composites is not diminished if we acknowledge that they are not well-polished, perfectly balanced, monolithic objects of art. The disruptive elements—the gaps, the vignettes, the contradictory chronology, the absence of recurring protagonists—are not flaws; they work either to subvert or reinforce the author's message. A larger pattern is often thereby established, one that makes room for both order and disorder.

Alternative Readings

Not all scholars, however, have felt the desire for totalization; recently more and more critics have acknowledged the basically open structure of the short story composite. Ingram's assumption that the short story composite possesses an intrinsic unity has thus been criticized by Kennedy who claims that it is rather the "ingenuity" of previous critics which has perceived connections that "imply a unified plan" and charges that "this insistence on unity has produced a restrictive and conservative theory of form which has canonized certain collections while ignoring others."[49] Even though Kennedy later discusses disunity and juxtaposition of stories, he unfortunately mars much of the impression by arguing in favor of a new term—the short story collection, as mentioned above—a term which implies too great a discontinuity, and which disregards the closural strategies of this fictional form.

While showing an awareness of the critic's urgent desire for unity and coherence and of the composite's loosely composed structure, Luscher in the end reveals his preferences by stating, for instance, that "in a short story sequence, we experience not only the pleasure of patterned closure in each story but also the rewards of discovering larger unifying strategies," and that "the reconciliation of an apparent disunity into a loose coherence provides satisfaction for the faculties which consistently seek form and pattern in artistic experience."[50] The implication of his title that the short story sequence is an "open book" is thus not given enough evidence in his discussion. The excitement of the disintegrated, the expectation of the indeterminate, the artistic pleasure of the unfulfilled—all characteristics of the short story composite—are in Luscher's piece unfortunately neither addressed nor examined to the extent one would have desired.

In discussing *Go Down, Moses*, Susan V. Donaldson gives an innovative reading of Faulkner's composite, pointing out initially that its tales are "bound not by unifying themes and principles but by disunity, discontinuity, and never-ending strife."[51] Donaldson argues that the history that Lucius Quintus Carothers McCaslin bequeaths to his descendant resembles a master narrative, against which the protagonists of the individual stories rebel. However, as she points out, "old narrative patterns

---

[49] Kennedy, "Toward a Poetics of the Short Story Cycle," 10-11.

[50] Luscher, "The Short Story Sequence: An Open Book," 158.

[51] Donaldson, "Contending Narratives: *Go Down, Moses* and the Short Story Cycle," in Evans Harrington and Ann J. Abadie, eds., *Faulkner and the Short Story* (Jackson: UP of Mississippi, 1992) 129.

... are not so easily circumvented," and the rebellion of, for instance, Lucas Beauchamp or Rider is only partially successful. However, even if the end of each individual story points to a failure of rebellion (and thereby exhibits a closural force), the whole of the composite "remains a battlefield of contending narratives, an unyielding contest between the individual stories of resistance and discontinuity and the all-encompassing narrative of the McCaslins" (147). Donaldson's article is to me one of the few that consistently and intelligently takes into account both the interplay between theme and structure and the tension between closure and open form that distinguish the short story composite.

In *Modern American Short Story Sequences*, referred to above, Susan V. Donaldson presents an equally exciting reading of another short story composite/sequence, Eudora Welty's *The Wide Net*. Donaldson argues that this composite both "offers and withdraws the possibility of unity," pointing to the coexisting desires for a single effect and for a dismantling of that totalizing moment. "Arranged in a loose sequence," she says, "the stories together ponder the tensions between the desire for illumination, mastery, and unity and the muted acknowledgment that such moments of revelation may be as elusive and as tantalizing as the ordering principle linking the tales themselves."[52]

A few other contributions to the same volume also argue for a revisioning of the short story composite. Hocks holds, for instance, that the five tales of Henry James' *The Finer Grain* make up a world of thematic discontinuity and structural continuity; the collection of stories "remains open-ended and contingent, although integrated, rather than formally 'unified'."[53] And Prigozy argues that even though Salinger's *Nine Stories* is characterized by numerous closural strategies, such as theme, recurrent characters, place, and stylistic repetitions, these connectives and surface similarities are deceptive and cannot conceal the basic discontinuity of the volume. "[T]he occasional links," she concludes, "hardly unify the whole collection."[54] Kennedy's essay, which concludes the volume, draws attention to how the short story sequence/composite downplays plot and an inclusive narratorial perspective and

---

[52] Donaldson, "Meditations on Nonpresence: Re-visioning the Short Story in Eudora Welty's *The Wide Net*," in Kennedy 1995, 98-99.

[53] Richard A. Hocks, "Henry James's Incipient Poetics of the Short Story Sequence: *The Finer Grain* (1910)," in Kennedy 1995, 15.

[54] Ruth Prigozy, "*Nine Stories*: J. D. Salinger's Linked Mysteries," in Kennedy 1995, 128.

how it to an equal degree privileges disjunction and indeterminacy in both theme and structure.[55]

Such alternative readings, which take the short story composite's open form into account, are, as we have seen, the exception rather than the rule. The by far most common way of coming to terms with the composite as a genre is still to marginalize the discontinuity and to ignore the multiplicity that are so central to the structure of this mode of narrative.

---

[55] J. Gerald Kennedy, "From Anderson's *Winesburg* to Carver's *Cathedral*: The Short Story Sequence and the Semblance of Community," in Kennedy 1995, 194-215.

Two:
Sketching the Generic Boundaries

What, then, is a short story composite, and what is it not? If it is living its life in the fictional no-man's land between the novel and the short story collection, in what way is it distinctive from these genres? It is my conviction that it is neither possible nor fruitful to draw exact boundaries between various forms of writing; such rigid categorization only checks and diminishes the dynamic force of literature, and particularly in the case of the short story composite—positioned between two well established genres, with both of which it shares narrative features—a strict classification would be counter to the variegated and open nature of this form of narrative.

There are no pure, perfect specimens of a genre, but rather, as Chatman points out, "all works are more or less mixed in generic character." While the novel and the drama require features like plot and character which are not essential to the lyric poem, "all three may utilize the feature of figurative language."[1] The short story composite is probably the mode of narrative that most explicitly and deliberately combines features from two established genres, the short story and the novel. What is also true, Chatman argues, is that "works ordinarily mix features in different dosages," creating qualitative differences within genres.[2] Also in this respect, the short story composite manifests a wide-ranging diversity in types of structure and measure of openness. But as readers we should not be disconcerted, writes Chatman, by the fact that texts are inevitably mixed: "It is their general tendencies that form the subject of rational inquiry," a guideline I have adopted also for this study of the short story composite as a separate genre.

Austin Wright's suggestion that we regard a genre as "a cluster of characteristics"—rather than "a category of works"—is a productive one,[3] since such an approach makes it possible for the critic to discuss how a work "partakes" of a certain genre and how the genre becomes an "ingredient" in the work. We may argue that one text possesses all

---

[1] Chatman, *Story and Discourse. Narrative Structure in Fiction and Film* (Ithaca, N.Y.: Cornell UP, 1978) 18.
[2] Chatman, *Story and Discourse*, 18.
[3] Wright, "On Defining the Short Story," in Lohafer and Clarey, eds., *Short Story Theory at a Crossroads* (Baton Rouge: Louisiana State UP, 1989) 47-50.

the conventions of the genre as we have defined it while another text possesses only some. Wright's relational approach facilitates a discussion of subgenres; he suggests a two-stage procedure, first identifying characteristics applicable to all the works of the genre, without which characteristics a work could not be considered to belong to that genre at all, then identifying conventions that tend to recur in most works of the genre. The latter investigation would lead to the discovery of subgenres, "composed of some of the properties of the [genre] as a whole but not others, and with some peculiar to itself."

Following Wright's suggestions, I will initially examine what critics have agreed constitutes the characteristics applicable to all the works of the short story composite and discuss the various attempts at bringing order to the immense variety within this mode of writing. In an effort to isolate such core features, I will suggest that a line be drawn between, on the one hand, the short story composite and the novel, and, on the other, the composite and the short story collection. Again inspired by Wright, I will then first discuss various subgenres—four major paradigms noticeable within the genre—and finally borderline cases and especially the question whether they, depending on the degree of closure/openness of the text and the reader's in/flexibility, meet or fail to meet certain basic generic requirements.

Basic Generic Characteristics

In charting the previously unexplored territory of the short story composite, critics have been, as we have seen, very insecure in determining the lay of the land. In their failed efforts to come up with an adequate generic term, most of them nevertheless exhibit a consensus when it comes to defining the bare essentials of the short story composite. Whether they suggest the term composite, cycle, cluster, or sequence, all agree with, say, Silverman that it designates "a group of stories written by one author, arranged in a definite order, and intended to produce a specific effect. Though every story of a composite can be understood in isolation, the stories have an added dimension when seen as co-ordinate parts of the larger whole."[4] The short story composite, then, is a form of narrative consisting of interlocking, autonomous stories, a narrative consciously constructed around the tension between simultaneous separateness and cohesion.[5] Most scholars also agree with Silverman that an

---

4 Silverman, "The Short Story Composite: Forms, Functions, and Applications." Diss University of Michigan 1970, *DAI* 31:12 (1970): 6633-A.
5 Ingram speaks in *Representative Short Story Cycles* of the balance between the "individuality" of the story and the "necessities of the larger unit" (15); to Mann the stories are both "self-sufficient" and "interdependent" (*The Short Story Cycle*, 15);

important characteristic of the short story composite is the successive modification or expansion of the text, i.e. that each individual story takes part in a cumulative process of meaning. As exemplary expressions of the genre have been suggested Joyce's *Dubliners*,[6] Welty's *The Golden Apples*,[7] Anderson's *Winesburg, Ohio*,[8] Faulkner's *Go Down, Moses*[9] and *The Unvanquished*.[10] This nomination of an ideal short story composite is, however, of limited help, since these works are so structurally diverse. From *Dubliners*, to *Winesburg*, to *Go Down, Moses*, to *The Golden Apples*, to *The Unvanquished*, there is a wide spectrum ranging from openness to closure; the intratextual links between the stories in *The Unvanquished* are both stronger and more numerous than in Joyce's book. These five works possess narrative structures so different that it is actually difficult to see how any of them could serve as a representative example of the genre.

Structural Variety

The plethora of terms discussed in the first chapter of this study is a sign of a critical confusion due to the genre's heterogeneity in structure and its varying degree of closure and openness. Kennedy is correct in his assumption that the proliferation in terminology "suggests that the difficulty of naming such aggregates may be related to the diversity of works to be subsumed by the generic label."[11] What, for instance, do works like Barth's *Lost in the Funhouse* and Steinbeck's *The Pastures of Heaven* have in common? To what extent does Doctorow's *Lives of the Poets* share generic structural features with Welty's *The Golden Apples*?

Aware of this diversity, some critics have sought to propose typologies of subgenres. Ingram's basis for categorization—the composition history and authorial intention of the composites—is divided into

—the *composed cycle*, conceived of as a cycle from the time the first story was written, and as a result, generally tightly organized.
—the *completed cycle*, generally less unified, conceived of only after some of the stories have been written.

---

to Creighton the stories are "detachable but interrelated" (*William Faulkner's Craft of Revision*, 85-87).
[6] Creighton, 85-87; Kennedy, ed., *Modern American Short Story Sequences*, vii.
[7] Mann, 150, Luscher, "The Short Story Sequence: An Open Book," 163.
[8] Luscher, 163, Ingram, 143-99, Kennedy 1995, vii, Dunn/Morris, *The Composite Novel*, 55.
[9] Luscher, 165, Creighton, 85-87.
[10] Ingram, 106-42.
[11] Kennedy, "Toward a Poetics of the Short Story Cycle," 13.

—*the arranged cycle*, the most loosely structured, conceived of by the author and/or the editor only after all of the stories have been written.[12]

This principle of classification seems questionable to me. Does it really matter, we may ask ourselves, whether we know how the composites initially were put together? Ingram's division is actually one of structure; he qualifies the texts of the three groups as follows: composed cycles are "more highly unified" than the two other forms; completed cycles have an intermediate position; and the arranged cycles constitute "the loosest composite forms." But these variations in structure exist in the *published* texts, and it is irrelevant what the authorial, or editorial, intention once harbored. Besides, as Mann correctly argues, Ingram's categories are not distinctive enough: "Completed cycles are frequently as well unified as composed ones."[13] Kennedy adds to this critique by pointing to the fact that Ingram's scheme of classification "privileges completed cycles —which supposedly best illustrate the development of the unifying concept—at the expense of the more numerous arranged cycles."[14]

Susan Garland Mann seeks to come to terms with the variety of the composite by suggesting a thematic systematization. She distinguishes primarily two groups of composites: one concerned with the maturation of a single protagonist or a "composite" protagonist, another expressing the theme of human isolation and the fragmentation of life.[15] The weakness of Mann's classification is that it adds but little to our understanding of the composite as a genre. A categorization based on theme is not distinctive in relation to the novel or the short story; identical themes may be found in each of these genres. Since the short story composite is distinguished by its narrative structure, a subdivision should, I believe, be based on divergencies in structure.

Maggie Dunn and Ann Morris differ to a degree from other critics by suggesting that the "composite novel," their term for the mode of writing under discussion here, is composed of interrelated autonomous shorter *texts*, i.e. not necessarily short stories. While this increases the proliferation even more, they simultaneously introduce a generic requirement that restricts the choice: to qualify as a composite novel, each of its texts should carry a title, which, according to Dunn and Morris, would exclude, for instance, Steinbeck's *The Pastures of Heaven*. These scholars subdivide "composite novels" according to the most prominent

---

[12] Ingram, 17-18, as paraphrased by Mann, 20.
[13] Mann, 20.
[14] Kennedy, "Toward a Poetics of the Short Story Cycle," 12.
[15] Mann, 7-14. Mann adds a third group of "other types" of short story cycles devoted to the "role of the artist," or concentrating on "a particular setting or community."

unifying feature: setting, protagonist, pattern/theme, and storytelling. The disadvantage of such a taxonomy is that the features chosen are shared by other genres and do not distinguish this mode of writing from, for instance, the novel or the short story. As in the case of Mann's book, what is lacking is a categorization according to structure.

Such a structural classification has been advanced by Lubbers who subdivides this form of narrative into short story sequences, short story cycles, and short story novels.[16] The sequence, to Lubbers, is often chronological and devoted to the development of a character. From the sequence he excludes the frame-tale and the composition of mere stories around a protagonist, like Doyle's *Adventures of Sherlock Holmes*. As examples of cycles he lists *Dubliners, Winesburg, Ohio*, and *The Pastures of Heaven*, works exhibiting more of a plan and a compositional whole, often unified by means of place, time, and theme. The short story novels are, according to Lubbers, "almost" novels, characterized by such a high degree of unity and closure that it is difficult to draw a line between this subgenre and the novel; as examples of such short story novels Lubbers lists *The Unvanquished, The Country of the Pointed Firs*, and Frank O'Connor's *Dutch Interior*.

The impossibility of absolute demarcation has caused several critics to place composites into a continuum from closure to openness, the nodes being the novel and the short story collection. As we have seen, Ingram positions his categories on a scale from "tightly organized" to "loosely structured." And even though she does not explicitly state it, Mann's categorization also rests on a sliding scale from unity to fragmentation. In a similar way, Luscher sees what he calls the short story sequences arranged along a continuum from collection to novel, finding works like *Winesburg* and *The Golden Apples* at midpoint,[17] as does Lubbers, whose scheme, simplified and translated, would look like the following: novel—short story novel—short story cycle—short story sequence—short story collection.

A Revised View of Structural Patterns

To see the genre of the short story composite as extending over a spectrum with a gradual transition from one subgenre to another is a sensible approach. It allows for various structural patterns to emerge without the rigidity of exact boundaries.

Of the three subgenres suggested by Lubbers I am in favor of two: the

---

16 Klaus Lubbers, *Typologie der Short Story* (Darmstadt: Wissenschaftliche Buchgesellschaft, 1977) 143-62. Lubbers' terms are "Kurzgeschichtensequenzen," "Kurzgeschichtenzyklen," and "Kurzgeschichtenromane."
17 Luscher, "The Short Story Sequence: An Open Book," 163.

sequence and the cycle. Since the term "short story novel" evokes too little of the genre's specificity, it should be avoided. While I would instead suggest that the short story composite within itself forms four general structural patterns, I hasten to repeat that they are not absolute but that overlappings occur, and, also, that there may well be short story composites that do not fit any of these patterns. But to generalize, on a scale from closure to openness, the four substructures that emerge are the *cycle,* the *sequence*, the *cluster*, and the *novella*. I suggest these terms in the belief that they are descriptive of the structural configurations they are meant to denote.

Both the cycle and the sequence are characterized by a comparatively high degree of unity and coherence, but to say that one is closer to the traditional novel than the other could be misleading. The term *cycle* suggests a short story composite that is basically organized cyclically — where in the last story there is a final resolution and a return to a beginning. As examples of this subgenre may be mentioned Welty's *The Golden Apples*, Jewett's *The Country of the Pointed Firs* (the 1896 edition, not Cather's 1925 edition), Steinbeck's *The Pastures of Heaven*, and Wilder's *The Bridge of San Luis Rey*. Welty's book starts with Katie Rainey as narrator and ends with her funeral; the last story, "The Wanderers," brings most of the protagonists of the preceding stories together. Jewett's and Steinbeck's composites are constructed around the arrival and departure of an observer, but they are different from, say, *Winesburg, Ohio* in that the individual stories are linked to each other and not only to the observer. The first and last stories of Wilder's book deal with the "accident" when the bridge breaks; the three intermediate stories, depicting the lives of the victims, are interdependent.

By *sequence* I mean, not the reader's sequential negotiation of the text as Luscher defines the term,[18] but a sequential narrative pattern where one story is added, as in a row, to the next, locking into it, but, taken together, not exhibiting a strong sense of unity and closure. In such a sequential structure one unit follows from another, as Smith says, "either logically, temporally, or in accord with some principle of serial generation."[19] Many such sequences consist of a series of chronologically ordered stories, such as Faulkner's *The Unvanquished* and Munro's *Lives of Girls and Women*, but the sequential order may also be of a different kind, as in Swados' *On the Line*, in which the lives of ten men working on an assembly line are portrayed in the very order in which they work along the line; the only connection between the first and the

---

[18] Luscher, "The Short Story Sequence: An Open Book," 148-49.
[19] Barbara Herrnstein Smith, *Poetic Closure: A Study of How Poems End* (Chicago: U of Chicago P, 1968) 109.

last story is thus provided by the setting, and there is no attempt at final resolution in the last story.

The *cluster*, a term only used in passing by other critics, to me depicts a rather loosely structured subgenre, in which stories seem to be striving in various directions; in which chronology is not strictly adhered to; in which the gaps between the stories are wide; and in which some stories are not easily integrated into a coherent whole. The cluster is thus less characterized by either cyclicality or sequentiality than the two forms discussed above. Three well-known examples of this mode of short story composite, exhibiting a fairly high degree of indeterminacy, are Hemingway's *In Our Time*, Faulkner's *Go Down, Moses,* and Erdrich's *Love Medicine*. These works possess an open structure, where in many cases the interconnections between the stories are not obvious, but will have to be constructed by readers, often with a constricting result. While there definitely is a measure of unity in these clusters, discontinuity and fragmentation emerge as the by far more characteristic features.

The last basic sub-pattern that I suggest is the *novella*, the model taken from the novella form of, for instance, Boccaccio's *Decameron*, consisting of a frame-tale, and a reappearing narrator, narrative devices linking otherwise unrelated stories. Modern variations on this pattern may be seen in Anderson's *Winesburg, Ohio*, Babel's *Red Cavalry*, John Horne Burns' *The Gallery*, Updike's *Olinger Stories*, and Cheever's *The Housebreaker of Shady Hill and Other Stories*, in which books a group of people, not necessarily familiar to each other, are depicted as a community. But there exist also even more loosely joined novellas such as Barth's *Lost in the Funhouse*, Coover's *A Night at the Movies*, and Godwin's *Mr Bedford and the Muses*, in which the intratextual links are scant, but where the collections are unified by theme and setting and by extradiegetic devices such as forewords and, as in Coover's case, by the simulated offering of a movie house.

However, as any reader familiar with short story composites will observe, classifications such as these tend to overlap. To take one example, I have labeled Anderson's *Winesburg, Ohio* a novella, but, since it is constructed around George Willard's arrival into and departure from the text, it might also be argued that it is cyclical; one might even propose that it is a sequence, since the characters George meets may be seen as stations, chronologically ordered, on his way to maturity. To me, however, the novella pattern takes precedence over the others, because I understand Anderson's book to be first and foremost about the individual fates of a small town, and I see George Willard as the vehicle into that world. Others may disagree with my classification of *In Our Time* as a cluster and argue in favor of either its cyclicality—on account of the final story, "Big Two-Hearted River," which depicts Nick's return—or its sequentiality, since several stories (but surely not all) are concerned with Nick's growth into manhood.

And what does one do, the skeptical reader may ask, with short story composites such as Doctorow's *Lives of the Poets*, in which the six first stories are not joined until, in the last story, it turns out that they were written by the protagonist of that story?[20] Where does such a structure belong, and how can it be designated? It would seem that the variety of the short story composite defies being pigeonholed into neat categories, even if, as I am convinced, certain general patterns can be discerned.

The Short Story Composite and the Novel

It is easy to understand why so few critics of the short story composite have sought to distinguish it from the novel, since an uncontestable definition of the latter is as difficult to produce as one of the former. While I will refrain from entering the quagmire of defining the novel, I would nevertheless wish to investigate whether it is posssible to indicate, in the continuum discussed above, a point or dividing-line between a fairly tightly structured short story composite and a novel. But to signal how hopeless a task this might be, one may only remind the reader of the fact that Faulkner called *Go Down, Moses*—a comparatively open work by most critical assessments—a novel,[21] while he said about the stories of *The Unvanquished*—characterized, according to critics, by fairly high degree of unity and closure—that "I realized that they would be too episodic to be what I considered a novel, so I thought of them as a series of stories."[22]

In comparison with the traditional novel, the short story composite puts less emphasis on causality, temporality, plot, and character. It is more multi-voiced and open-ended; it defuses closure and resolution of plot. However, such openness is true of many modernist and postmodernist novels as well. Komar points out that "any reader contemplating contemporary literature is struck by the frequent appearance of novels in which the narrative text is fragmented, split up into several separate (and often seemingly unrelated) lines of narration, a form char-

---

[20] Paul Auster's *New York Trilogy* exhibits a similar structure in that in its last part, "The Locked Room," the narrator claims to have written the two preceding parts, "City of Glass" and "Ghosts."

[21] See Joseph L. Blotner, *Faulkner: A Biography* (New York: Random House, 1974) 1102.

[22] Frederick L. Gwynn and Joseph L. Blotner, eds., *Faulkner in the University: Class Conferences at the University of Virginia, 1957-1958* (New York: Vintage, 1959) 252.

acteristic of the works of Joyce, Dos Passos and Faulkner."[23] This textual fragmentation and "multilinearity" characterize also many works in the generations after the modernists. But these narrative strategies of discontinuity are shared, as I indicated above, by the short story composite as well. The difference between the composite and this "multilinear" form of novel, however, is that the stories of the composite are autonomous; they are completed units, characterized by closure. And between these closed units are inserted gaps or interstices of considerable width. The novel may be characterized by fragmentation, by the juxtaposition of several plot lines, by the use of multiple narrators—all features shared by the short story composite—but it is not composed of self-sufficient units.

To sum up, it would appear that the only two distinctive features of the short story composite in relation to the novel are the closed structure of each of the interdependent stories in combination with the significant temporal and spatial gaps between them; chapters or segments/sections of novels, traditional or experimental, are more open-ended, deliberately seeking linkage and coherence with other parts of a more or less continuous narrative. Then, in addition, in comparison with the traditional novel, the short story composite exhibits a greater polyphony and openness, but these are less distinctive features when we speak also of later developments of the novel.

As a test case I would like to compare Anne Tyler's *Dinner at the Homesick Restaurant*, generally accepted as a novel, with Faulkner's *The Unvanquished*, considered a "representative" short story composite by Ingram, but held to be more of a novel by Lubbers.[24] By choosing two narratives that are situated so close to each other on the scale, I hope to find the features that make these books fall on either side of the dividing-line.

Most readers regard *Dinner at the Homesick Restaurant* as a novel, but one may, in fact, launch a rather convincing argument for its being a short story composite. Like the composite, *Dinner at the Homesick Restaurant* consists of narrative units, chapters, that can actually be read as independent stories. There are temporal gaps between the stories/chapters—between Chapters 2 and 3 there is an ellipsis of six years—and in the plot there are hermeneutic gaps of considerable importance—Jenny's marriage to Sam Wiley, for instance, is more or less omitted from

---

[23] Kathleen L. Komar, *Pattern and Chaos: Multilinear Novels by Dos Passos, Döblin, Faulkner and Koeppen* (Columbia, S.C.: Camden House, 1983) 1.
[24] Lubbers, 158. Even though Lubbers deals with Faulkner's book under the rubric of "Kurzgeschichtenromane," he writes: "De facto handelt es sich um einen Roman, der seine Existenz dem Prinzip der imaginativen Amplifizierung verdankt."

the story. The focalization shifts from one chapter to the next; the ten chapters are told through the central consciousness of, in this order, Pearl, Cody, Jenny, Ezra, Cody, Pearl, Jenny, Luke, Ezra, and Cody. There is also a shift from the past tense, in nine of the stories, to the present tense, in "Beaches on the Moon." Each chapter has a title, as is common in the short story composite, and the title of the book is taken from the last story, making it similar to, for example, *Go Down, Moses* and *Lives of the Poets*. Certain stories are less well integrated, like "Dr Tull Is Not a Toy," which is devoted almost entirely to one of the characters, Jenny. Plot is de-emphasized; turning-points may occur in some of the stories/chapters, but there is no climax in the plot of the novel. Information about family relations and events is repeated in subsequent chapters, information necessary for the chapters/stories to function autonomously, but "unnecessary" for the progress of the novel, a narrative device distinctive of the composite.[25] While all these narrative elements then seem to make *Dinner at the Homesick Restaurant* into a composite, in my judgment, it is not.

Even though I as a scholar interested in short story composites have developed a capacity for "detecting" such composite structures almost everywhere, I would have to admit that there is something in *Dinner at the Homesick Restaurant* that resists the label of composite. In spite of a structure that to a considerable extent resembles that of the short story composite, *Dinner at the Homesick Restaurant* possesses a degree of continuity and coherence that makes it impossible for me to define it as anything but a novel. Many narrative strategies contribute to this impression of a novelistic pattern. The book contains comparatively few protagonists, and it presents the development of character that one often associates with a novel. Even though the focalizers alternate between the chapters, each new section contains information on the other characters, complementing and modifying their portraits, as so often happens in, for example, a Faulkner novel. Surrounded by the frame of Pearl's, the mother's, illness and death, the plot—if one can talk about plot in this plotless book—progresses chronologically; there are considerable gaps in the continuity of events, that is true, but the narrative is basically not anachronic. Certain events and metaphors create a sense of progression and wholeness, such as Ezra's repeated, thwarted attempts to arrange a family dinner which will not be interrupted in the middle; in the last section, the title story, it is implied that he may finally succeed. Certain

---

25 Anne Tyler, *Dinner at the Homesick Restaurant* (New York: Berkley Books, 1983) 70, 73, 125, 175, 212, 215, 222, 272-73, 290-91. Just to mention one example, on page 125 we are told that Jenny is Ezra's sister, a piece of information we have been in the possession of since the first chapter.

key events are retold again and again, instances of what Rimmon-Kenan terms "repetitive frequency,"[26] such as the archery accident in which Pearl is shot, an incident which is described four times from different points of view, a repetition that adds to the narrative's sense of unity. The "redundant" information about e.g. family relations discussed above not only establishes each chapter as a self-sufficient story, it, paradoxically, also adds to the linking between the chapters. The transitions from one chapter to the next is not characterized, as in most short story composites, by recalcitrance. The reader does not have to reorientate him/herself completely or familiarize him/herself with a new context. In *Dinner at the Homesick Restaurant* there is always a reference to a name, a place, an event at the beginning of a new chapter, making it clear that the plot from the preceding chapter/story continues in one way or another. In sum, then, there are too many and too strong intratextual connections between the ten sections to ultimately leave us with the impression that this is a short story composite.

Faulkner's *The Unvanquished* is a sequence of tightly interlocking, yet independent stories. As we have seen, Faulkner himself regarded it not as a novel, but a series of stories; certain critics have agreed with Faulkner, others have argued in favor of it being a novel. Waggoner and Howe referred to the book as a novel, while Swiggart, for instance, saw little thematic unity.[27] Critics of the short story composite have been equally divided: Ingram discusses *The Unvanquished* as one of his representative composites, while Lubbers critiques Ingram for doing so, claiming that it de facto is a novel.

A number of generic features most often identified with the novel are apparent in the text of *The Unvanquished*. It has been termed a *Bildungsroman*[28] in that it traces the development of Bayard Sartoris into maturity. Bayard is not only the unifying protagonist but also the narrator of all the stories. While numerous characters, like Ringo, Drusilla, Granny, John Sartoris, recur in several stories, the book is also unified by a chronological story line, by the setting of Yoknapatawpha County, and by the events of the Civil War and the Reconstruction.

At the same time it is obvious that in writing this series of stories Faulkner took pains to create discrete narrative units characterized by a

---

[26] Shlomith Rimmon-Kenan, *Narrative Fiction: Comparative Poetics* (London: Routledge, 1983) 57-58.
[27] See Hyatt H. Waggoner, *William Faulkner: From Jefferson to the World* (N.p.: U of Kentucky P, 1959) 170; Irving Howe, *William Faulkner: A Critical Study*, 2nd rev. ed. (New York: Vintage, 1962) 42; Peter Swiggart, *The Art of Faulkner's Novels* (Austin: U of Texas P, 1962) 36.
[28] Frederick R. Karl, *William Faulkner: American Writer. A Biography* (New York: Weidenfeld & Nicolson, 1989) 525.

fairly strong sense of closure. Each story develops its own plot that reaches a resolution. There are temporal and causal gaps between the stories; a year has passed between "Ambuscade" and "Retreat," three years between "Skirmish at Sartoris" and "An Odor of Verbena." Certain stories, like "Skirmish at Sartoris," are less well integrated into the whole. All the stories thus become self-sufficient, in part due to Faulkner's incorporation of "summaries" of previous events necessary for the individual story to function independently but appearing repetitive if we view the book as a novel.[29] While it contains numerous analeptic passages like these "summaries," there are no examples of prolepsis, advance mention, or other forms of foreshadowing, a narrative feature not uncommon in novels, and the stories exist simultaneously on two narrative levels—as detached units and as integrated segments. Ingram describes well this interplay between the discrete units circumscribing a single action and their relation to the continuity of the work: "Each story develops its own action, but the significance of *The Unvanquished* accumulates from story to story through the achievement of successively higher viewpoints embodied in the gradually maturing reflections and actions of Bayard Sartoris."[30]

In my view, then, in comparison with *Dinner at the Homesick Restaurant, The Unvanquished* is characterized by a higher degree of autonomy in the stories, by the width of the gaps between the stories, by the comparative lack of connectives and a continuous, coherent story line.

The Short Story Composite and the Short Story Collection

Let us now turn to the other end of the continuum, to the point where a short story composite becomes so discontinuously structured that it loses its generic specificity and must be defined as a collection of stories. A short story collection almost always possesses a measure of unity. The author carefully makes a selection and creates a specific order or structure among the stories; the selection is often made on the basis of similarities in theme. Stories may also share a resemblance in setting, tone, and style. But such unifying elements alone do not make a collection into a composite. "It is not enough," as Mann says, "simply to depict a particular class of people at a particular time and in a particular geographic setting."[31] If, as we saw above, the composite is distinguished from the novel by the autonomy of the stories and the intervening gaps, in relation to the short story collection the composite is characterized by

---

[29] This narrative feature will be further discussed in the following chapter.
[30] Ingram, *Representative Short Story Cycles*, 134.
[31] Mann, 16.

the connectedness and intratextuality between stories, a form of totalization not characteristic of the collection.

How many intratextual links, and what *kind* of unifying strategies, are
necessary before we experience a collection as a composite? If time, setting, and depicting a group of people are not enough, as Mann claims,
would, for instance, Anderson's *Winesburg, Ohio* cease to be a composite if the introductory "Book of the Grotesque" and the figure of George
Willard were excised from the narrative? Is it Willard who makes the
book a composite? While considering an "aggregate" like Freeman's *A
New England Nun* not to be a "true short story sequence" because its
form is neither "complex" nor "sequential,"[32] Luscher finds *Winesburg,
Ohio* a supreme example of the sequence. It is true that Freeman's book
is more loosely constructed, but is there really such a difference between
Freeman's and Anderson's books? The form of *Winesburg* is not especially complex, nor does the text undergo much sequential modification
as we read it. While Luscher excludes *A New England Nun* from the
composite canon, Mann includes Godwin's *Dream Children*, because, it
seems, "all the protagonists are dreamers."[33] Is this theme so strongly
present in the book that—together with the unifying title—it is turned
into a composite? I am personally equally hesitant concerning both
Luscher's exclusion of Freeman as of Mann's inclusion of Godwin. Was
it not Mann who held that "to depict a particular class of people," e. g.
dreamers, is not enough?

Are connectives between stories other than thematic and geographic
ones absolute genre specifics? Intratextual links of another nature than
theme and setting seem to be required, such as narrator, characters, specific places, events, symbols recurring in several stories of the composite.
The repeated appearance of narrator, character, and event seems more of
a distinctive feature than place and symbol, unless the latter are of a very
specific nature, like a very restricted neighborhood.

The title of the book may also indicate whether it is a short story
composite or collection; however, only general tendencies may be observed on the issue of titling, since there are exceptions, as I will make
clear. Most often collections of stories are named after one of the stories
of the book, whereas short story composites as a rule carry titles that aim
at expressing the whole work, as a novel usually does. Composites like
*The Country of the Pointed Firs, Winesburg, Ohio, In Our Time, The
Pastures of Heaven, The Golden Apples,* Naylor's *The Women of Brewster Place,* Kingston's *The Woman Warrior,* and Lee Smith's *Oral History* indicate through their titles that they are intended to possess more

---

[32] Luscher, 163.
[33] Mann, 196.

cohesion than a short story collection. There are, however, exceptions to this general tendency; certain narratives that undeniably are composites take their titles from one of the stories, like *Go Down, Moses, Lost in the Funhouse, Lives of the Poets*, and Erdrich's *Love Medicine*, but as far as I can judge these make up a small minority.

There seem to be even fewer short story collections with titles embracing the whole work. But again there are exceptions; works like Dreiser's *A Gallery of Women*, Fitzgerald's *Flappers and Philosophers*, and Hemingway's *Men Without Women* do not become composites merely because they carry titles not referring to one of the collection's stories. All one can ultimately say seems to be that the general tendency is that the composite has a unifying title whereas the collection has not. However, to make this a distinguishing feature or the basis on which a classification can be made is futile, since too many exceptions exist.

As in the discussion above of the novel, I would like to select two works for comparison, Hubert Selby, Jr.'s *Last Exit to Brooklyn*, a loosely structured short story composite of the cluster type, and Richard Ford's *Rock Springs*, a short story collection characterized by a certain coherence. *Rock Springs*[34] possesses the totalizing elements of setting and theme. All the stories, except one, are situated in a limited part of Montana. Places like Great Falls, Havre, Deer Lodge Prison, Clark Fork River, and Rock Springs recur in more stories than one. Two of them, "Winterkill" and "Communist," are narrated by "Les," but Ford never makes clear whether it is the same person. Thematically, the stories exhibit a strong resemblance: They are all about ordinary, lower-class people in their thirties or forties, disillusioned and often unemployed. More often than not they are divorced and have very unsteady relations to the other sex; the stories exude a general distrust of lasting relations. The characters—only sketchily drawn—are not really cynical, only weary and uncommitted.

Do these connectives make *Rock Springs* qualify as a short story composite? In my opinion they do not: the places that recur are mentioned in passing; little emphasis is placed on them as narrative elements, and so, as a unifying device, they are not very significant. But had Ford wished to produce a composite, very few changes in the text would have been necessary; if he had let the action of the stories take place in one town, say Rock Springs, the collection would better have qualified as a composite similar to *Winesburg, Ohio* or *The Country of the Pointed Firs*. With the exception of possibly Les, no protagonists turn up, even cursorily, in other stories, and there is neither frame-tale nor unify-

---

34 Richard Ford, *Rock Springs. Stories* (New York: Atlantic Monthly Press, 1987).

ing narrator or observer like George Willard. Grantedly, there is thematic coherence in the book, but themes like human isolation, lack of communication, and the bleakness of existential fatigue are too universal to
create a definite sense of wholeness.

Like *Rock Springs*, Hubert Selby, Jr.'s *Last Exit to Brooklyn*[35] has a
very open structure. Distinctive of the stories and sketches depicting a
world of drug addicts, criminals, homosexuals, prostitutes, and trans-
vestites is fracture and disjunction rather than integration and oneness.
While one story, "The Strike," is by its length so dominant that it threat-
ens to dwarf the others, another story, "The Baby Makes Three," is so
marginally integrated that it could be termed a "fringe" story.[36]

And still there are more connectives between the individual stories,
and more significant ones, in this narrative than in Ford's *Rock Springs*.
The title, for example, is not taken from one of the stories. Each story/
section is introduced by an epigraph from the Bible. There is a "Coda"
called "Landsend," which serves as a sort of resolution. All the stories
take place in a rather small area of Brooklyn, and as focal point for the
neighborhood people — and for the book — serves the bar called The
Greeks, mentioned in almost all the stories. Certain characters turn up in
more than one story: Tony, Harry, Vinnie. While they may be the protagonist of one story, they have a marginal position in others. Vinnie, for
instance, plays a central role in "The Queen Is Dead," but in "Another
Day Another Dollar" and "Tralala," his is a peripheral presence. It is not
the fact that Selby has stated that in writing this book he was inspired by
Dubliners, *Winesburg, Ohio* and Babel's *The Red Cavalry*[37] that makes
Last Exit to Brooklyn a short story composite, but the numerous threads,
pointed to above, that hold the stories together.

To sum up, the specificity of the short story composite in relation to
the novel consists in the autonomy of its discrete stories and the interstices between them, and in relation to the short story collection it is determined by the intratextuality between the stories. As a consequence of
these distinctions, the stories of the composite exist simultaneously as
self-contained entities and as interconnected parts of a larger whole. The
reader experiences a "doubleness" present in the individual stories. Ultimately the most characteristic feature of the short story composite is this
"double" existence of the stories, and the tension that emerges from that
doubleness.

---

[35] Hubert Selby, Jr., *Last Exit to Brooklyn* (New York: Grove Press, 1965).
[36] See Chapter Six on "The Fringe Story."
[37] In conversation with the present author.

Borderline Cases

The discussion above concerns borderline texts, short story composites close to being either a novel or a collection. But there are other kinds of borderline cases, where the classificatory endeavor does not emanate from the question of openness or closure, but from whether the book fulfills the basic generic requirements, namely being a work consisting of autonomous yet interlocking short stories. Different kinds of such borderline texts exist: one type in which all but one of the stories are self-sufficient, and another type in which it is questionable whether the separate narratives can be defined as short stories. With Austin Wright's relational genre model we can say that many of these texts "partake" of the short story composite and that the short story composite is an "ingredient" in these works.[38]

While certain texts consist of a series of independent, yet interlinked stories, they also contain one narrative that is too dependent on the other stories to function autonomously. This is true of the frame-tale novella type of composite, where the frame itself seldom exists independently of the subsequent or embedded stories. Godwin's "Author's Note," placed after the stories of *Mr Bedford and the Muses,* is a case in point, as is the frame of "Dawn" and "Dusk" in Naylor's *The Women of Brewster Place.* Another example is "The Book of the Grotesque" in *Winesburg, Ohio.* Even though such framing texts are contingent on the stories, they make up the unifying raison d'etre of this form of narrative and should not disqualify the whole work from being defined as a composite. More problematic is the narrative that fulfills all requirements except that one story is not autonomous. To take one example, Lee Smith's *Oral History* consists of four sections, of which the third one, it seems to me, is so dependent on the other sections that it functions less well separately. Does this make Smith's book a novel rather than a composite?

Having thus far shied away from defining the short story, I will not attempt to do so now. There are, however, two types of books of united narratives of which one may question, on the basis of length, whether these narratives are actually short stories. The first kind is the composite of sketches—very short pieces without much of a plot—and the second type is the work which consists of several stories long enough to resemble short novels.

In her annotated list of short story composites Mann includes Langston Hughes' books about Jesse B. Semple, such as *Simple Speaks His Mind.* These works link narratives which are sketches, or skits, consisting of witty dialogue, but with little plot or character development in the

---

[38] Wright, "On Defining the Short Story," in Lohafer and Clarey, eds., *Short Story Theory at a Crossroads,* 48.

separate narratives. Concerning the assessment of such short pieces, I find Wright's position a sensible one: "I include no lower limit to length since extremely short pieces have been called short stories often enough to suggest that any specific lower limit is a tendency rather than an absolute."[39] Sandra Cisneros' *The House on Mango Street* is a case in point. Cisneros presents a series of vignettes, all told by Esperanza, about her youth, her dreams, fears, shames. There are recurring figures like Sally, Minerva, and Mamacita. Cisneros' book thus shares the interlocking strategies with the short story composite. Even though the sketches are more like prose poems, the book in my mind contains the basic characteristics of a short story composite.

It is equally difficult to judge whether works like Auster's *New York Trilogy*, Stein's *Three Lives*, or Wharton's *Old New York* ought to be included in the composite canon.[40] They all consist of longer tales, so long in fact that it is doubtful whether they can be defined as short stories. It has often been claimed that, to qualify as a short story, a text should not exceed the length of Joyce's "The Dead" or Conrad's "Heart of Darkness."[41] We must ask ourselves where the line concerning the length of a text should be drawn. Should we decide that works such as these are short story composites, the problem arises what to do with a book like Dos Passos' *U.S.A*, whether it should be counted as a composite, which is actually what Mann does. But if one includes Dos Passos' novel trilogy, then one would also have to consider all examples of the *roman fleuve* and saga novel, which seems absurd. Therefore, I am willing to include the works by Auster, Stein, and Wharton into the canon of short story composites but would exclude Dos Passos' *U.S.A*. on account of the length of the individual narrative units.

Constructed Short Story Composites
There is yet another question concerning composites that should be addressed, the fact that a number of existing composites have been constructed or re-constructed after the original publication. There are mainly two types of such composites: those that were constructed, expanded or modified by the author him/herself and those that were constructed by an editor. The former are obviously short story composites in the proper sense, the latter, in my opinion, are not. Let me make clear the reasons for such a judgmental statement.

In the 1930 edition of *In Our Time* Hemingway made certain minor

---

39 Wright, "On Defining the Short Story," 50.
40 The works by Stein and Wharton are included in Mann's "Annotated list."
41 See, for instance, Wright, "On Defining the Short Story," 51.

changes. He added, at the beginning of the book, the section "On the Quay of Smyrna," and he changed the typography of what has been called the "interchapters," so that they in the 1930 edition no longer are units placed in-between the stories—which can connect with both the preceding and the following story—but are placed as a preamble to the following story. The original and the 1930 editions are then different texts, but they are both composites, since Hemingway himself was the initiator of the alterations.

The other type, the editor-constructed composite, was never intended by the author to be a composite, at least not with the structural pattern that it now has. While *The Nick Adams Stories* may thus be a short story composite, it is not Hemingway's; it may be Philip Young's, the editor's. This "chronological sequence," presented in five neat sections, may create greater "coherence" and a more "consistent character,"[42] as Young claims, but it certainly makes for a totalizing construct to which I refuse to believe Hemingway himself would have consented. Critics of the composite have been divided concerning the status of such compilations as that of Young. Mann does not include *The Nick Adams Stories*, Luscher and Kennedy object to it, and Lubbers defines it as a sequence without showing an awareness of its problematic nature.[43] Flora is in favor of Young's assemblage but objects to the chronological pattern of the stories that Young suggests.[44]

A less extreme example of a constructed composite is Willa Cather's 1925 edition of Jewett's *The Country of the Pointed Firs*, into which Cather inserts into Jewett's 1896 text three stories before the concluding "The Backward View." These three stories do not belong in the composite; they break the original pattern of the narrator arriving at Dunnet Landing at the beginning of the summer and leaving at the end, since the action of these stories takes place after the action of "The Backward View," a fact of which Cather seems unaware or inconsiderate.

There are many such composites about which one may have doubts whether they should be considered authentic composites, intended to be thus structured. The stories of Flannery O'Connor's *Everything that Rises Must Converge* were evidently meant to form some sort of composite, but since O'Connor died before she could finish it, and the book in its present form was constructed by her editor, one must be doubtful about its status. Kennedy questions the kind of compilation made in *Every-*

---

[42] Ernest Hemingway, *The Nick Adams Stories*, ed. by Philip Young, (New York: Charles Scribner's Sons, 1972) 5-6.
[43] Luscher, 160; Kennedy 1988, 12-13; Lubbers, 146-47.
[44] Joseph M. Flora, *Hemingway's Nick Adams* (Baton Rouge: Louisiana State UP, 1982) 14-15.

thing that Rises Must Converge:

> although the dying author contemplated a second collection [Kennedy's term
> for composite], she left no instructions for its arrangement, nor did she mention
> a conceptual scheme. Her editor simply placed the title story first, then pre-
> sented the other eight narratives in the order of their magazine publication. Is
> the book nevertheless a cycle in the same sense that her deliberately arranged *A
> Good Man* is?[45]

A case parallel to O'Connor's book, Fitzgerald's *Pat Hobby Stories* was
intended as a series, but, as the editor Arnold Gingrich states, had Fitzgerald not died, he would have revised and reshuffled the order of the
sequence.[46] And what about Fitzgerald's *The Basil and Josephine
Stories*, which Mann includes in her list? These stories were collected by
two editors, Bryer and Kuehl, and published years after Fitzgerald's
death. It has also been argued that the sequence "The Old Order," a series of stories about Miranda, in *The Collected Stories of Katherine Anne
Porter* constitutes a composite,[47] a totalizing project without the sanc-
tion of the author. Yet another example of such a constructed composite
is Harold Frederic's *Stories of York State*, edited by Thomas F. O'Donnell, which gathers seven of Frederic's stories about "his onetime neigh-
bors in Mohawk Valley towns and villages,"[48] stories which have not
earlier appeared in the same volume.

As a final example of the work of overly ambitious editors one may
mention Robert Altman's compilation of a few of Raymond Carver's
stories, *Short Cuts*, and the movie by the same name based on that collection. Since Carver never put these seven stories and one poem together, if this is a composite, it is not Carver's; the fact that Altman has con-
sulted with Carver's widow Tess Gallagher gives no legitimacy.[49] In the
movie, Altman takes even greater liberties by explicitly interweaving the
story lines of the individual stories and by even inventing new characters
and a new setting—and as a film director he has of course the right to do
whatever he likes—but this product, great as it may be as a movie, is no
longer a recreation of Carver's work. Besides, Altman's movie is not
structured as a short story composite. The various stories are not told

---

[45] Kennedy 1988, 12.
[46] Arnold Gingrich, "Introduction" to F. Scott Fitzgerald, *The Pat Hobby Stories*
(New York: Charles Scribner's Sons, 1962) xx.
[47] Mann, 203.
[48] "Editor's Foreword," *Harold Frederic's Stories of York State*, ed. by Thomas F.
O'Donnell (Syracuse, N.Y.: Syracuse UP, 1966) vi.
[49] Robert Altman, "Introduction; Collaborating with Carver," in Raymond Carver,
Short Cuts (New York: Vintage Books, 1993) 8.

one at a time as completed units but are presented throughout the movie in short sequences alternating between the story lines, making it resemble rather a multilinear novel like Dos Passos' *Manhattan Transfer*.

Three:
Coherence and Closure in the Short Story Composite

The short story composite profits from being discussed in terms of closure and openness on two levels: first, as a genre the short story composite exhibits various degrees of openness, as we have seen, from the fairly closed form resembling a novel to the relatively open form not unlike a collection of stories; second, each individual short story composite, wherever it may be found on the continuum from closed to open form, exhibits a tension between closural and anti-closural strategies, a co-existence specific to the genre.

The individual short story composite is constructed from an intricate combination of centripetal and centrifugal narrative forces. While it is characterized by an openness that the traditional novel does not possess, without a measure of coherence and a sense of closure, to state the obvious, the short story composite would not exist at all. It is only on account of the unifying narrative elements that what might have been a collection of stories gains the status of short story composite. I will in this chapter focus on the totalizing strategies of the short story composite, and devote the next chapter to a study of the centrifugal, discontinuous forces that are of equal significance to this genre. This division into closure and openness is obviously arbitrary, since no clear distinction can be drawn between an open and a closed text, nor between unifying or fragmenting forces within texts, but my emphasis will, as earlier, be on tendencies, in this case the processes that seem to pull the text apart and those that seem to work towards unity and harmony. It should further be pointed out that many of the unifying features discussed in this chapter are not distinctive solely of the short story composite but may be found in all narratives.

As the previous chapters have made clear, I sense that the critical concern with unity and continuity in the short story composite has been overdetermined, leaving, until recently, its basically fragmentary structure without much consideration. This skewed interest illustrates Kermode's paraphrase of Hershel Parker that "there are so many professional interpreters around, and most of them continue to assume that if a text appears to lack coherence it is their business to demonstrate that the reality is otherwise."[1]

The Order of Things

The desire to enclose seems to be a fundamental human need. To fend off a seemingly chaotic and incomprehensible reality, gestalt psychologists assure us, humankind seeks—by means of philosophy, religion, art, morals, conventions, games, and so on—to establish order, unity, and meaning.[2] Many literary scholars have followed suit by stating that "the impulse to enclose, in short, is a basic property of the mind, inseparable from man's humanness," that "our minds inveterately seek structure," and that "stereotyping *is* perception's normal mode of operation."[3] Smith summarizes the argument succinctly:

> It would seem that in the common land of ordinary events—where many experiences are fragmentary, interrupted, fortuitously connected, and determined by causes beyond our agency or comprehension—we create or seek out 'enclosures': structures that are highly organized, separated as if by an implicit frame from the background of relative disorder or randomness, and integral or complete.[4]

What may be seen then as a fundamental human need has expressed itself in cultural and literary conventions. For centuries after Aristotle's suggestions concerning the ideal unity, coherence, and completeness of literature, writers and critics have followed their instincts and the demands of their culture to structure the world into a harmonious whole.[5]

---

[1] Frank Kermode, "Sensing Endings," *Nineteenth-Century Fiction* 33:1 (June 1978): 144-45.

[2] See Wolfgang Köhler, *Gestalt Psychology* (New York: Liveright, 1947) 204, and Wilhelm Worringer, *Abstraction and Empathy: A Contribution to the Psychology of Style* (New York: International UP, 1953) 44.

[3] Philip Stevick, *The Chapter in Fiction. Theories of Narrative Division* (Syracuse: Syracuse UP, 1970) 10; Seymour Chatman, *Story and Discourse: Narrative Structure in Fiction and Film* (Ithaca, N.Y.: Cornell UP, 1978) 45; Michael Holquist, "Stereotyping in Autobiography and Historiography: Colonialism in *The Great Gatsby*," *Poetics Today* 9:2 (1988): 461.

[4] Barbara Herrnstein Smith, *Poetic Closure. A Study of How Poems End* (Chicago: U of Chicago P, 1968) 2.

[5] See, for instance, G. N. Giordano Orsini, *Organic Unity in Ancient and Later Poetics. The Philosophical Foundations of Literary Criticism* (Carbondale: Southern Illinois UP, 1975) 77-90.

Whether natural or habitual, the human need for gestalts has deeply affected our view of literature. Every critical approach to literature, Stevick holds,

> begins with the prior fact of the mind, accustomed to respond to experience in certain ways, and thus predisposed to respond in certain analogous ways to works of art. Of these analogous responses perhaps none is more important— in experience, in art, in the relation between the two—than the impulse to shape materials into intelligible and satisfying forms. In both the perception of experience and the response to art, one seeks to enclose, to perform the act which, at its simplest, is that basic gestalt formation by which an observer sees three dots and perceives the possibility that they may become corners of a triangle.[6]

The tradition of organicist criticism from Aristotle to Kant to Coleridge to the New Critics has convincingly advocated the integral unity and the internal purposiveness of the work of art,[7] so much so that they for a long time were, and often still are, taken as natural ingredients rather than culturally constructed conventions. The reader's need for a masterplot, characterized by strong closure, made itself apparent over the centuries, first in the form of sacred/providential plots, later, since the eighteenth century, in the emphasis on human plots to order and explain existence.[8]

Man's need for gestalt formation also functions as a conservative force. "The central interest of all human beings," according to Peckham, "is to create a predictable world," and the "goal of social training is to produce predictability," with the consequence that innovation is usually met with resistance.[9] Frames of intelligibility such as literary conventions mold the reader into accepting certain textual patterns and configurations. Over the centuries, as readers we have assimilated certain generic conventions; we have come to expect closure from literary texts. When we recognize a text as, say, Greek tragedy, to take an example from Kenshur, "we expect certain kinds of relationships, namely, causal relationships between a series of described events," and we are then

---

[6] Stevick, *The Chapter in Fiction*, 9-10.

[7] Murray Krieger, *A Reopening of Closure: Organicism against Itself* (New York: Columbia UP, 1989) 43-46, 51.

[8] Peter Brooks, *Reading for the Plot: Design and Intention in Narrative* (Cambridge, Mass.: Harvard UP, 1984) 6, 268.

[9] Morse Peckham, "Art and Disorder," in Richard Kostelanetz, ed., *Esthetics Contemporary* (Buffalo, N.Y.: Prometheus Books, 1978) 100.

predisposed to read the text in that way. Kenshur continues: "All our expectations regarding the types of relationships that will be drawn between the elements of a text are in fact determined by the type of text that we take it to be."[10]

In the historical evolution of genres, some were more fit for survival than others; the novel, for instance, subsumed the romance. And this reductionism had consequences for criticism and college curricula, in which, according to Martin, "the immense range of prose narrative tended to be narrowed down to the novel and the short story."[11] As Iser points out, texts were thus referred to an already existing frame of reference "by means of which the sharpness of a text was inevitably dulled."[12] This means, on the one hand, that over time certain forms of literature with strong closural force have come to be preferred—even though exceptions have always existed—and, on the other, that once genres have been established, the tendency is to categorize texts within such constructed generic boundaries, even if the specific text resists such categorization. Critics have tended to seek unity in apparently disunified texts, and since these critics rarely specify, according to Kenshur, "what sorts of resemblances constitute unity, their attempts to find unifying resemblances can scarcely fail. In short, since resemblances among parts can always be found, it is always possible to claim that any assemblage is 'unified'."[13] The critical treatment of the short story composite is a case in point. Often scholars approaching this form of narrative have attempted to make it align with an already accepted genre, usually the novel. When their expectations of closure, associated with the traditional novel, have not been immediately fulfilled, they have felt a strong urge to impose such closure and unity even on texts that quite explicitly profess indeterminacy and open-endedness. In their wish to make sense of a "chaotic" form, the critics "naturalize" the text by refusing it to remain alien.[14]

---

10 Oscar Kenshur, *Open Form and the Shape of Ideas. Literary Structures as Representations of Philosophical Concepts in the Seventeenth and Eighteenth Centuries* (Lewisburg: Bucknell UP, 1986) 20.

11 Wallace Martin, *Recent Theories of Narrative* (Ithaca, N.Y.: Cornell UP, 1986) 21.

12 Wolfgang Iser, "Indeterminacy and the Reader's Response in Prose Fiction," in J. Hillis Miller, ed., *Aspects of Narrative* (New York: Columbia UP, 1971) 2.

13 Kenshur, 24.

14 See Raman Selden, *A Reader's Guide to Contemporary Literary Theory* (Brighton: Harvester Press, 1985) 13-14.

Plot, Closure, and Coherence

Until recent decades, then, the critical demand for unity and coherence in the text has led to a number of presuppositions: that the text possesses infallibility and complete interpretability; that the inclusion and placing of any particular element of the text can be justified; that the initial equilibrium of the plot may be disturbed on the condition it be returned to final equilibrium; that if gaps and anomalies appear in the text they are due to the failure of the interpreter's skills, and that the more aspects of a work are explained the more successful the interpretation; that works which, in spite of repeated sincere interpretive efforts, resist totalization are at least partial failures.[15]

Closure as a term has been variously used as a synonym for unity and coherence[16] and, more particularly, as denoting the totalizing thematic and textual strategies employed at the end of texts. Smith defines the concept of literary closure in the following way:

> Closure occurs when the concluding portion of a poem creates in the reader a sense of appropriate cessation. It announces and justifies the absence of further development; it reinforces the feeling of finality, completion, and composure which we value in all works of art; and it gives ultimate unity and coherence to the reader's experience of a poem by providing a point from which all the preceding elements may be viewed comprehensively and their relations grasped as part of a significant design.[17]

Closure is characteristic not only of poetry but of all literary texts; it is, indeed, located not merely in the reader's experience but also in the text, as a function of the intentions of the author:

> The writer ... wishes ... that we have no further expectations at the end of the play, novel, or poem, no 'loose ends' to be accounted for, no promises that go begging. The novelist or playwright is likely to end his work at a point when

---

[15] See Krieger, *A Reopening of Closure*, 3, 32-33; Tzvetan Todorov, *The Poetics of Prose* (Ithaca, N.Y.: Cornell UP, 1977) 111; Wendell V. Harris, "Unity" in *Dictionary of Concepts in Literary Criticism and Theory* (New York: Greenwood Press, 1992) 424.

[16] See, for instance, Mariana Torgovnick, *Closure in the Novel* (Princeton, N.J.: Princeton UP, 1981) 6.

[17] Smith, *Poetic Closure*, 36.

either nothing could follow (as when the hero dies) or everything that could follow is predictable (as when the hero and heroine get married).[18]

Discussing Smith's use of the term "closure," Gerlach assures us that it is not applied evaluatively. "More closure," he claims, "is not better closure; the nature and degree of closure has no bearing on the quality of the work as a whole."[19] I am not quite convinced by his assertion. At this stage of Smith's career more closure probably *was* better closure, as it was, and still is, for so many other critics. In the last section of *Poetic Closure*, Smith does discuss "anti-closure," and she has later continued to do so, in, for instance, *On the Margins of Discourse*; but, judging from her rhetoric in *Poetic Closure*, at this point in time she still seemed to consider closure the norm and the ideal of poetry.

Critics have often tended to avoid addressing the issue of openness in art. To generalize, one may claim that the concept of openness as such arouses in many critics suspicion and defensiveness. They point out that all literary texts, however "modern" in technique and thematic irresolution, must come to an end. Making clear his lodestar, Richter writes that "however 'unlimited' the flux of experience portrayed, however expansive the ethical framework, novelists have never quite managed to get around Aristotle's dictum that a work of art must be 'whole, complete, and of a sufficient magnitude'."[20] Richter is not alone among critics in sketching a rather extreme scenario as he takes exception to openness in literature on the basis that it expresses an "open experience" of modern man:

> The ultimate extension of such a view would be that, for a novelist to express a vision of life as chaos, his novel ought to be as chaotic as possible, with no plot at all, inconsistent characters, incomplete thought, and ungrammatical or unfinished sentences—but such a work, if thus written, would not express chaos, for it could express nothing at all. To be expressive, a discourse must minimally be coherent; to be expressive as an aesthetic object, a work must minimally be one whole object, not a fraction of one.[21]

It does not seem to matter to Richter that, as a rule, advocates of open form in literature have not claimed that art should express "a vision of

---

18 Smith, *Poetic Closure*, 35.
19 John Gerlach, *Toward the End. Closure and Structure in the American Short Story* (N.p.: U of Alabama P, 1985) 8.
20 David H. Richter, *Fable's End. Completeness and Closure in Rhetorical Fiction* (Chicago: U of Chicago P, 1974) 4.
21 Richter, 6-7.

life as chaos." With a similar argument and adhering to the same classic norm, Kermode dismisses the "cut-out writers" and the "card-shuffle writers." "A novel which really implemented this policy," he writes, "would properly be a chaos. No novel can avoid being in some sense what Aristotle calls 'a completed action'."[22]

Smith acknowledges in *Poetic Closure* that tension and disruption in a text may instill pleasure in the reader, but only on certain conditions. Openness and indeterminacy are acceptable as a "teasing" of our tensions, as a deferral of "the immediate fulfilment of our appetites and expectations." If there is a "promise of eventual resolution," discontinuity may be a "source of pleasure" (3). Using terms which show that she regards openness as a digression and delay rather than an essential component of literature, Smith writes that

> every disruption of our expectations causes some kind of emotion, and ... the emotion is not unpleasant if we are confident of the presence of design in the total pattern. As we read a poem we are continuously subjected to small surprises and disappointments as the developing lines evade or contradict our expectations. But far from annoying us, this toying with and teasing of our expectations is a major source of our 'excitement'—that is, our pleasure—in literature. If the surprises and disappointments are not finally justified, so to speak, by the total design, then to that extent the poem is a poor one. (14)

Like Smith, other critics appropriate openness into a larger scheme of closure. Barthes argues, for instance, that the "dilatory area" between the beginning and the end of the narrative is a space of retard, postponement, error, and partial revelation that only delays fulfillment of the reader's desire for the end.[23] The term "open work" is avoided by many critics and the concept is often incorporated into the text's closural strategies. By widening closure to include also "the honesty and the appropriateness of the ending's relationship to beginning and middle," Torgovnick manages to make the term all-inclusive. In her discussion of different kinds of closure, she suggests terms like "incomplete closure," "tangential closure," and the "closural strategy" of "linkage," all of which, it seems to me, are just other words for various kinds of openness.[24] In a similar way Lohafer employs the term "deferred cognitive

---

[22] Frank Kermode, *The Sense of an Ending. Studies in the Theory of Fiction* (New York: Oxford UP, 1966) 138.

[23] Roland Barthes, *S/Z* (New York: Hill and Wang, 1974) 75-76.

[24] Torgovnick, 6-13.

closure" for what brings the reader to an "awareness of ramified implications" in a story.[25]

Wright suggests the term "recalcitrance" to designate what would appear to be the concept of openness. He deplores the fact that recalcitrance has been elevated by modern critics, under the name of discontinuity or disruption, a development which has tended to "reject the form that is its reason for being." *Form* is defined by Wright as "a work's unique principle of wholeness." In his discussion of five different forms of "final recalcitrance," Wright makes it particularly clear that he is concerned with what another critic might have termed "open-endedness."[26] From the negative connotations of the term "recalcitrance" and from his Aristotelian view of form as wholeness, it is apparent that Wright's concept of open form resembles that of Smith; he views the discontinuity and resistance of the text only as strategies meant to delay the ideal closure intended by the author.

Closure and Coherence in the Short Story Composite

Human beings evidently harbor a deeply seated desire to induce order and to make literary texts not simply end, but conclude.[27] In all narratives, even such an open work as, say, Gertrude Stein's *Lucy Church Amiably*, there is a measure of coherence and closure. Texts with a complete absence of closure would not make sense. But we must, on the other hand, keep in mind that all literary works also possess a degree of openness.

In spite of the fact that coherence and closure are required genre specifics, in the light of the aesthetic judgments concerning closure above, the short story composite fares less well. In general, this is not a genre characterized by a strong closural force. It poorly fulfills the reader's expectations of finality, coherence, and resolution of conflict. Its endings seldom lead to "retrospective patterning" of the whole work.[28] The writers of short story composites are apparently less willing to follow their natural human impulse to enclose. To some extent they reject the unity and continuity of the traditional novel. They do not, however, see openness as leading to complete chaos, nor do they view it as serving as a

---

25 Susan Lohafer, *Coming to Terms with the Short Story* (Baton Rouge: Louisiana State UP, 1983) 97.

26 Austin M. Wright, "Recalcitrance in the Short Story," in Susan Lohafer and Jo Ellyn Clarey, eds., *Short Story Theory at a Crossroads* (Baton Rouge: Louisiana State UP, 1989) 116-27.

27 See, e.g., Smith, *Poetic Closure*, 2.

28 Smith, *Poetic Closure*, 13; see also Torgovnick, *Closure in the Novel*, 5.

detour on the road to an end. In an evaluation based primarily on closure the composite would end up as inferior art. Indeed, this may explain the marginalization of the genre. Maybe the critical overcommitment to totalizing phenomena in the short story composite has been
caused by its form being unconsciously apprehended as a threat to the
powerful interpretive convention privileging the text's organicism and
harmony. The structure of the composite challenges, it seems, our traditional conception of narratives.

Nevertheless, the short story composite does possess a measure of
closure. Some composites are characterized, as we have seen, by considerably more closure than others, some to such an extent that it makes
them resemble novels. But the "average" composite is more open than
the "average" novel and more closed than the short story collection.
Luscher points out that, in comparison to other genres, "the short story
sequence will ultimately be a looser one, involving us in a more wide-
ranging search for patterns of action and meaning."[29]

Specific to the short story composite is the tension between openness
and closure. To generalize, one may claim that the composite is an open
work consisting of closed stories. Having finished one of the stories, the
reader's sense is often one of closure; having read the whole composite,
his or her final impression is one of openness. As I hope to show below,
the resolution and completeness of each autonomous story is the basic
strategy in the creation of openness in the totality of the work; the "indeterminacy spots" between stories contribute to the strengthening of
closure in the stories. Simultaneously, the connectives between stories,
however tangential, forge a sense of a whole. The individual stories thus
come to possess a double function, a coexistence as independent entities
and as partially integrated segments of a totality.

Starting with the totality of the short story composite, the complete
unit consisting of subordinate parts/stories, we find that, on the one hand,
there are numerous narrative strategies in the composite which work in
favor of closure, and, on the other, that the closural force varies significantly from one end of the continuum to the other. Critics like Ingram,
Mann, and Dunn/Morris have charted many of such unifying elements as
setting, focalizer, character, theme, myth, metaphor, and tone. Below I
will pay particular attention to the way and degree to which such centripetal forces as end-orientation, retrospective patterning, intratextuality,
narrativity, and framing are manifested in the short story composite.

---

[29] Robert M. Luscher, "The Short Story Sequence: An Open Book," in Lohafer and
Clarey, eds., *Short Story Theory at a Crossroads*, 157.

Most narratives are both prospective and retrospective, both oriented forward and backward.[30] But some narratives possess a higher degree of this double orientation than others, the novel much more so than the short story composite. Generally speaking, the composite is less prospective in its orientation; it is, as a composite, not as end-oriented as the short story or the novel. The unifying force in the short story composite is rather a retrospective one, a repeated backward glance from one story to the preceding one/s. However, the end of a composite serves a less retrospective function than the end of a novel.

End-Orientation
Narrative is conventionally held to be striving for an ultimate finality. At the end of Aristotle's plot waited *anagnorisis*, the recognition that brought illumination and secured the tragic effect. The passion for meaning, according to Barthes, ignites the reader's desire for the end.[31] "Reading a narrative is waiting for the end," Prince postulates, "and the quality of the waiting is the quality of the narrative."[32] And paraphrasing Sartre, Brooks states:

> The very possibility of meaning plotted through sequence and through time depends on the anticipated structuring force of the ending: the interminable would be meaningless, and the lack of ending would jeopardize the beginning. We read the incidents of narration as "promises and annunciations" of final coherence, that metaphor that may be reached through the chain of metonymies: across the bulk of the as yet unread middle pages, the end calls to the beginning, transforms and enhances it.[33]

This drive forward through the text is, however, seriously disturbed and diverted in the short story composite. Its paratactic structure of autonomous, closed stories with wide interstices leaves the reader's desire for an end challenged, creating in her or him an insecurity concerning how the composite will actually conclude. The numerous story lines of the individual stories, the metonymies if you like, seldom merge into the metaphor Brooks is envisioning. Even at the next to last story in a composite, the reader often has little sense of how the end will be consti-

---

[30] See Martin, *Recent Theories of Narrative*, 127.

[31] Roland Barthes, "Introduction to the Structural Analysis of Narratives," *A Barthes Reader*, ed. Susan Sontag (New York: Hill and Wang, 1982) 261, 267.

[32] Gerald Prince, *Narratology: The Form and Functioning of Narrative* (Berlin: Mouton, 1982) 157.

[33] Brooks, *Reading for the Plot*, 93-94.

tuted. To take just two examples, in Welty's *The Golden Apples* there is no single plot that unites the stories and drives the reader toward a resolution; the last story, "The Wanderers," does bring a fair degree of closure to the composite, but while reading the next but last story, "Music from Spain," located not in Morgana like all the other stories but in California, we have little or no awareness of how the whole composite will end. On the other hand, a "sequence" like *The Unvanquished* exhibits greater prospective movement in its following the growth of one protagonist, Bayard Sartoris, but remains nevertheless less forward-oriented than the traditional novel.

Certain narrative strategies work in favor of resolution. By pointing forward, *prolepsis* and *foreshadowing* prepare the reader for what is to come. By prolepsis Genette means "any narrative maneuver that consists of narrating or evoking in advance an event that will take place later."[34] The author is telling the future before its time, sometimes even notifying the reader about what he or she is doing. Genette makes a distinction between *external* and *internal* prolepsis based on whether the event is taking place without or within the "first narrative." He further divides internal prolepsis into *completing* prolepsis, which fills in ahead of time a later blank, and *repeating* prolepsis, which doubles a narrative section to come (71). The latter, also called *advance notice*, refers briefly in advance to an event that will later be told in full. Such repeating prolepses are sometimes employed at the end of novel chapters to give notice of what is to come. All forms of prolepsis are explicit in the sense that the reader is made aware of their futurity. The short story composite never openly orients the reader forward from one story to another, and hardly ever looks forward at all. Prolepsis, it is true, is not a common device in any narrative, but in the composite it is always absent. Such statements as "we shall meet him again, ... much later in the course of our story"[35] are an impossibility in a short story composite, which insists on the discreteness of its stories.[36] This absence of prolepsis is yet another anti-closural factor which contributes to the composite's open-endedness.

---

[34] Gérard Genette, *Narrative Discourse: An Essay in Method* (Ithaca, N.Y.: Cornell UP, 1980) 40. Chatman's term for this strategy is *flashforward*, see *Story and Discourse*, 64.

[35] Example from Proust used by Genette in *Narrative Discourse*, 74-75.

[36] An exception to the rule may be found in "Mother" in Anderson's *Winesburg, Ohio*, in which George Willard informs his mother that he eventually will leave town, thereby telling in advance what will happen in "Departure." See Anderson, *Winesburg, Ohio* (New York: Viking Press, 1960) 47.

Genette makes a clear distinction between *advance notice*, or repeating prolepsis, and *advance mention*. The latter is not really a prolepsis but rather a form of "preparation" (75), giving hints to the reader of what might come. This narrative "seed" is only fully understood in retrospect, when the anticipation is satisfied. In the creation of suspense, which prepares the reader for the resolution, these seeds, or "anticipatory satellites,"[37] are a necessary ingredient. *Foreshadowing*, as this strategy is also termed, thus contributes to closure.

This strategy of "preparation" and anticipation does occur in short story composites, but to a much smaller degree than in the novel. In the traditional narrative of resolution, suspense is created by the reader's urge to know "what will happen next." In composites, as in many modernist texts, the plot is rather one of revelation, where the goal is not primarily to resolve events but to reveal a state of affairs.[38] The *delay* of the text creates suspense of two different types, *future-oriented* and *past-oriented*, the former keeping alive the question of what the final outcome will be, the latter giving rise to questions like "What happened?","Who did it?," "What is the meaning of all this?" Short story composites are not concerned with resolving problems and coming to an end. They are rather unsuspenseful narratives revealing an incomplete world; the reader is encouraged to ask how characters, themes, and symbols of one story are related to those of the preceding ones. The very structure of the text obviates the plot-centered continuities on which foreshadowing rests.

Narrative "seeds" are planted also in short story composites even if the practice is less common than in traditional novels. The seemingly random introduction of Ike McCaslin at the beginning of "Was" in *Go Down, Moses* leads the trained reader to expect this character to play an important part later in the book. The repeated focus on the wall in Naylor's *The Women of Brewster Place* makes us anticipate that wall to be central in the resolution of the composite. However, numerous short story composites refuse to employ such anticipatory satellites.

Because of its discontinuous structure, its multiple focalizers and themes, the short story composite often does not make use of such a closural device as advance mention or foreshadowing. In the well-balanced novel, the end is contained in the beginning; not so in the composite where the reader in the beginning gets few indications of how the text will develop and even fewer of how it will end. Taking part of the first stories of *In Our Time*, the reader gets signals of a *Bildungszyklus*, but

---

[37] See Chatman, *Story and Discourse*, 59.

[38] See Chatman, *Story and Discourse*, 48.

this initial preparation ceases when we reach the non-Nick stories. Moreover, the first stories contain no anticipatory satellites in the form of objects, symbols or events which in retrospect will turn out to be part of a unifying strategy. To take another example: initially we cannot know that Virgie Rainey will play such a central role at the end of Welty's *The Golden Apples*. It is true that she is a central character in "June Recital," but then she disappears completely—not even her name is mentioned— for the next four stories, only to resurface as the focalizer of the last story. If the composite had followed the same anticipatory strategy as the traditional novel, it would have been more "natural" for Welty to choose either King MacLain or his son Ran as focalizer of the closing story, since they have been continuously present. Welty, however, rejects such a pattern of preparation and predictability and marginalizes both King and his son in "The Wanderers."

Retrospective Patterning
Arriving at the end of a narrative means, according to many critics, experiencing a sense of finality, a regained equilibrium, and a stasis which equals the expectation of nothing. This desire for closure is an "internalized expectation" of patterns we have experienced in life.[39] At the same time, the sense of ultimate composure of the ending, that metaphoric moment, triggers an orientation backward through the text. We value endings of texts, Torgovnick suggests, because in reading them we make use of the very process that characterizes life in general, a "retrospective patterning" aimed at making sense of past events; appreciating endings is "one way of evaluating and organizing personal experience."[40]

The critical agreement on the retrospectivity of narratives seems almost unanimous. According to Leitch, a primary function of narrative endings is to "provide or confirm a teleology or retrospective rationale for the story as a whole," and stories which lack such endings, he points out, are often considered unsatisfactory.[41] The totalizing final metaphor, Brooks writes, determines the meaning of the preceding metonymies of the text:

---

[39] Lohafer, *Coming to Terms with the Short Story*, 96.
[40] Torgovnick, *Closure in the Novel*, 5.
[41] Thomas M. Leitch, *What Stories Are: Narrative Theory and Interpretation* (University Park: Pennsylvania State UP, 1986) 43.

It is the role of fictional plots to impose an end which yet suggests a return, a new beginning, a rereading. Any narrative, that is, wants at its end to refer back to its middle, to the web of the text: to recapture us in its doomed energies.[42]

Maybe any narrative desires this retrospectivity, but certain narratives like the short story composite, it seems to me, desire it less than others. The short story composite possesses a comparatively strong retrospective force, a feature I will return to in a moment, but this backward totalizing glance is not cast in particular at the end of the whole composite. The last story of a composite does not to the same degree as the ending of a novel make the reader reassess the whole work; it does not attempt to tuck in all the loose ends of the various stories. The final stories of Amy Tan's *Joy Luck Club*, Ursula LeGuin's *Orsinian Tales* or Louise Erdrich's *Love Medicine* evoke little retrospective desire. In other composites, however, like Doctorow's *Lives of the Poets*—in which the last story solves the riddle of the connection between the preceding ones— the retrospective process is made the structuring principle of the whole composite. But in general the short story composite exhibits at its end a less strong backward orientation than the traditional novel.

But if retrospectivity is comparatively insignificant at the end of the short story composite, it is the more actively in use in the continuous reading process. Barbara Herrnstein Smith writes that

> the reader's experience is not only continuous over a period of time, but continuously changes in response to succeeding events. As we read, structural principles, both formal and thematic, are gradually deployed and perceived; and as these principles make themselves known, we are engaged in a steady process of readjustment and retrospective patterning.[43]

The reader views, according to Iser, the "themes" (perspective segments) succeeding each other in the narrative against the "horizon" of what has gone before, readjusting his understanding of the past action as he or she goes along. Iser writes:

> Our attitude toward each theme is influenced by the horizon of past themes, and as each theme itself becomes part of the horizon during the time-flow of our reading, so it, too, exerts an influence on subsequent themes. Each change

---

[42] Brooks, *Reading for the Plot*, 29, 109-10.
[43] Smith, *Poetic Closure*, 10.

denotes not a loss but an enrichment, as attitudes are at one and the same time refined and broadened.[44]

Luscher makes such retrospective patterning the basis for his definition of the short short story sequence/composite: "a volume of stories, collected and organized by their author, in which the reader successively realizes underlying patterns of coherence by continual modifications of his perceptions of pattern and theme."[45] However, even though such sequential modification is central to the short story composite, it is not exclusive to this form of narrative and therefore less appropriate as a ground for definition. On the other hand, one can argue that the *degree* of continuous retrospective patterning is one of several generic features of the short story composite. The reader becomes even more implicated than in a novel in the attempt to close the narrative, by connecting recurring elements and filling the gaps of its fragmented structure. It is consequently not so much the retrospective patterning that defines the short story composite as the *degree* to which the reader becomes involved in trying, often unsuccessfully, to unify the text. Because of the autonomy of the individual stories and the often considerable gaps between them, the reader is faced with a more demanding task than when reading a novel in overcoming the resistance of the new context and perspective of each story and forming retrospectively a pattern of connectives. There are simply not that many backward links in most composites, nor a very clear horizon, to speak with Iser, against which to posit the new themes. In the subgenre I call "sequence" such interlockings may yield a comparatively unified pattern, but in most short story composites long stretches of the horizon are hidden from view.

For all their autonomy, the individual stories interlock with preceding and subsequent stories, creating bridges and enjambments, which to a degree strengthen the reader's expectations of ultimate cessation. The separate story transcends its own boundaries to establish more jointure with previous than subsequent stories. Proceeding from one story to the next, the reader experiences an expansion or modification which causes the earlier stories to gain an added dimension. In his discussion of horizon and theme, Iser holds that every perspective segment/theme of the text is a "two-way glass":

---

44 Wolfgang Iser, *The Act of Reading: A Theory of Aesthetic Response* (Baltimore: Johns Hopkins UP, 1978) 96-103.
45 Robert M. Luscher, "The Short Story Sequence: An Open Book," in Lohafer and Clarey, eds., *Short Story Theory at a Crossroads*, 148-49.

each segment appears against the others and is therefore not only itself but also a reflection and an illuminator of those others. Each individual position is thus expanded and changed by its relation to the others, for we view it from all the perspectives that constitute the horizon.[46]

If the "perspective segment" is expanded to mean a short story, Iser's statement sheds light on the "double existence" of the stories in the short story composite—while being themselves they yet function as reflections and illuminators of all the stories that constitute the horizon.

Hemingway's "Big Two-Hearted River," for instance, sheds light on earlier stories of *In Our Time*, particularly those explicitly about Nick, making these stories transcend their boundaries as discrete items; and the preceding stories, the horizon, affect the reading of the last story of the composite. Simultaneously, it must be remembered, "Big Two-Hearted River" exists as a self-sufficient story, originally published as a discrete narrative. This "doubleness" is occasionally deliberately exploited by authors of composites. In "The Wanderers," the concluding story of *The Golden Apples*, for example, Welty foregrounds this doubleness by playing with the question of knowledge:

> Eugene, for a long interval, had lived in another part of the world, learning while he was away that people don't have to be answered just because they want to know. His very wife was never known here, and he did not make it plain whether he had children somewhere now or had been childless. His wife did not even come to the funeral, although a telegram had been sent. A foreigner? "Why, she could even be a Dago and we wouldn't know it." (458)

Welty here asks readers to close the story by giving them an epistemological advantage. She knows that we know from "Music from Spain" that Eugene lived in California, with his wife Emma, who was not a foreigner, and with his daughter Fan, who died young. Our preknowledge thus changes the story we are reading at the moment. The story thus exists on two textual levels at the same time, as autonomous item and as part of a totality.

This often intricate weave of stories, a weave on more than one textual level, may be regarded as a deliberate encouragement from the author to the reader to close the work, but only, I would argue, to a degree. The reader is always invited to fill up the empty spaces of a text, to take what Eco calls "inferential walks."[47] The reader is supposed to speculate a-

---

[46] Iser, *The Act of Reading*, 98.
[47] Umberto Eco, *The Role of the Reader: Explorations in the Semiotics of Texts* (Bloomington: Indiana UP, 1984) 214-17.

bout the fulfillment of the sentence or the fabula; he or she is expected, and allowed, to try to fill the "holes" of the text. He or she is on occasion even lured into writing his or her own "ghost chapter."[48] But it seems to me that the use of this closural strategy is generally not very pronounced in short story composites. Many critics have tried to take rather lengthy "inferential walks" in order to fill up the often very obvious spaces of a composite. Some have even endeavored to construe "ghost chapters" between the stories in order to establish the wholeness and finality that satisfy their need for order. I am convinced, however, that these critics by and large have accepted an invitation that was never expressly extended by the author. By creating wide, often unbridgeable gaps between stories, the authors of short story composites seem rather to resist too much co-authorship from the reader. The spaces are not meant, it seems to me, to be completely filled; the Aristotelian norm of coherence and resolution is questioned and the desire for an end thwarted. The narrative thus resists being naturalized to the same degree that often happens in a novel; the reader is less successful in filling in gaps or adjusting events and existents into a coherent whole.[49]

Intratextuality, Narrativity, Framing
One dimension of retrospective patterning is what Todorov terms "intratextuality" and "figuration."[50] There may exist, Todorov points out, intratextual links between one text and another by the same author. These links make up a figuration; the reader reads the text as a palimpsest, a commentary on an earlier text by the same author. In many cases the second text stands in a syntagmatic relationship to the first in that it reacts actively; the first, external text provokes or modifies the latter. It seems to me that Todorov's schema may not only be applied to an author's *oeuvre*, but also to a narrative like the short story composite which has a structure that resembles an *oeuvre* in that it consists of autonomous, interlocking texts by the same author. The sense of coherence in a composite is dependent on intratextuality and the stories exist in general in a syntagmatic relationship.

One centripetal narrative force is what Prince terms narrativity, the assumption that some narratives tell a better story than others,[51] a characteristic intimately related to and dependent on closure, end-orientation, and retrospective patterning. A high degree of narrativity is the re-

---

[48] Eco, *The Role of the Reader,* 252-56.
[49] Chatman, *Story and Discourse*, 49.
[50] Todorov, *The Poetics of Prose*, 241-45.
[51] Prince, *Narratology*, 145-60.

sult, according to Prince, of the narrative's emphasis on, for instance, events, temporality, an ongoing conflict, concreteness, and relevance of content. It is also dependent on whether the narrative has a "complete structure" of beginning, middle, and end:

> A narrative where there is no continuant subject, no relationship between beginning and end, no (ex-planatory) description of a change in a given situation, a narrative made up of middles, as it were, has practically no narrativity. (151)

The digressive elements of a narrative, those that cannot be "meaningfully" related, are narratively "inert," threaten narrative coherence and "impair" narrativity (159). The narrative that lacks a "point" has a "low degree of narrativity indeed" (159). Applying Prince's rules of what makes a good story to the short story composite, one must draw the conclusion that it no doubt has a low degree of narrativity. Each short story may have a high degree of narrativity, but taken together as a composite they do not. With its lack of emphasis on continuing plot, unifying chronology, "complete structure" of beginning-middle-end, with its many digressive elements and its "pointlessness," the composite scores less well in Prince's totalizing schema than do most novels. But as Prince himself acknowledges, a high degree of narrativity does not necessarily make a better narrative.

The structure of the short story composite, more paratactic in nature than that of the novel, often demands a frame to create closure. As Smith puts it, "a generating principle that produces a paratactic structure cannot in itself determine a concluding point. Consequently, the reader will have no idea from the poem's [composite's] structure how or when it will conclude."[52] Therefore a paratactic structure is often enclosed by a frame.[53] There are instances of such framing in all subgenres of the short story composite, but the most common subgenre in which such enclosing takes place is the "novella," narratives like *Winesburg, Ohio*, *Lost in the Funhouse*, *A Night at the Movies*, and *Olinger Stories*. However, several narratives of the subgenre "cycle," such as *The Pastures of Heaven* and *The Women of Brewster Place*, gain closural strength from such frames. This totalizing strategy seems less prevalent in what I term "sequences" and "clusters."

---

[52] Smith, *Poetic Closure*, 100-101.
[53] Viktor Shklovsky has shown in *Theory of Prose* (Elmwood Park, IL: Dalhey Archive Press, 1990) how early collections of stories and loosely constructed novels were held together by means of "framing" and "threading" devices (65-69).

The closural strategies discussed above are present in short story composites to a higher or lesser degree. A small number of composites are characterized by a relatively high degree of closure. These are works possessing a strong presence of causality, temporality, and retrospective structuring, often ending with inversion of problem and resolution of conflict. These semi-closed works are mostly to be found in the sub-genres I term "sequences" and "cycles."

John Steinbeck's *The Pastures of Heaven*[54] contains numerous unifying elements which contribute to the reader's sense of partial finality at the end of the book. The twelve sections/stories are numbered like chapters in a novel, instead of given individual titles. The independent stories are enclosed within a frame, sections One and Twelve, the first of which introduces Las Pasturas del Cielo and invests the valley with paradisiacal expectations, while the last section takes the reader out of the valley, showing him the illusory quality of these dreams of an edenic existence. In the stories within the frame we are exposed to the tragedies and sufferings of many individuals and families in the midst of the valley's beautiful opulence. The unity of place and the recurrence of characters, like the Munroe family, also serve to create continuity and coherence. In addition, the book possesses a sense of temporality and causality: the individual stories are often put into a historical context, and the actions of a character in one story find illumination and explanation in another. The description, for instance, of the school teacher Mary Morgan's background in section Eight explains her actions in sections Four and Six, a very explicit example of retrospective patterning.

At the same time, the closural force of *The Pastures of Heaven* is never allowed to become as strong as it is in most novels. Instead of having a major character whose psychological growth is recorded, Steinbeck uses a multiplicity of characters of lesser stature. Instead of depicting a major conflict to be resolved, he presents multiple conflicts which are seldom brought to a resolution.

To take a more recent example, Gloria Naylor in *The Women of Brewster Place* (1982)[55] employs, like Steinbeck, the closural strategy of framing; the composite is introduced by a section in italics, "Dawn," and closed by a coda, "Dusk," also in italics. "Dawn" describes the birth of Brewster Place, a street in New York, and its development from a neighborhood of Mediterranean immigrants to a black ghetto. It tells of how Brewster Place has become walled off from the main street and become

---

[54] Steinbeck, *The Pastures of Heaven* (New York: Brewer, Warren and Putnam, 1932).

[55] Naylor, *The Women of Brewster Place* (New York: Viking Press, 1982).

a "dead-end street"; throughout the composite the wall and the dead-end street are symbols of the black female experience. The concluding section, "Dusk," depicts the death of Brewster Place, how its residents move out and the area is condemned.

The last chapter, immediately preceding the coda, called "The Block Party," serves to reinforce the book's sense of closure. Six of the seven stories within the frame are devoted to the fates of individual black women; the further the reader proceeds into the book, the more intratextual links emerge between protagonists and locales. One person, Mattie, appears in all the stories and thus serves as one of the main agents in the ongoing retrospective process. In the last story, Naylor brings all the women of the preceding stories together. She shows what women could do if they join forces; they start demolishing the hated wall that has closed them in as blacks and above all as women. This bringing together of the women gives the reader clear closural signals, which are then strengthened even further in the ensuing coda.

The ending of the book, however, does not provide the reader with the sense of metaphoric finality that it first seems to promise. Tearing down the oppressive wall in the final story appears to be the fulfillment of a long dream, but instead it turns out to be merely a dream, which takes place in Mattie's sleep. The initial sense of cessation is thereby challenged; nothing has been resolved for the women of Brewster Place, no real progress has been made. The title of the coda, "Dusk," points in two directions: at first sight it seems to announce the completion of the day, and thus a sense of finality and fulfillment, but it soon becomes clear that it also represents the perpetual dusk in which the black women of Brewster Place—and The United States—have to continue living. It is true that Brewster Place is dead, but neither the individual nor the social problems are dead. Mattie and her friends have moved to another Brewster Place, but the morning light is nowhere in sight.

In addition to this lack of resolution, Naylor's book is characterized by such generic features of the composite as gaps between the stories, absence of one central character or focalizer, lack of major conflict and decisive turning-point. Taken together, such unifying and disunifying elements create a book that, when viewed side by side with other short story composites, gives the impression of being comparatively closed, but which, against the backdrop of traditional novels, remains relatively open.

The final story of William Faulkner's *The Unvanquished*,[56] "An Odor of Verbena," creates in the reader "a sense of appropriate cessation," to

---

56 Faulkner, *The Unvanquished* (1934; New York: Random House, 1965).

use Smith's phrase. The composite exhibits both prospectivity and retro-spectivity. We have followed the growth of the book's focalizer, Bayard Sartoris, to the resolution of the conflict and the inversion of disintegra-tion into tentative stability. Bayard refuses not out of fear but out of newly gained maturity to take revenge on his father's murderer. He thereby breaks the pattern of violence and corruption prevalent in the preceding stories. As readers we have few further expectations, and there are few loose ends to be accounted for. This sense of completion has been prepared for by such unifying factors as the strict chronology ad-hered to, the use of the same focalizer throughout, and the retrospective patterning caused by the many back-references between the stories. Compared to, for instance, Faulkner's own *Go Down, Moses, The Un-vanquished* then stands out as a work of a rather high degree of integra-tion and closure. Nevertheless, its stories are autonomous, and there are considerable breaks in the chronology, anti-closural features which make the book a short story composite rather than a novel.

One particular narrative strategy that contributes to the sense of coher-ence in *The Unvanquished* is the retrospective linking or enjambment that takes place in the repetition of "unnecessary" or "redundant" infor-mation. This reiteration of material may be seen as either a closural force or as a device creating openness, depending on the perspective from which it is regarded. In all the stories of *The Unvanquished* except the last, Faulkner gives a synopsis of central aspects of the plot up to that point. Thus, the first paragraphs of, for instance, "Raid," "Vendée," and "Skirmish at Sartoris" contain recapitulations, with added details, of pre-vious events. Such "repeating analepses" or "recalls"[57] contribute ac-tively to the strengthening of the text's retrospectivity. This information is "unnecessary" if we see the book as a sequence of stories to be read consecutively; as we already possess this information, it serves as a strong linking device between the stories, a strategy that ultimately works toward an increased sense of closure. On the other hand, looking at these repeating analepses from the point of view of the individual story, they are necessary for an understanding if we are to read that story as an autonomous text. When thus regarded, the reiteration serves to make the story relatively self-sufficient and independent of the other stories; it thereby satisfies our need for closure in the individual story. It thereby becomes a device that widens the gaps between the stories and thus reinforces the anti-closure of the composite as a whole. The double function of such repeated synopses is not exclusive to Faulkner but may be found in many other composites such as Welty's *The Golden Apples*,

---

[57] See Genette, *Narrative Discourse*, 54.

Susan Kenney's *In Another Country*, and Jayne Anne Phillips' *Machine Dreams*.[58] In the first pages of the concluding story of *The Golden Apples*, "The Wanderers," Welty reminds the reader of family relations and previous events already familiar to him; Phillips repeats in "Anniversary Song: Jean, 1948" information about the female protagonist which has already been given in previous sections devoted to Jean. Without such "redundant" material these stories could not be able to achieve autonomy.

Like *The Unvanquished*, Susan Kenney's short story "sequence" *In Another Country*[59] is made to cohere by means of surplus information and by the use of one single narrator and a linear chronology. The focalizer, Sara, becomes central to an extent that is unusual in composites; in most composites a multiplicity of characters compete for the central focalizing position. Her experience of and relationship to her father and his death, to the mental disorders of her mother, and to the serious illness of her husband Phil, give the book a high degree of unity and closure. At the same time, *In Another Country* remains a comparatively open work. The final story, "The Death of the Dog and Other Rescues," does end in the death of the family dog, but the more burning question of whether Phil, the husband and father, will survive is not resolved. Even though the self-sufficient stories are fairly well integrated, there are significant temporal and causal gaps between them. The theme of the instability of life and the unreliability of experience—"it's all done with mirrors" is an echo heard throughout the book—is illustrated in the semi-open form of the composite.

In the majority of short story composites, however, the closural strategies are much less prominent than in the ones discussed so far. It is true that Hemingway's *In Our Time* can be seen as cyclical in that Nick returns to America to recuperate after his shattering war experience, if this is the way to read the story. But if we look at the book in its entirety, it is characterized by less coherence than a novel. The first Nick stories point to a prospective movement, but the reader's sense of end-orientation is soon diverted in the non-Nick stories and at as late a stage in the narrative as "My Old Man" the end of the composite can certainly not be predicted. The intratextual links are likewise much more common in the first part of the book than in the latter. Even though there is a certain sense of "appropriate cessation" or finality, Hemingway leaves many loose ends unaccounted for; the end does not really provide "a point from which all the preceding elements may be viewed comprehensively

---

58 Phillips, *Machine Dreams* (London: Faber and Faber, 1984) 101, 106.
59 Susan Kenney, *In Another Country* (New York: Penguin, 1985).

and their relations grasped as part of a significant design."[60] The critical disagreement on the structure and design of *In Our Time* testifies to the relative absence of final coherence. Still, it is clear that "Big Two-Hearted River" functions as not merely an end but a close to the book; it lends a measure—though a limited measure—of closure to Hemingway's composite.

E. L. Doctorow's *Lives of the Poets*[61] constitutes another example of tenuous closure. The reader finds few links between the first six stories of the volume; they simply do not seem to connect or interlock. But well into the title story, which concludes the book, it dawns on him or her that the writer protagonist of that story, Jonathan, is the author of the preceding stories, since allusions occur in passing to events already dealt with.[62] However, the closural force never becomes particularly strong. A careless reader could easily miss the offhand references to the other stories, and to one of them, "The Water Works," there is, as far as I can judge, no reference at all. One might say that Jonathan's dilemma in the final story comes to a tentative resolution, but that is a resolution which does not include the remainder of the stories. The openness of the whole work remains; the expectations of the reader concerning the first six stories are not fulfilled when the stories are seen as part of the composite.

When it comes to such loosely joined works as John Barth's *Lost in the Funhouse*[63] and Robert Coover's *A Night at the Movies*,[64] the closural element is restricted almost entirely to the framing device and thematic similarities. One may ask oneself if Barth's book would have been experienced as a composite if the frame had not been explicitly present in the "frame tale," or if Barth himself had not insisted on the "serial nature"[65] of the volume. One may further wonder if Coover's stories had been seen as a series of interrelated stories if the author had not supplied the title and the explanatory table of contents, which make

---

[60] Smith, *Poetic Closure*, 36.

[61] Doctorow, *Lives of the Poets* (New York: Random House, 1984).

[62] Hemingway evidently played with the possibility of a similar structure for *In Our Time*. See Debra A. Moddelmog, "The Unifying Consciousness of a Divided Conscience: Nick Adams as Author of *In Our Time*," *American Literature* 60:4 (December 1988): 591-610.

[63] John Barth, *Lost in the Funhouse. Fiction for Print, Tape, Live Voice* (New York: Doubleday, 1968).

[64] Robert Coover, *A Night at the Movies; Or, You Must Remember This* (London: Paladin, 1987).

[65] See "Author's Note," *Lost in the Funhouse*, ix-xi.

the stories part of the billing of a movie house. In a similar way one may question if the reader would have been acute enough to experience *Mr. Bedford and the Muses*[66] as a composite if Gail Godwin had not produced closure by explaining in an afterword, "Author's Note," how the stories are interconnected by representing different kinds of muses.

Closure in the Composite Story

The short story composite as a genre is thus more open than closed. In a continuum from closure to openness, a majority of the composites would fall closer to the latter pole than the former. The separate stories of the short story composite, however, are not characterized by the openness that characterizes the whole work. With few exceptions, the self-sufficient story has a large measure of closure, and in this respect the story in the short story composite is distinguished from the chapter in the novel, which by comparison is open in its signals to the reader that there will be a continuity. Even if chapters in novels often express completion, as Stevick has shown,[67] by means of devices such as ending with a cadence, or narrowing or broadening the focus, the degree of closure is limited in comparison to that of the story in the composite. In the separate stories of the composite, as Susan G. Mann puts it, "the sense of closure is still more definite than the end of chapters in contemporary novels."[68]

The short story, as Gerlach points out, is generally end-oriented; the structure of the whole is determined by the anticipation of the ending.[69] According to Lohafer, the short story is the most "end-conscious" of literary forms: it binds the reader more closely to the sentence[70]; it is distinguished by "its shorter span, its 'foregrounded' end."[71] The short story has thus been considered to possess what Leitch calls *imminent*

---

[66] Gail Godwin, *Mr. Bedford and the Muses* (New York: Viking, 1983).

[67] Stevick, *The Chapter in Fiction*, 47-57.

[68] Mann, *The Short Story Cycle*, 18.

[69] Gerlach, *Toward the End. Closure and Structure in the American Short Story*, 3. See also Wallace Stegner, *Teaching the Short Story* (Davis, Cal.: Department of English, UC, 1965) 11, and Hans H. Skei, *William Faulkner. The Novelist as Short Story Writer: A Study of William Faulkner's Short Fiction* (Oslo: Universitetsforlaget, 1985) 21-22.

[70] Lohafer, *Coming to Terms with the Short Story*, 50.

[71] Lohafer, "Introduction to Part III," in Lohafer and Clarey, eds., *Short Story Theory at a Crossroads*, 110. See also Norman Friedman, "Recent Short Story Theories: Problems in Definitions" in in the same volume, 28-29.

teleology in that the reader anticipates a revelatory ending.[72] Short stories tend to focus on a central problem or an "epiphanic moment"[73] and to strive for what Poe called the "single effect"; conflicts are resolved and there are few possible loose ends left untied. In elaborating various forms of "terminations," Gerlach makes the following distinction between the novel and the short story:

> The novel customarily announces its theme clearly and advances and develops it symphonically—repeating, doubling, contrasting, breaking apart, and reassembling the theme; the short story, merely in showing it has a theme, sometimes comes to its end, the completion of its purpose, as if in merely revealing a leap from the particular to the general, the story has fulfilled its purpose and might cease.[74]

Short stories are, obviously, not closed by definition—one may only point to the stories of Coover's *Pricksongs and Descants*, Barthelme's *City Life*, LeGuin's *Searoad* or Welty's *The Wide Net* [75]—but the short story seems more dependent on compressed finality than the novel. As Gerlach points out, one composite may consist of both open ("incomplete") and closed stories. In Anderson's *Winesburg, Ohio,* for instance, "Hands" presents little growth of character and no resolution, whereas the other stories in the same volume do. Some of the stories in Hemingway's *In Our Time* are "compressed" stories highlighting a small incident, forcing the reader to imagine a larger context. "Hemingway's endings," Gerlach comments, "are not the goal toward which all of the story is clearly directed."[76] Nevertheless, even open stories like "The Doctor and the Doctor's Wife" and "The End of Something" appear to possess relatively much closure when seen in contrast to the open form of the whole of *In Our Time*.

The individual stories in a composite may even appear more closed as a result of the temporal and causal gaps between the stories. The measure of closure at the end of a story is enhanced when the reader con-

---

[72] Thomas M. Leitch, "The Debunking Rhythm of the American Short Story," in Lohafer and Clarey, eds., *Short Story Theory at a Crossroads*, 131-32.

[73] See Friedman, "Recent Short Story Theories," in Lohafer and Clarey, 21-22.

[74] Gerlach, *Toward the End. Closure and Structure in the American Short Story*, 12.

[75] Susan V. Donaldson says about the stories in *The Wide Net* that they "question the possibility of achieving any sort of resolution. If they shimmer with anticipation and yearning, it is because that anticipation ultimately remains unfulfilled." See Kennedy, ed., *Modern American Short Story Sequences*, 104.

[76] Gerlach, 110.

tinues to the next and realizes that there is little linkage back to the preceding story; the implicit "enjambment" from one chapter to another so common in a novel is missing. The reader must address a new context, maybe a new focalizer and new characters; he or she must, in short, familiarize him/herself with a new world. The first sentences of a story are composed of anticlosural elements; they are characterized by a high degree of "recalcitrance," i.e. the material resists being shaped by the reader. We often find ourselves catapulted into a new world full of initially obscure references.[77] This re-orientation demanded of the reader also reinforces his or her impression of closure in the preceding story. One could very well imagine that the following story at its beginning deliberately referred back to the preceding one, a device which would strengthen the impression of that story's continuity; this, however, is not a practice common to the short story composite. Thus a double perspective is noticeable. The sense of resolution at the end of a story in a composite closes the separate story, but this sense of finality simultaneously may make the whole work more open, since the closure at the end of each story widens the gap to the next one.

At the beginning of a short story composite, the reader is often not given enough signals to know what to expect after the first story. With little preknowledge the reader is faced with generic expectations of whether the book will turn out to be a novel, a short story collection, or a composite. Arriving at the second story, the reader of the average composite receives signals that instead of reading a novel, s/he is rather faced with a collection of stories. In most composites the second story resists the first. As the first sentences of a story show recalcitrance, later to be overcome, so the first stories of a composite exhibit quite extensive anti-closural strategies. Not until the first few linkages appear, usually far into the second or third story, does the reader begin to suspect that the text is not a collection of stories but a composite. At the beginning, however, of the second, autonomous story, when he or she has not yet encountered the first conjoining elements and when the process of retrospective patterning has not been activated, s/he experiences a deepened sense of closure in the first story. Miller argues that a given apparently closed text may easily be reopened; Trollope, Gaskell, and Woolf first published novels characterized by closure only to later publish novels

---

[77] See Lohafer, *Coming to Terms with the Short Story*, 52-55, and Wright, "Recalcitrance in the Short Story," in Lohafer and Clarey, eds., *Short Story Theory at a Crossroads*, 117-18.

which continue the plotlines of the previous ones.[78] In the same manner, the second story of a short story composite could easily reopen the first, but in most composites this does not happen; this "reopening" usually takes place later in the composite.

If we look in more detail at the beginning of three short story composites—Faulkner's *Go Down, Moses*, Welty's *The Golden Apples*, and Erdrich's *Love Medicine*—we can analyze how the tensions between closure and recalcitrance have been resolved in these books. I have chosen three fairly "representative" composites; a study of, for instance, the opening stories of Godwin's *Mr. Bedford and the Muses* or Doctorow's *Lives of the Poets* would have yielded a different pattern, one characterized by even greater recalcitrance.

The original title of Faulkner's book, *Go Down, Moses and Other Stories*,[79] told the reader to expect a collection of stories named after the concluding title story; since the excision of the latter half of the title, the reader no longer knows what to expect. The introductory section of "Was," the first story of *Go Down, Moses*, is not well integrated into the story. Later in the book we realize that this section about Ike McCaslin serves as an introduction to the whole composite, but at the outset of "Was" this is not clear. The rest of the plot tells of how Uncle Buck and Cass chase the runaway Tomey's Turl, how they are fooled by Mr. Hubert and Sophonsiba, and how, with the help of Uncle Buddy, they get out of their dilemma. The plot is characterized by several closural strategies. It starts off with a farcical indoor hunt of the fox which is repeated at the end as a frame to the action. The parallel hunt of Tomey's Turl also comes to an end and the characters return home, again forming a pattern of circularity. In addition, the pervasive theme of men being chattel to be bought and sold strengthens this sense of coherence. At the end of the story the reader thus receives strong signals of finality.

When he or she reaches "The Fire and the Hearth," the reader must overcome great resistance of the text. S/he will not know for many pages that there is a substantial chronology gap between the stories. The characters of "Was," who have become familiar to him, are no longer present, and when they appear later in "Fire" it is only in passing references. It takes six pages until the reader knows for sure that the focalizer is not the same as in the preceding story; the "he" of the story is no longer Cass but Lucas Beauchamp. And it takes more than fifty pages of

[78] J. Hillis Miller, "The Problematic of Ending in Narrative," *Nineteenth-Century Fiction* 33:1 (June 1978): 4.

[79] Faulkner, *Go Down, Moses* (1942; New York: Modern Library, 1955).

reading before the reader is informed that the focalizer is the son of Tomey's Turl and Tennie, two of the central figures of "Was." If Faulkner had striven for novelistic coherence, he could easily have made such information available in the first paragraphs without impairing the story's artistic quality. But in "Fire" Faulkner deliberately establishes a new world and infuses the text with a recalcitrance which widens the gap to the preceding story, a fact which in turn makes that story initially seem more autonomous.

As a discrete item, "Fire," as well as "Was," is characterized by a pronounced sense of closure. The hunt for the gold, which makes Lucas possessed, ends in his awareness of its destructiveness and in the complete renouncement of the divining machine. Edmonds comes to a parallel insight concerning racial injustice and takes action in favor of Molly. The plot is thus resolved in a rather traditional manner.

Arriving at the third story, "Pantaloon in Black," the reader experiences a radical disruption; as critics have observed, the reader feels that he is entering a disparate entity. The break with the preceding story is considerable, even if, a couple of pages into the story, there are two references in passing to Roth and Lucas. Rider and Mamie have not been mentioned before; they have a very tangential relationship to the two preceding stories. The discreteness of "Pantaloon" thus points up the space between this story and "Fire" and thus reinforces the sense of resolution of the latter.

At the beginning of *The Golden Apples*[80] the reader gets signals of novelistic coherence. Welty supplies a note about the town of Morgana being fictitious, which makes the reader expect the town to be the setting of the entire book. She further presents the reader with a table of contents in which the chapters/stories are numbered and from which the title of the book is absent, showing that the book is not named after one of the stories. As a third step into the work, we meet a list of the "main families in Morgana, Mississippi," which further strengthens our expectations of entering a novel. This anticipation is, however, frustrated as we proceed in our reading.

At the end of the first story, "Shower of Gold," the reader experiences a sense of closure. Katie Rainey has concluded her story to the anonymous passer-by who presumably will then leave. She has described the possible arrival and departure of King MacLain, and she has suggested an explanation to what happened. Coming to "June Recital," the second story, however, the reader encounters a new world with which he or she

---

[80] Eudora Welty, *The Golden Apples,* in *The Collected Stories of Eudora Welty* (New York: Harcourt Brace Jovanovich, 1980).

must make him/herself familiar. The point of view is no longer first person singular; the focalizer is not Katie, but somebody called Loch; the characters of the first few pages have not been mentioned in "Shower of Gold." After four pages of reading we realize that also this story is about the town of Morgana, and after five pages a character from the preceding story, Fate Rainey, is mentioned in passing.

It is clear that Welty's recalcitrant and anti-closural strategies here are deliberate. At the beginning of "June Recital," we read: "Next door was the vacant house" (275), after which follows a lengthy description of the house which will play a central role throughout the story. However, it is not until section two of the story, when Cassie takes over as focalizer, that we are informed that it is the MacLain house, which was also the setting of "Shower of Gold." Welty thus deliberately withholds the information and thereby creates resistance in the text. Welty's narrative strategy here closely resembles that of Faulkner in *Go Down, Moses*. The recalcitrance of the first part of "June Recital" contributes to creating more space between this story and "Shower of Gold."

Erdrich's *Love Medicine*[81] is subtitled "a novel," but is named, like a short story collection, after one of the stories. In the introductory story, "The World's Greatest Fishermen," we meet numerous people from the same family, that will reappear later in the book. The death of June Kashpaw brings them together back home. But the homecoming, as a unifying device, is set off against the internal strife within the family, particularly, as we see in retrospect, between June and her husband Gordie, and between their son King and his white wife Lynette. Central to the story is the baking of pies and how, in his frustration, King smashes them; the pies come to stand for a sense of community and for human relations and how easily they break. At the end of the story King and Lynette reach a temporary reunification and take leave. Albertine, the narrator, in a parallel act, tries to put the smashed pies back together and does a fairly good job of healing, even though she knows that "once they smash there is no way to put them right"(39). The story thus comes to a close, but the sense of closure is not as strong as in the opening stories of *Go Down, Moses*, or *The Golden Apples*.

The second story of *Love Medicine*, "Saint Marie," is told by Marie Lazarre and takes place almost fifty years earlier. References in the first part of the story to "going up there on the hill" and "Sacred Heart Convent" echo phrases in the preceding story, but these links are not strengthened and the initial expectations are not fulfilled. The reader sees little resemblance to "The World's Greatest Fishermen." For one

---

[81] Louise Erdrich, *Love Medicine* (New York: Holt, Rinehart, and Winston, 1984).

thing, "Saint Marie" is entirely different in tone. It is a story of a small format involving, in fact, only two people, Marie and Sister Leopolda, and their struggle for power. The plot focuses on a psychological and religious issue and relegates questions of Indianness, reservation life, and social injustice to the background. It seems as if not a single person from the first story reappears in this one. It is only later in the book, well into the third story, that we understand that Marie Lazarre and Grandma Kashpaw from the first story are one and the same. Through the separateness and self-sufficiency of "Saint Marie," the preceding story also becomes a more completed and closed narrative. From the third story and onwards, more and more links to preceding stories are established, but the autonomy of each story is never sacrificed for the coherence of the larger whole.

As I hope the discussion in this chapter has demonstrated, the short story composite possesses intricate patterns of closure. The overall pattern that emerges is a *sinusoidal* structure, to borrow Eco's term, a tension-resolution dialectic consisting of "tension, resolution, renewed tension, further resolution, and so on,"[82] but with the difference that in the composite there is a distinct break between resolution and renewed tension. What is ultimately striking in this sinusoidal structure is the tension between the individual stories and the total composite, between the closural and anti-closural strategies that I have drawn attention to above, between the centripetal and the centrifugal forces at work. The resulting double perspective discussed repeatedly in this chapter of simultaneous closure and openness, depending on whether the reader focuses on the discrete story or on the composite, makes the short story composite such a vital, variegated, and potentially renewable narrative form.

---

[82] Eco, *The Role of the Reader*, 132.

Four:
Indeterminacy and Open Form in the Short Story Composite

Narrative "openness" is an open term. It designates the partial negation or absence, or the depreciation, of unifying, cohering designs and devices in the text. Expressions of this counterforce are therefore often characterized by a prefix of negation or opposition—indeterminacy, anti-closure, anti-teleology, discontinuity—demonstrating their dependence on the ordering processes they intend to challenge. Ultimately it is not only a matter of critical preference whether and when to term a text "open"; there also exist numerous different conceptions of openness based on theme, structure, temporailty, or reader implication.

The discussion in the preceding chapter made clear, I hope, that even though numerous closural strategies are at work in the short story composite, these strategies are, in comparison with the traditional novel, often minimized. Although, in effect then, the question of openness has already been addressed, I nevertheless need to go over more or less the same ground but to do so with a new set of spectacles. If in the last chapter I focused on the centripetal narrative forces, those that attempt to hold the text together, here I want to emphasize the major centrifugal, disrupting strategies that characterize the composite. Certain repetitions and overlappings will necessarily occur, but it is my hope that the shift of perspective will bring new light to an understanding of the genre.

During the course of this century the autonomy of literature and the integral unity and purposiveness of literary texts have been questioned to an ever increasing degree by authors and critics alike. As Krieger, de Man, and Hillis Miller have shown,[1] the long tradition of organicism carrying within it the subversive forces of variety, ambiguity, and irony, resulted in an inevitable challenging of the naturalness of artistic unity and coherence, and initiated the debate over narrative indeterminacy, openness, and anti-closure.

---

[1] Murray Krieger, *A Reopening of Closure*, 36-37, 39, 41, 49; Paul de Man, *Blindness and Insight: Essays in the Rhetoric of Contemporary Criticism*, Second ed., revised (Minneapolis: U of Minnesota P, 1983) 21, 27-28, 229-45; J. Hillis Miller, "Stevens' Rock and Criticism as Cure, II," *Georgia Review* 30:2 (Summer 1976): 333, 334, 345.

The Open Work

As all literary texts possess closure, they also exhibit a degree of openness. According to Iser, all literary texts demonstrate a general "indeterminacy" in that they cannot be referred to any "identical real-life situation." The text can be identified neither with the reality of the outside world, nor with the reader's own experience.[2] This indeterminacy causes gaps to open up which give room for a free play of interpretation. The reader is thereby invited to participate; the indeterminate elements of the text are thus, according to Iser, "the switch that activates the reader in using his own ideas in order to fulfill the intention of the text" (43). Openness consequently resides both in the text itself and in the reader's participation. In no way are the indeterminate elements to be regarded as a defect; they are "a basic element for the aesthetic response" (12).

The issue of thematic indeterminacy and interpretive openness has been dealt with by several critics. Robert M. Adams' early study in literary openness is not concerned with fragmentation or discontinuity in form; to Adams literary openness means that a major conflict has been left unresolved, so that a work of art may be completely unified structurally and still be open.[3] Euripides' *The Bacchae,* one of Adams' examples, is deliberately contradictory, presenting conflicting ideas which the author refuses to mediate. The play "is saying two different things at once, and one token of this fact is precisely that scholars ... show no signs of reaching agreement" (29). Like Iser, Adams refuses to see openness as a flaw; it is not an impeachment of, for instance, John Donne to "think him a divided and fragmentary sensibility"(10).[4]

As basic to the definition of an open work, critics like Eco and Kenshur emphasize, on the one hand, the structure of the text itself and, on the other, the reader's implication in the text. Eco holds that all texts in a sense are open, but what he calls an "open work" or "open text" has a

---

2 Wolfgang Iser, "Indeterminacy and the Reader's Response in Prose Fiction," in J. Hillis Miller, ed., *Aspects of Narrative* (New York: Columbia UP, 1971) 8-9. Narrative aspects and events not selected for treatment have also been termed "indeterminacies," *Unbestimmtheiten*; a verbal narrative may, for instance, choose not to present some visual aspect, such as a character's clothes. See Seymour Chatman, *Story and Discourse: Narrative Structure in Fiction and Film* (Ithaca, N.Y.: Cornell UP, 1978) 30.

3 Robert M. Adams, *Strains of Discord. Studies in Literary Openness* (Ithaca, N.Y.: Cornell UP, 1958) 13.

4 For a similar study of thematic openness, see Alan Friedman, *The Turn of the Novel* (New York: Oxford UP, 1966).

higher degree of openness. "So-called open texts," he writes, "are only the extreme and most provocative exploitation ... of a principle which rules both the generation and the interpretation of texts in general."[5] To Eco, an open text has a "halo of indefiniteness" and is "pregnant with infinitive suggestive possibilities,"[6] lending itself to multiple interpretations. In the interpretative process the reader is a collaborator in organizing and structuring the text.[7] In *The Role of the Reader* Eco writes that the "type of cooperation requested of the reader, the flexibility of the text in validating (or at least in not contradicting) the widest possible range of interpretive proposals—all this characterizes narrative structures as more or less 'open'."[8] To illustrate the interplay between the openness of the "text" and the collaboration of the reader/spectator/listener, Eco uses examples from architecture and music. Baroque form, for instance, is built on a play between "solid and void, light and darkness, with its curvature, its broken surfaces, its widely diversified angles of inclination," all of which leads in the spectator to an effect of "indeterminacy." And modern music is often left unfinished by the composer in order for the performer, and presumably the listener, to "complete" it.[9]

In Kenshur's view, an open work is one that resists the reader's application of coherence and a "correct configuration."[10] The discontinuous work contains gaps, which, "whether logical, narrative, grammatical, or typographical, prevent the separate parts from combining into unified wholes" (13). This incompleteness of the open work is not accidental but reflects rather the "incompleteness of our knowledge, and even the necessity of such incompleteness"(16). Kenshur thus connects openness not primarily with theme, but with the fragmented structure of the text and the impossibility of making complete sense. The open work is seen by the reader as consisting of not only "disconnected" but also "unconnectable" fragments (22).

---

[5] Umberto Eco, "Introduction," *The Role of the Reader* (Bloomington: Indiana UP, 1984) 4-5.

[6] Umberto Eco, "The Poetics of the Open Work," *The Open Work* (Cambridge, Mass.: Harvard UP, 1989) 9.

[7] Eco, "The Poetics of the Open Work," 12.

[8] Eco, "Introduction," *The Role of the Reader*, 33.

[9] Eco, "The Poetics of the Open Work," 7, 12.

[10] Oscar Kenshur, *Open Form and the Shape of Ideas. Literary Structures as Representations of Philosophical Concepts in the Seventeenth and Eighteenth Centuries* (Lewisburg: Bucknell UP, 1986) 17.

Bakhtin and his disciples see certain narratives, like the novels of Tolstoy and Dostoevsky, as possessing an openness of time, an indeterminism and a less strict causality. Bakhtin also finds such texts to be polyphonic in the sense that the author enters into a special relationship with his or her characters, in which the characters gain a degree of independence and the author partially loses control and becomes a "character" of his/her own story. Bakhtin writes: "By the very construction of the novel, the author speaks not *about* a character, but *with* him." The hero's freedom is thus an aspect of the author's intention:

> A character's discourse is created by the author, but created in such a way that it can develop to the full its inner logic and independence as *someone else's discourse*, the word of the *character himself*. As a result it does not fall out of the author's design, but only out of a monological authorial field of vision. And the destruction of this field of vision is precisely a part of Dostoevsky's design.[11]

Morson summarizes Bakhtin's view of this dialogic and indeterminate field of vision as follows:

> Readers intuit that Dostoevsky's heroes also retain the power to mean directly. *It is as if each major character could be the organizing point for the novel.* In a sense, the work seems to oscillate between several possible novels, each somehow intended by a different character. It is this peculiar plurality that creates that special sense of palpitating contradictoriness we recognize as quintessentially Dostoevskian.[12]

Morson introduces the concept of *sideshadowing* to be able to explain the openness of Tolstoy's and Dostoevsky's texts. In sideshadowing, he writes, "two or more alternative presents, the actual and the possible, are made simultaneously visible. This is a simultaneity not *in* time but *of* times: we do not see contradictory actualities, but one possibility that was actualized and, at the same moment, another that could have been but was not" (*Narrative and Freedom*, 118).

In the following pages I will discuss different strategies of openness as they appear in the short story composite. I will not deal with the universal "indeterminacy" of texts, the fact that texts are ultimately uniden-

---

11 Mikhail Bakhtin, *Problems of Dostoevsky's Poetics*, ed. and transl. by Caryl Emerson (Minneapolis: U of Minnesota P, 1984) 63, 65.
12 Gary Saul Morson, *Narrative and Freedom: The Shadows of Time* (New Haven: Yale UP, 1994) 94.

tifiable or unverifiable in Iser's terms; nor will I here pay much attention to the reader's collaboration in the construction of the literary text, even though this process is always present as an underlying assumption in my discussion. The main emphasis of the discussion below will rather be on the thematic and structural anti-closural forces situated in the text itself. Some of these strategies are characteristic of all open literary works; others, I believe, are specific to the genre of the short story composite. I will address the composite as a totality rather than focusing on the individual stories. Although it is certainly true that some of the separate stories exhibit an open form, my interest lies not in the short story proper, but rather in the loose jointure of the stories into a larger whole. The underlying conviction of the discussion that follows is that in a continuum from closure to openness, the average short story composite finds itself closer to the latter than the former pole. Most composites are characterized by so many anti-closural elements that the genre, it seems to me, must be designated an open form. The analysis below isolates five anti-closural strategies which I consider central to the composite: 1. anti-teleology, 2. discontinuity, 3. family resemblance, 4. multiplicity, and 5. potentiality.

Anti-teleology

In the previous chapter I quoted Prince as saying that a narrative made up of middles has practically no narrativity. The short story composite is such a narrative of "middles." No narrative can show either its beginning or its ending, as Hillis Miller has pointed out,[13] but the composite makes this state of in *medias res* a structuring principle. It does not subscribe to the strategy of end-orientation; when dealing with this kind of narrative, the tool of "the anticipation of retrospection" that Brooks suggests we apply to narratives[14] is simply not very useful. Looking at the middle ground between beginning and ending as a dilatory space, a teasing of the reader, a delay or deceleration of the text, is not very helpful either, since the composite does not privilege the beginning and the end over the middle.

The short story composite is rather "anti-teleological" in its nature, to use Meyer's term for avant-garde art. This form of art, he argues, "directs us toward no points of culmination—establishes no goals toward which to move." And because this art presents a "succession rather than a pro-

---

[13] J. Hillis Miller, "The Rhetoric Ending in Narrative," *Nineteenth-Century Fiction* 33:1 (June 1978): 4

[14] Brooks, *Reading for the Plot*, 23.

gression of events, it is 'essentially static'."[15] The short story composite is not anti-teleological to the same degree as the works of art Meyer refers to, such as a Jackson Pollock painting, but it partakes of the same tendency and is no doubt more "static" than the traditional novel.

Short story composites often refuse to fulfill the reader's expectations of an end. A characteristic of closure is that the reader at the end senses that nothing of importance has been left out. At the end of a composite the reader is not certain; important information may very well have been left out. Another closural feature is a sense of well-rounded circularity. Conversely, the final story of some short story composites so disrupts the possible preceding plot development as to function as an anti-closural unit. It may present new characters or themes, be set in new localities, be different in tone. The effect of such disruption is that these composites seem to take off in a new direction rather than make the narrative come to a close. Such lack of resolution is noticeable in, for instance, *Go Down, Moses* and *Dubliners*.

As referred to above, Morson has introduced the term "sideshadowing" to describe the indeterminate status, the simultaneous actual and possible presents, of the middle of certain texts. But Morson's term is less felicitous, it seems to me, because the simultaneity of alternatives it proposes to discuss is an illusion. Sideshadowing does not really multiply stories, as Morson claims, since the choices have already been made; the alternatives have already been discarded, and the multiple, possible stories end up, as the plot moves along, on the garbage heap of the past. Sideshadowing does point to the multiplicitous nature of a text, but it is dependent on the closure of the end, and cannot therefore serve to describe the openness of the short story composite, in which the stories make up not an illusory but an actual multiplicity not ultimately subsumed under a totalizing ending.

Texts that are characterized by an open structure, like a polyphonic novel, cannot have an "effective" ending, and this is why, according to Bakhtin, Dostoevsky usually resorted to "a conventionally literary, conventionally monologic ending."[16] This is also true of such an open narrative as the composite with the difference that, since this narrative consists of autonomous stories, its author does not feel the need, like Dostoevsky, to resort to conventional closure.

If openness means that a major conflict is left unresolved, most short story composites are open. This is so simply because most composites

---

[15] Leonard B. Meyer, "The End of the Renaissance? Notes on the Radical Empiricism of the Avant-Garde," *Hudson Review* 16:2 (Summer 1963): 173, 183.

[16] Bakhtin, *Problems of Dostoevsky's Poetics*, 39.

contain no major conflict, but multiple conflicts which may or may not be resolved separately as the composite progresses. However, at the end of the composite the denouement is most often minimized. There may be a resolution of the last story, but, as we saw in the previous chapter, while it in certain instances may serve as a denouement to more stories than the last, seldom does the last story act as a resolution to the whole composite. I pointed to how "Big Two-Hearted River" functions as a conclusion of sorts, offering a resolution to the conflict that has ruptured Nick's life. But this story does not serve as a resolution to the many conflicts presented in stories like "Mr and Mrs Elliot," "Out of Season," "Cross-Country Snow," and "My Old Man." The ending of Anderson's *Winesburg, Ohio*, "Departure," constitutes a similar denouement to the continuous story about George Willard, but it refuses to serve as a resolution to the preceding twenty stories. The story of "Departure" is actually, as Fussell has shown, "pointedly anti-climactic."[17] While there is a multiplicity of crises in Anderson's book, it does not present a pervasive, major conflict which can be resolved. "Crossing the Water," the last story of Erdrich's *Love Medicine*, makes clear the family relations of one of the characters, Lipsha, but although the story refers back to characters appearing in several earlier stories, it does not serve as a denouement to all the story lines of the book.

Endings enable us to define through retrospection the "geometry" of a narrative text.[18] Reading a short story composite entails casting a continuous backward glance, an implicatory process in which the reader links one story to the preceding ones, thereby establishing a tenuous coherence in the work. However, the ending of the composite does not start a readjustment of the whole work, as often happens in the novel. As has been illustrated by the examples above, it may add new threads to the network being woven between the stories and thus serve as a partial retrospective patterning, but it seldom functions to create overall coherence.

Morson points out that, since in life we do not experience foreshadowing, this narrative strategy "appears as the most artificial, and therefore most recognizable, of literary devices." He also underlines the illusory, constructed nature of closure: "In our own lives, most of us know by experience that there is never a point when all loose threads are tied up together, at least not until the end of history or the Last Judgment. Real time is an ongoing process without anything resembling literary

---

[17] Edwin Fussell, "*Winesburg, Ohio*: Art and Isolation," in Sherwood Anderson, *Winesburg, Ohio*, Viking Critical Library (New York: Viking Press, 1966) 392.
[18] See Smith, *Poetic Closure*, 14, and Torgovnick, *Closure in the Novel*, 5.

closure."[19] Taking Morson's point, one could argue that a narrative like the short story composite, with its virtual lack of foreshadowing and its depreciation of closure, is more realistic, more closely rendering the indeterminacy of our lives, than both the short story and the novel.

Discontinuity

Maybe the most genre-specific feature of the short story composite is that of seeming negation and absence. Even though there is always a measure of linkage between stories in a composite, what really stands out in this form of narrative is the disruption created by the gaps between the stories. The composite thereby rejects the ideals of continuity and coherence that orient the traditional novel.

All continuous narratives have holes, gaps, ellipses, and indeterminacy spots,[20] some to be filled by the author at a later stage in the narrative, others to be inferred by the reader, others still to remain permanently open. The short story composite, however, is unique in the respect that between the narrative sequences it always inserts interstices of considerable width. In some cases these sequences are unconnectable, i.e. the breaks are not, it seems, intended to be bridged. In the following I am concerned with the holes between the stories, not with possible ellipses in the plot lines of the individual stories.

Ellipsis may be *frontal*, consisting of a break in temporal continuity, or *lateral* (*paralipsis*), an omission of one or more components in a situation; in both cases, the gap is *hermeneutic*, i.e. information has been left out.[21] Ellipsis may also be *definite* or *indefinite*, depending on whether its duration is specified, and *explicit* or *implicit*, i.e. openly stated ("two years later") or unannounced but inferable from chronological lacunae.[22] Finally, breaks may be either *temporal* or *spatial*, achieving either a gap in time or a change of setting.[23]

The gaps between stories in short story composites can be temporal or spatial, or both at the same time. The break between the first story, "In France," of Andrea Lee's *Sarah Phillips* and the second, "New African," covers eleven years and shifts the scene from France to Philadel-

---

[19] Morson, *Narrative and Freedom*, 7-8.

[20] For a discussion of these terms, see Lohafer, *Coming to Terms with the Short Story* (Baton Rouge: Louisiana State UP, 1983) 48; Rimmon-Kenan, *Narrative Fiction*, 127-29; Genette, *Narrative Discourse*, 106-09.

[21] Rimmon-Kenan, *Narrative Fiction*, 128-29.

[22] Genette, *Narrative Discourse*, 106-109.

[23] Genette, *Narrative Discourse*, 89.

phia. In Erdrich's *Love Medicine* and Faulkner's *Go Down, Moses*, the duration of the ellipses often exceeds a decade.

Hemingway's *In Our Time* is characterized by its spatial breaks with their changes of setting from Michigan to various European sites and back to the United States. In a similar way, the stories of such works as Barth's *Lost in the Funhouse*, Coover's *A Night at the Movies*, and Doctorow's *Lives of the Poets* involve multiple changes of scene; the shifts of setting from one story to the next are fundamental. Since there is little continuous plot in these composites, discontinuities are not generally interpretable as temporal ellipses.

The inter-story gaps of many short story composites are, however, neither temporal nor spatial. In these books the interstices are of a different nature. Such static works as Anderson's *Winesburg, Ohio* and LeGuin's *Searoad* are *uni-temporal*, in that they exhibit little chronological progression, and *uni-spatial*, in that they keep the same setting throughout. In a sense, the breaks of these books are spatial in that there is a change of scene within the larger setting of the town. But such spatial breaks are less radical than, for instance, the ones surrounding "Music from Spain," in Welty's *The Golden Apples*, which takes place in San Francisco, while the preceding and the following stories are acted out in Morgana, Mississippi. In general, however, Anderson's and LeGuin's composites minimize the importance of time and place. The gaps of these books, and also of Godwin's *Mr. Bedford and the Muses*, are what might be called *character breaks*. Each story is devoted to the fate of a character, and the reader is asked to leap from one to the next. Space and time here function rather as aspects creating coherence; these characters coexist at the same time and in the same setting.

Lateral ellipsis, or paralipsis, may obviously take place within a discrete story but seldom in the composite as a totality, since stories seldom refer back or forth to other stories. For the same reason, ellipsis in composites is hardly ever explicit; such open references outside of the separate story as "two years later" are extremely rare if they occur at all. The reader is always implicitly made aware of omission in time. The explicit ellipsis is a novelistic strategy not employed by the short story composite.

Psychoanalysis views ignorance as an integral part of the very structure of knowledge. Ignorance is not a passive state of absence but rather an "active refusal of information."[24] Meyer states that "silence is just as real, just as much a part of existence as sound," and Rauschenberg once

---

[24] Shoshana Felman, *Jacques Lacan and the Adventure of Insight* (Cambridge, Mass.: Harvard UP, 1987) 79.

said that "a canvas is never empty."[25] Analogously, the gaps between composite stories are not to be regarded as passive states of absence, but rather as dynamic components of the composite's specific narrative structure. Iser's statement that "it is only through inevitable omissions that a story will gain its dynamism"[26] is particularly true of the genre I am discussing here. The gaps implicate us as readers. During the ellipsis events may take place which sometimes are elucidated later, but which are often left unexplained, making the gap permanent.[27] Chatman analyzes a comic strip, i.e. frames divided by spaces, showing a king losing his money at his own royal casino. The major event, the loss of the money, takes place in the space between two frames.[28] The burden of inference is thus left to the reader. Resembling the frame-space structure of the comic strip, the same often happens in the short story composite, with the difference that the gap in many cases remains open. To take an example, in "Music from Spain" in Welty's *The Golden Apples* we find that Eugene MacLain, one of the major characters, has left Morgana and is now living in San Francisco. When we last met him he was around twenty and single; in San Francisco he is married and middle-aged. We are never informed of what has happened to him, why he moved to the West Coast. We may infer that he did so in order to find his father, King MacLain, who is rumored to have gone west, but we do not know. In the following story, also the last one, it is made clear that Eugene moved back to Morgana where he died, but we are told neither why he returned, nor what has happened to his wife. As readers we are invited to participate in "completing" the story without being given the necessary information to be able to do so.

In Hemingway's *In Our Time*, a central issue, most critics would agree, is war, its cause and effect. But the author prefers to let the action of the war take place in the spaces between the interchapters and the stories. In the middle of the book we meet Nick in a vignette after he has been injured, but we are not allowed to witness the cause of his injury. Likewise, in "Soldier's Home" and "Big Two-Hearted River," we see only the effect of war on two young men, and we are forced to infer the cruelty, violence, and humiliation that caused their atrophied state of existence. We may also infer that the war is the cause of the boredom and corruption of the stories about post-war Europe, or we may try to take

---

25 Meyer, "The End of the Renaissance?", 178.
26 Wolfgang Iser, "The Reading Process: A Phenomenological Approach," *New Literary History* 3:2 (1972): 285.
27 See Rimmon-Kenan, *Narrative Fiction*, 128.
28 Chatman, *Story and Discourse*, 38.

inferential walks of a different nature. The end result of our unifying efforts is that we are uncertain; the gaps are never closed, they remain permanent. Todorov holds that in James' short stories "the narrative is always based on the *quest for an absolute and absent cause.*" The absence of the cause is the "text's logical origin and reason for being."[29] It would be to go too far to make such an absolute claim for the short story composite, but the reader does become involved, as in reading a James story, in the quest for the absent causes residing in the interstices between the stories.

In its rejection of coherence, the short story composite consequently assumes a structure of *parataxis* and *asyndeton.* The connectives and conjunctions "normally" used in narratives are absent. "As we move from story to story," Kennedy writes, "we experience a partitioning of fictional scenes."[30] It has been pointed out that Hemingway, in *In Our Time*, employs a paratactic style. The terse sentences of "Indian Camp," for instance, omit all connectives: "The sun was coming up over the hills. A bass jumped, making a circle in the water. Nick trailed his hand in the water. It felt warm in the sharp chill of the morning."[31] This paratactic, or maybe asyndetic, style is extended to the structure of the whole of Hemingway's composite; the interstices between the stories correspond to the omission of conjunctions between sentences.

Much of the uniqueness of the short story composite is constituted in its specific *rhythm.* There are few narratives where the *speed* is so varied, where the combination of maximum *acceleration* and *deceleration* is so pronounced.[32] Genette distinguishes between four basic forms of narrative movements: the two extreme poles of *ellipsis* and *descriptive pause* and the intermediate forms of *scene* and *summary.* The narrative's tempo, according to Genette, is "a continuous gradation from the infinite speed of ellipsis, where a nonexistent section of narrative corresponds to some duration of story, on up to the absolute slowness of descriptive pause, where some section of narrative discourse corresponds to a nonexistent diegetic duration."[33]

---

[29] Todorov, *The Poetics of Prose*, 145.

[30] J. Gerald Kennedy, "From Anderson's *Winesburg* to Carver's *Cathedral*: The Short Story Sequence and the Semblance of Community," in Kennedy, ed., *Modern American Short Story Sequences*, 196.

[31] Hemingway, *In Our Time* (New York: Charles Scribner's Sons, 1958) 21.

[32] See Genette, *Narrative Discourse*, 93-94, and Rimmon-Kenan, *Narrative Fiction*, 51-53.

[33] Genette, *Narrative Discourse*, 93-94.

The short story composite consists of repeated ellipses of often long duration and stories which comprise all four of the narrative movements. Most often the stories have a short diegetic duration; there is a rather high correlation between story-duration and text-duration.[34] The short story is often characterized by its intensity and conciseness, a highlighted moment or an epiphany. The composite combines such narratives of slow speed with the complete acceleration of the interstices. The stories often cover no more than a day or two, while the time elapsing in the gaps amounts to years or even decades.

Eudora Welty's *The Golden Apples* serves as a case in point. The book covers a time-span of more than forty years. The combined story-duration of the individual stories, however, is merely two weeks; the rest of the time passes in the ellipses. The book thus consists of a string of highlights of slow tempo (with occasional analepses) separated by long intervening gaps of fast speed. An outline of the rhythm of *The Golden Apples* would look something like this:

"Shower of Gold"	1 day[35]	12 pp.[36]
	Ellipsis: 15 years	
"June Recital"	1 afternoon[37]	52 pp.
	Ellipsis: 1 year	
"Sir Rabbit"	2 afternoons[38]	11 pp.
	Ellipsis: 2 years	
"Moon Lake"	3-4 days	33 pp.
	Ellipsis: 11 years	
"The Whole World Knows"	2-3 days	18 pp.
	Ellipsis: 11-13 years	
"Music from Spain"	1 day	34 pp.
	Ellipsis: 5 years	
"The Wanderers"	2 days	34 pp.

---

[34] See Rimmon-Kenan, *Narrative Fiction*, 52.

[35] If one takes Katie Rainey's telling of the story as story-duration, it would be only an hour. However, I consider King's possible visit to demarcate the story's duration.

[36] From *The Collected Stories of Eudora Welty* (New York: Harcourt, Brace Jovanovich, 1980).

[37] However, analepses of considerable duration are included in the story. If one incorporates the recollections of the focalizers Cassie and Loch, the story-duration is five or six years.

[38] I consider the first section of this story an analepsis, since it takes place prior to "June Recital." The ellipsis of approximately one year concerns the time between "June Recital" and the second section of "Sir Rabbit."

The separate stories thus form a pattern of discontinuous glimpses of life in Morgana, Mississippi. One of the stories, "Moon Lake," constitutes a *mise en abyme* in that it is characterized by the same paratactic structure of ellipsis and scene/summary. The six sections of the story are unconnected fragments, where the length of the interstices remains undetermined. The gaps are here shorter, maybe a few hours or a day, but the structure of the story parallels that of the entire composite.

One effect of the composite's discontinuity on the reader, I would argue, is the creation of a sense of verisimilitude. Narrative structure, Morson claims,

> falsifies in several distinct but closely related ways. It violates the continuity of experience imposing a beginning and an ending; it reduces the plurality of wills and purposes to a single pattern; it makes everything fit, whereas in life there are always loose ends.[39]

The narrative structure of the short story composite escapes, at least more so than the novel, this kind of accusation. By means of the gaps (and other strategies), the plurality of wills and purposes is not reduced and it resists making everything fit. As a consequence, one may again argue that the composite is truer to life than most novels and short stories. Paradoxically, however, in cases when composites depict the discontinuity of life—and there are many of those—the discontinuous structure may be seen to reinforce that theme and consequently serve as a means of giving added coherence to the work as a whole.

Family Resemblance
The concept of family resemblance may, in two ways, serve as an illustration of the open structure of the composite and of the tangential relationship between its stories. The first application of the concept I would like to make, and which I do not intend to develop further, is that the short story composite resembles a family in that the urge of the stories/family members to come together and emphasize the similarities between them is counterbalanced by the desire of each story/family member to establish its/his/her own individuality apart from the others.

My second application is more suggestive: Wittgenstein's family resemblance concept, which has been applied by literary scholars to genre

---

[39] Morson, *Narrative and Freedom*, 38-39.

theory,[40] might be used to explain the composite's irregular, seemingly arbitrary structure. To illustrate the heterogeneous character of language Wittgenstein proposed an analogy to games, pointing to the fact that there is nothing in common to all games but that they possess "similarities, relationships, and a whole series of them at that," similarities and relationships that remind us of those of a family:

> I can think of no better expression to characterize these similarities than "family resemblance"; for the various resemblances between members of a family: build, features, color of eyes, gait, temperament, etc, etc, overlap and criss-cross in the same way.[41]

The individual members of the family are thus related in various ways "without necessarily having any single feature shared in common by all."[42] Fogelin has suggested what he terms a "crude representation" of Wittgenstein's idea:

O_1	O_2	O_3	O_4	O_5	O_6
A	B	C	D	E	F
B	C	D	E	F	A
C	D	E	F	A	B
D	E	F	A	B	C

Fogelin comments on his table in the following manner: "O_1 through O_6 represent a set of objects; the letters represent properties they possess. Here each object shares three features with two others in the group, but there is no single feature that runs through the lot."[43]

Let us assume that the objects represented as O_1, O_2, etc., are the individual short stories of a short story composite. While each story possesses a series of properties—characters, settings, themes, events—some of which are shared by other stories, in many composites there is no single property shared by all stories.

To enumerate all properties of all stories in a composite in order to test this idea would be an almost sisyphean task. I therefore decided to

---

[40] For an overview of such an application, see David Fishelov, "Genre Theory and Family Resemblance—Revisited," *Poetics* 20 (1991): 123-38.

[41] Ludwig Wittgenstein, *Philosophical Investigations* (Oxford: Oxford UP, 1978) 31-32.

[42] Alastair Fowler, *Kinds of Literature. An Introduction to the Theory of Genres and Modes* (Cambridge, Mass.: Harvard UP, 1982) 41.

[43] Robert J. Fogelin, *Wittgenstein* (London: Routledge & Kegan Paul, 1987) 133.

select only one property, characters, in two composites, Welty's *The Golden Apples* and Kenney's *In Another Country*, to see what structural patterns would emerge. Having read Kenney's composite, I knew beforehand that to me it was characterized by stronger closure and unity than that of Welty, an impression that was confirmed by this investigation. If my calculations are correct, *The Golden Apples* presents exactly one hundred different characters, many of whom are marginal. It turns out that two characters, the twins Ran and Eugene MacLain, appear or are mentioned in all the stories, and so one might claim that Wittgenstein's family resemblance is a less appropriate analogy. But since Ran and/or Eugene are of marginal significance in a few stories, like "June Recital" and "Moon Lake," one could argue that they possess a negligible relationship to those stories. King MacLain recurs in six of the seven stories, his wife Snowdie only in four. Characters comparatively central to the composite as a whole, such as Katie Rainey and her daughter Virgie, appear only in three, respectively two, stories, while a relatively marginal figure like Lizzie Stark comes back in six stories. Fifty-five of the one hundred characters are present in only one story. In the first story of the composite, "Shower of Gold," we meet thirteen characters, and in the last story, "The Wanderers," all of these thirteen come back (plus about forty more), attesting to the closural, or framing, capacity of the end of this particular composite.

Kenney's *In Another Country* is so tightly structured that applying the family resemblance concept proved to make little sense, mainly because the same person, Sara, acts as focalizer in all the stories. In addition, her father Jim is referred to in all six stories and her husband Phil in five of them. Of the book's thirty-one characters, eighteen appear in only one story. It might have been more fruitful to study Anderson's *Winesburg, Ohio*, in which no single narrative feature is present in all the stories: George Willard unifies most stories but not all, not all stories are set in Winesburg, and no theme runs through the entire composite. Applying the concept of family resemblance to Harvey Swados' *On the Line* might also give interesting results, since this composite is constructed around an intricate relay-race type of relationship between the characters.[44] The tentative conclusion to be drawn from this limited investigation is that while the family resemblance concept is a helpful tool in understanding the majority of composites, it is less so when it comes to those characterized so much by unity and closure that they, on the continuum from short story collection to novel, are close to the latter.

---

[44] For a more detailed discussion of *On the Line*, see Chapter Five.

Multiplicity

In the last one hundred years fictional narratives have become increasingly more open; they have undergone a development towards greater and greater discontinuity and multiplicity. The narrative text of today is often centrifugal in that it expresses multiplicity, rather than unity, of time, place, and action. It is polyphonic, rather than monologic, in that it consists of a plurality of independent and unmerged voices and consciousnesses, and in that it advocates, not evolution, but *coexistence* and *interaction*.[45] In postmodern narratives this development has resulted in what Marcotte calls *intersticed prose*—"short, paragraph-like segments, separated by a space"—a device "which questions all our assumptions concerning the nature of narration, emphasizing timelessness, discontinuity, reality depicted in a series of tableaux or static shots, with concurrent underplaying of the linear and the dramatic." This development is connected to other tendencies in recent prose such as "contempt for character motivation, historical and logical continuity, causality."[46]

The short story composite may be seen as part of this process towards plurality, multiplicity, and polyphony. The composite rejects coherence and speaks in favor of open-endedness; it questions the monologic and advocates a multi-voiced text. As a result, many unifying phenomena—such as temporality, causality, character, narrator, theme, and plot—are reduced in importance.

Because of its rejection of end-orientation and resolution, the short story composite puts less emphasis on evolution and successiveness, on teleology itself. Because of its paratactic nature, its gaps and interstices, it plays down the unbroken continuity of temporal progression. This depreciation of *temporality* is shared by other kinds of fictional narrative of the last one hundred years. The authors of such narratives of "open time" seek to find strategies that elude foreshadowing and closure, creating texts that rather than resolve events reveal a state of affairs. "Thus a strong sense of temporal order," Chatman maintains, "is more significant in resolved than in revealed plots."[47]

Many composites are "timeless" or "static" in that temporal progression is minimized. In Anderson's *Winesburg, Ohio*, Jarrell's *Pictures from an Institution*, Barth's *Lost in the Funhouse*, and Coover's *A Night at the Movies*, to mention a few, there is little progression in time from one story to the next. In Anderson's and Jarrell's books the stories seem to take place at approximately the same time. White's rather fruitless at-

---

45 See Bakhtin, *Problems of Dostoevsky's Poetics,* 6-8, 29-30.
46 Edward Marcotte, "Intersticed Prose," *Chicago Review* 26 (1974/75): 31-36.
47 Chatman, *Story and Discourse*, 48.

tempt to construct a chronology for *Winesburg, Ohio* proves the static character of that composite.[48] In Barth's and Coover's composites the temporal relations are unclear; the stories do not take place at the same time, but it is impossible to know if there is a progression. In *Lost in the Funhouse*, "Petition" is dated 1931 and "Life-story" occurs in 1966, but the way in which they and the other "atemporal" stories are interrelated is something Barth leaves to the reader to speculate about.

While other composites clearly express temporal development, their references to time are inexact. In such works as Welty's *The Golden Apples* and Kenney's *In Another Country*, the chronology is straight but vague. As readers we may be able to infer approximately how long a period of time has elapsed from one story to the next. But, as we have seen, there are large chunks of time not explicitly accounted for by the text.

Still other composites make use of very exact dating of each story; as examples one may mention Jayne Anne Phillips' *Machine Dreams* and Louise Erdrich's *Love Medicine*. Most of the individual stories of these books carry a date in the title or within parenthesis below the title, a much more exact dating than most novels make use of. While time is a factor in these works, the *progress* of time is not. The gaps between the stories break up the continuous evolution of plot and create a very fragmentary chronology.

In the process of subordinating temporality, the modern text also made *causality* suffer. The traditional narrative rests on the idea of causality, "on a series of steps toward a recognizable end," to use Gerlach's words.[49] But in the short story composite the end is no longer clearly recognizable, nor is the *series* of steps depicted in any detail. Making light of the causal context, instead the emphasis is on the independent state of the moment. Sometimes the reader is expected to supply the cause; at other times, due to a lack of information, the reader's power of inference fails.

This denial or disparagement of causality also means a disvaluation of the possibility of prediction. The short story composite often omits the causal nexus between key events, i. e. stories; the result is that changes that have occurred since the preceding story may be seen as not impossible, but neither inevitable. The reader does not know whether nothing else but what did happen could have happened. Such causal indeter-

---

[48] See Ray Lewis White, Winesburg, Ohio: *An Exploration* (Boston: Twayne Publishers, 1990) 54-55.

[49] John Gerlach, *Toward the End. Closure and Structure in the American Short Story* (N. p.:U of Alabama P, 1985) 91.

minacy makes it virtually impossible to predict the development or the final outcome of the story line.

The multiplicity and polyphony of the short story composite characterize such narrative elements as theme, plot, character, and focalization. In comparison to the traditional novel, less emphasis is placed on the unifying force of these narrative components.

As scholarly journals bear witness every month, critics tend to argue over the nature of *the* theme of all narratives, but the short story composite, more than most other narratives, thwarts their efforts by presenting the world through separate and discrete stories. What is, for instance, the central theme of Faulkner's *Go Down, Moses*? Is it racial relations? Life as a hunt or quest? Life as a commodity to be bought and sold? The defilement of the wilderness? Whichever theme one chooses, there is always one or more stories that do not seem to fit in. We feel the same uncertainty about Erdrich's *Love Medicine*, Hemingway's *In Our Time*, and Welty's *The Golden Apples*, all of which are characterized by a multiplicity of themes. The world depicted in such composites is not a universe but a multiverse. For other, more coherent works, however— Faulkner's *The Unvanquished*, Naylor's *The Women of Brewster Place*, and Kenney's *In Another Country*—it would presumably be easier to come to an agreement on the dominating theme.

Because of the short story composite's disjointed structure and its minimization of temporality and causality, plot is never allowed to become a prominent narrative element. Even if two events in traditional narratives seem unrelated, we infer, as Chatman says, "that they may be [connected], on a larger principle that we will discover later." Accustomed to the Aristotelian concept of unity, we expect the working out of plot to be "a process of declining or narrowing possibility. The choices become more and more limited, and the final choice seems not a choice at all, but an inevitability."[50] But the short story composite violates this expected formal arrangement of incidents; it often broadens the choice as the book progresses and skirts that inevitable resolution endorsed by organicists.

A natural consequence of a multi-story narrative is also the fact that no character is allowed to become dominant. In narrative—by means of repetition, similarity, contrast—character is a construct combining increasingly broader traits into cohesion.[51] This "fleshing-out" process is not present to the same degree in the composite, in which the depicted traits are often so few and so scattered as to discourage cohesion. Be-

[50] Chatman, *Story and Discourse*, 46.
[51] Rimmon-Kenan, *Narrative Fiction*, 39-40.

sides, there are usually so many characters of equal stature that no one is allowed center stage.[52] These many competing voices force the author partially out of control, making the short story composite a polyphonic text in the Bakhtinian sense. As we saw from Morson's summary of Bakhtin's argument earlier in this chapter how characters in certain texts, like those by Dostoevsky, retain the power to mean directly and that the potentiality of each character to "write his own novel" creates in such texts a sense of contradictoriness and oscillation between alternatives. Such polyphony, it seems to me, also characterizes many short story composites.

It is true that characters reappear in several stories, but can one really claim that Mattie in Naylor's *The Women of Brewster Place*, Ike in *Go Down, Moses*, or Ran MacLain in *The Golden Apples* are the main protagonists of their respective composites? Although there are certainly composites where a protagonist is allowed to develop, as in Faulkner's *The Unvanquished*, and Alice Munro's *Lives of Girls and Women*, as a rule the composite is characterized by a multiplicity of cameo portraits.

Critics acknowledge the dominance in modern narratives of character over action and the fact that narratives emphasizing action/plot leave little space or need for complexity of character.[53] The short story composite is a modern narrative, but neither does it privilege character over action, nor action over character. This either-or formula seems, like so many other critical paradigms established to explain the novel, to fail to make us understand the short story composite.

Multiple focalization further adds to the open form of the composite. Advocating unity and coherence, Lubbock held that it is doubtless the author's "purpose to shift the point of view no more often than he need; and if the subject can be completely rendered by showing it as it appears to a single one of the figures in the book, then there is no reason to range further."[54] Obviously, most writers of short story composites found reason to range further. Within the same book they often shift back and forth from external to internal focalization, and the latter is often multiple, in that it employs several first-person narrators.[55] Books like Erdrich's *Love Medicine* and Welty's *The Golden Apples* make use of a varied strategy of focalization. Other such works are LeGuin's *Searoad* and Phillips' *Machine Dreams*.

---

52 See Mann, *The Short Story Cycle*, xii.

53 See Martin, *Recent Theories of Narrative*, 116, 117.

54 Percy Lubbock, *The Craft of Fiction* (London: Jonathan Cape, 1921) 74.

55 See Genette, *Narrative Discourse*, 189-90.

Machine Dreams is characterized by its many voices and its varying modes of focalization. Initially, this shift from one focalizer to another and from first-person to third-person narrative may be confusing, but a closer look reveals that Phillips' book is built up according to a rather strict plan; the multiplicity is thus not allowed to fragment the narrative too much. Phillips starts out with two seemingly unrelated, first-person narratives, reminiscences by Jean and Mitch, two of the four main characters. Then follows a section of war letters, without comments, from Mitch to various people mentioned in the preceding story. After this we are presented with five third-person narratives with Jean, Mitch, and their children Danner and Billy as focalizers. Exactly in the middle of the composite Phillips returns to a first-person reminiscence, again by Jean, after which follow another five third-person stories with Danner and Billy as focalizers. The end of the book is characterized by reversed repetition: there is a section of war letters, this time from Billy, and thereafter a first-person narrative, with Danner as intradiegetic narrator.

This structure of focalization becomes even more varied by the fact that passages within the stories are presented through voices different from the principal narrator. In "The Secret Country: Mitch," for instance, the first-person narrative shifts from Mitch to Ava, and to Reb. And in "War Letters: Billy, 1970," the final messages are not by Billy but by his friend Robert informing the family of Billy's death in Vietnam.

Phillips' short story composite is a telling illustration of the polyphony and multiplicity of the genre. Not only does it utilize multiple focalization, but it also gives evidence of the genre's depreciation of temporality and causality and of the reduced emphasis on theme, plot, and character.

Potentiality
The paratactic structure of the short story composite leads to what might be termed narrative potentiality, as opposed to the narrative necessity that characterizes traditional novels. Modern narratives have experimented with various forms of potentiality. B. S. Johnson's *The Unfortunates* (1969) consists of a box in which the introductory and concluding sections are set, whereas the other sections/chapters are interchangeable. Marc Saporta's *Composition N.1* (Paris 1962) and Julio Cortazar's *Hopscotch* (1967) employ the same idea of making the order of the chapters variable. The short story composite belongs among such open works that question the rigidity of traditional narrative; even if it does not choose such radical solutions as the narratives mentioned above, it nevertheless admits the *potentiality* of omitting, adding, and reversing stories within the composite.

Smith argues that in paratactic structure, "(where the principle of generation does not cause any one element to 'follow' from another), thematic units can be omitted, added, or exchanged without destroying the coherence or effect of the poem's thematic structure."[56] The same kind of potentiality seems present in the short story composite; its open structure possesses the interminability and exchangeability that Smith describes. Shklovsky points out that certain narratives, like the picaresque and the adventure story, are potentially limitless since motifs can be accumulated *ad infinitum*. Such narratives can only come to an end by means of a framing story or the "crumpling" of time.[57] This potential limitlessness is distinctive also of the short story composite.

If yet another character study had been added to Anderson's *Winesburg, Ohio,* it would have made the total text longer and the picture of Winesburg fuller, but it would not significantly have affected either the interrelationship among the other stories, or the resolution of the book. The same holds true for *In Our Time, Go Down, Moses, Lost in the Funhouse, Lives of the Poets,* and numerous others. Welty could easily have added stories to *The Golden Apples*; as it is, this composite contains germs that could easily have been developed into entire story lines. The fates of both Mrs and Mr Morrison—she taking her own life and he locking himself up in a corner room, looking out at the world through a telescope—could have been made into fascinating stories which would fill voids in the present text but which would not really alter the whole of the composite. In 1993, Louise Erdrich published a new edition of *Love Medicine,* expanded with several new stories. In a sense, of course, this is not the same text as the 1984 edition, but in general the composite is not drastically changed, a fact on which Erdrich presumably would be the first to insist. The generic structure of the short story composite is consequently such that it often allows for additions.

It would also be possible in many composites to remove or exchange certain stories without greatly impairing the final impression of the work. One needs, however, to discriminate between stories. According to Barthes and Chatman, plot consists of *kernels,* major events which "cannot be deleted without destroying the narrative logic," and *satellites,* which can be (logically) omitted, even if the omission impoverishes the narrative esthetically.[58] This terminology could be applied to the stories

[56] Smith, *Poetic Closure,* 98.

[57] Shklovsky, *Theory of Prose,* 42, 52.

[58] Chatman, *Story and Discourse,* 53-54; Barthes, "Introduction to the Structural Analysis of Narratives," in *A Barthes Reader,* ed. by Susan Sontag (New York: Hill and Wang, 1982) 265-69. Boris Tomashevsky's corresponding terms are "bound mo-

of many composites, in which certain stories may be seen as kernel stories. It would affect the meaning of *Go Down, Moses* if stories like "The Bear," "Fire and Hearth," or "Delta Autumn" were omitted. But the deletion of "Pantaloon in Black" would have less impact on the whole, and would even please certain critics, since, according to them, it disrupts the unity of the work.[59] "Pantaloon in Black" could therefore be regarded as a satellite story. In *The Golden Apples,* I would view "Shower of Gold," "June Recital," and "The Wanderers" as kernel stories without which the book would suffer considerably. The other four stories are satellites and any of these could be taken out without greatly affecting the composite as a whole. Let me make clear, however, that if one undertook such an excision of satellite stories in order to increase textual coherence and unity, the specificity of the short story composite as an open work would also disappear. Let me also emphasize that I do not consider the stories referred to above as satellites of a lesser *quality* as stories, merely that they are less central to the total composite. In the same way, certain stories could be lifted from *Lost in the Funhouse, Winesburg, Ohio, Love Medicine,* or *A Night at the Movies* and these composites would not change logically in any radical way.

Within short story composites, stories can be added and omitted because of the genre's indeterminate form. Potentially, on account of this openness, the order of stories can often be reversed as well. Such reversals would be more difficult in composites employing a continuous chronology such as *The Golden Apples,* Kenney's *In Another Country,* or *The Unvanquished,* but it would be perfectly possible in *Winesburg, Ohio, Searoad,* or in the middle section of *In Our Time.*

Concluding Analogy

Let me attempt a final illustration of the anti-closural strategies discussed in this chapter by pointing to, maybe, an unexpected analogy in visual art: Pieter Brueghel's "The Fight between Carnival and Lent" (1559). In discussing the function of chapters in novels, Stevick has drawn attention to this painting: "No one assumes, in looking at such a painting by Brueghel, that all the rustics visible on the day in which he painted his picture are captured within his frame. Part of the effect of such a painting must be the suggestion that the scene would have continued if

---

tifs" and "free motifs"; see "Thematics" (1925) in Lee T. Lemon and Marion J. Reis, eds., *Russian Formalist Criticism: Four Essays* (Lincoln: Nebraska UP, 1965) 61-95.
[59] See, for instance, Stanley Tick, "The Unity of *Go Down, Moses,*" *Twentieth Century Literature* 8:2 (1962): 68-73.

the frame were larger."[60] Brueghel's work is characterized by a lack of finality, unity, and coherence; it is an open work.

The openness of "The Fight between Carnival and Lent," and other early Brueghel paintings like "Children's Games" (1560), exhibits interesting similarities to that of the short story composite. Brueghel's painting is a framed work of art, consisting of numerous scenes or "stories," simultaneously independent and interconnected. A myriad of scenes are linked by the overall theme of the fight between Carnival and Lent.

In this painting, as in the short story composite, there is a rejection of final resolution; the action spills over, as Stevick indicates, into a possible world outside the frame. Like the figure by the church entrance, some characters are depicted as being more outside than inside the frame. Always present is the possibility of adding or omitting characters.

Brueghel's picture, again like the composite, possesses a paratactic structure; there are spatial gaps between the separate stories. The trio in the middle, for instance, is enacting a separate story from the cripples on the left or the fishmongers on the right. And the man sitting in the window in the background invites us to speculate about his individual fate, separate from that of the people playing games below him in the square. The multiplicity of stories and individuals presented prevents, as in the composite, any single character or group of characters from becoming dominant. The eye is encouraged to roam from one group to the next and to infer their interconnectedness. Perhaps one might even speak of multiple "narrators" as Lassaigne and Delevoy suggest in their reading of the painting (and the similar "Children's Games"):

> Renouncing the grandiose vision of the Renaissance artists which, starting from a single, unvarying, immobile point of sight, penetrates deeply into space, he represents these fables as they would be seen by a number of spectators, viewing them from different angles. In a host of episodes—soldiers' pranks, peasant dances, mountebanks doing their turns, mock fights, ludicrous incidents of daily life—he conjures up bustling crowds of small, typical, yet always personalized figures. All disport themselves upon a single plane like that of medieval tapestries, and there is no attempt to graduate them in perspective.[61]

With a few substitutions this analysis could illustrate the structure of works like *Winesburg,Ohio*, *Love Medicine*, and Selby's *Last Exit to Brooklyn*.

---

[60] Philip Stevick, *The Chapter in Fiction. Theories of Narrative Division*, 67-68.
[61] Jacques Lassaigne and Robert L. Delevoy, *Flemish Painting: From Bosch to Rubens* (New York: Skira, 1958) 48.

The title of Brueghel's painting, "The Fight between Carnival and Lent," brings to mind Bakhtin's concept of the "carnivalization of literature." In the carnival, Bakhtin points out, the division between performers and spectators ceases to exist, the normal order of life is suspended as is the distance between people. The carnival has the logic of the world upside down.[62] The carnivalization of literature entails the assimilation into literary texts of the openness, instability, and multi-levelled structure of the carnival. Like Bakhtin's foremost example, Dostoevsky, most authors of short story composites shape their narratives in accordance with the carnivalization principle.

Brueghel's painting does not, however, depict only the carnival, but also the fight between Carnival and Lent. Symbolized in the painting by the lines of people emerging from the cathedral, Lent represents order and tradition. The advocates of Lent have arrived to supervise the carnival and to prevent the instability and disruption from going too far. Even in this respect one may see an analogy to the short story composite. The carnivalization process, with its emphasis on multiplicity and separateness, is checked by "Lentian" forces that wish to establish order, coherence, and closure. In the short story composite a balance is thus struck between coherence and disruption, between closure and open form.

---

62 Bakhtin, *Problems of Dostoevsky's Poetics*, 122-25.

Five:
E Pluribus Unum:
The Americanness of the Short Story Composite

With reference to the creation of *Winesburg, Ohio*, Sherwood Anderson stated in his *Memoirs* that, as "the novel form does not fit an American writer," he had invented his own form of a "new looseness" in the Winesburg book. In a note he pointed to a parallel between the composition of his narrative and that of a much larger structure. "Do we not live in a great, loose land of many states," he wrote, "and yet all of these states together do make something, a land, a country. I submit that the form of my Winesburg tales ... may offer a suggestion to other writers." [1]

The aim of this chapter is to investigate whether Anderson's suggestion, in fact, is a valid one, whether there is a degree of correspondence between the form of narrative that Anderson employed, the short story composite, and what over the years has been constructed as an American identity. Ever since colonial times Americans, as well as visitors to the new continent, have been concerned with establishing a "dominant value profile"[2] for America, and if a link between this national "ethos" and the short story composite could be convincingly suggested, it would follow that this form of narrative could be held forth as more "American" than other literary genres. And if, in turn, the short story composite could be projected as yet another expression of a more general American cultural pattern, constructed or not, we might expect a larger number of short story composites to be written in the United States than in any other country.

Undoubtedly there are many pitfalls in such a project, since so many of its presuppositions are questionable. To begin with, what Michael Kammen wrote in 1980 is surely still valid:

> No contemporary historian with any self-protective antennae sensitively extended can comfortably or casually write about "national character." That phrase,

---

[1] Quoted from James Schevill, *Sherwood Anderson: His Life and Work* (Denver: U of Denver P, 1951) 96.
[2] Term used by Cora Du Bois in "The Dominant Value Profile of American Culture," *American Anthropologist* 57:6 (December 1955): 1232-39.

along with "climate of opinion" and "spirit of the age," has become for many persons an object of intellectual scorn.[3]

Secondly, the generic boundaries of the short story composite are not easily drawn, as I have shown, even though its structure of interlinked autonomous stories constitutes a core of genre specificity. And thirdly, it would be a virtually impossible task for any one scholar quantatively to prove the percentage of short story composites to be higher in the U.S. than in other countries.

Although the following thoughts, then, are submitted with a substantial degree of hesitation, I remain convinced that, as Giambattista Vico said, "to each type of culture necessarily belong some characteristics not found in any other,"[4] and I would also contend that in literature a country's culture is formulated, expressed, and maybe even defined.

The United States—A Contrapuntal Civilization

The United States has frequently been characterized as a "contrapuntal civilization,"[5] and many scholars involved in defining American culture have thus pointed to the existence of opposition, paradox, and contradiction as fundamental ingredients contributing to the specificity of the nation. In the section of his *Childhood and Society* called "Reflections on the American Identity," Erik Erikson observes that "it is a commonplace to state that whatever one may come to consider a truly American trait can be shown to have its equally characteristic opposite."[6]

Going on to state, however, that this is probably true of all "national characters" or "national identities," Erikson joins numerous other commentators on American culture who have been equally wary of proposing that opposition and contradiction are features exclusive to the United States. What has been claimed, however, is that there seems to be a higher *degree* of paradox and contradiction in American society. Kammen, for instance, holds that "Americans alone are not *the* people of paradox: we are one among many, though perhaps more paradoxical than most because of our numerical size and social diversity." (Kammen, xiii) Phrasing it only slightly differently, Erikson suggests that "[t]his dynamic country subjects its inhabitants to more extreme contrasts and abrupt changes during a lifetime or a generation than is normally the case with other great nations" (Erikson, 258).

---

3 Michael Kammen, *People of Paradox* (Ithaca, N.Y.: Cornell UP, 1980) xi.

4 Quoted from Kammen, xii.

5 See, for instance, Kammen, 116.

6 Erikson, *Childhood and Society* (St. Albans: Triad/ Paladin, 1977) 258.

In the general attempts at constructing the United States as a contrapuntal civilization, specific attention has been paid to expressions of coexisting fusion and fragmentation, i.e. to the conjunction of centripetal and
centrifugal forces in American society and the American "character." According to many scholars, tensions seem to exist between the autonomy of
the states and the unity of the nation, between the diversity of various ethnic groups and the ideals and rhetoric of the nation, between the individualism that the United States is so well-known for and the harmonizing,
levelling desires of democracy, between the self-fulfillment of the private
sphere and the commitment to public causes. Erikson highlights still other
polarities such as "open roads of immigration and jealous islands of tradition; outgoing internationalism and defiant isolationism; boisterous competition and self-effacing cooperation" (Erikson, 258).

Scholars have used somewhat divergent terms to describe this conjunction of centripetal and centrifugal forces. The French sociologist Raymon
Aron speaks of a "dialectic of plurality and conformism"[7] as lying at the
core of American life, and Sacvan Bercovitch argues that the American i-
dentity is characterized by a "conjunction of opposites," stating more specifically that "fusion and fragmentation ... are the twin pillars of liberal hegemony in the United States."[8] This doubleness is distinguished by Kammen as a "biformity," i. e. a paradoxical coupling of opposites without loss
of identity in either and he argues in favor of a view of America as characterized by a combination, a biformity, of conflict and consensus. He
states that "[c]onservatism *and* liberalism, individualism *and* corporatism,
hierarchy *and* equalitarianism, emotionalism *and* rationalism, autonomy
and co-operation are all integral to the mutuality of pluralism" (Kammen
89, 92).

Biformities in American Society

Several of the biformities suggested by Kammen constitute simultaneously
unifying and diversifying social components, and yet further biformities in
the political, economic, ethnic, and religious spheres might be added. Let
me dwell briefly—and rather superficially, I am afraid—on a few such representations of fusion and fragmentation, highlighted by various analysts
of American society.

---

[7] Quoted from Kammen, 292.

[8] Bercovitch, "Fusion and Fragmentation: The American Identity" in Rob Kroes, ed.,
The American Identity: Fusion and Fragmentation, European Contributions to American Studies 3 (Amsterdam: U of Amsterdam, 1980) 19.

The United States is precisely that: a nation of comparatively autonomous yet united states. The balance between the diffusion of power to the
states and the concentration of authority in the federal government has varied over time. The *dual federalism* of the 19th century—which meant that
the "state governments and the federal government existed within distinct,
separate, and equal spheres" and that "tension rather than cooperation
characterized the relationship between these two spheres"—later gave way
to an increasing centralization of federal authority which culminated in the
cooperative federalism of the New Deal.[9] But however the balance was
weighted, the tension remained between the unifying force of the federal
government and the diversifying powers of the individual states.

This constitutional structure of biformity finds its parallel in the American double commitment to the local and the national, a biformity shared
with citizens of most other nations. In the United States, however, the construction of national unity has been of greater concern, it has been argued,
than in most other nations in order to keep such a vast, young, and eth-
nically diverse country together. The historian Michael Zuckerman, for example, points to the importance of consolidating the national identity in the
years after the achievement of national independence:

> The very fragmentation of the country that had occurred in the colonial era
> made all the more imperious, and poignant, the craving for social solidarity that
> attended the creation of the nation. And since that craving could not be satisfied
> in a social reality that was already too heterogeneous for successful central-
> ization, it had to be gratified in symbolic ways. The symbols would begin to be
> forged in the maelstrom of revolution.[10]

By means of religious and political rhetoric, metaphors, and icons—concepts like the city upon a hill and the New Canaan; rituals like flag worship, oath-taking, and the presidential inauguration; figures like Columbia,
Uncle Sam, and the Statue of Liberty—the federal forces have managed,
against all odds, to create cohesion around the American Way of Life, a
cohesion which has but little foundation in the social, ethnic, and religious
reality underlying the surface homogeneity.[11]

---

9 Tony Freyer, "Federalism" in Jack P. Greene, ed., *Encyclopedia of American Political History* (New York: Charles Scribner's Sons, 1984) Vol. II, 550-57.
10 Zuckerman, "Identity in British America: Unease in Eden," in Nicholas Canny and
Anthony Pagden, eds., *Colonial Identity in the Atlantic World 1500-1800* (Princeton:
Princeton UP, 1987) 157.
11 For a discussion of the rhetoric of nationalism and the creation of an American
identity, see Bercovitch, 19-45.

It was of the utmost significance not only to create a conjunction be-tween federal and state authority and between the citizen's commitment to national as well as local interests, but also to find a means of bridging the growing cultural and ethnic diversities, of constructing a biformity of coexisting ethnic and national pride. The widespread and long-lived belief that by means of the construction of a national sense of belonging the ma-ny could become one has, of course, not come true. As Kammen puts it, "[a]bove all factors ... the greatest source of dualisms in American life has been unstable pluralism in all its manifold forms: cultural, social, sequen-tial, and political. *E pluribus unum* is a misbegotten motto because we have *not* become one out of many. The myth of the melting pot is precisely that: a myth" (Kammen, 293-94).[12] The nineteenth-century assimilationists were convinced that the diversity and homogeneity would give birth to a synthesis, a new human breed. Americans, John Higham claims, "fashion-ed an image of themselves as an inclusive nationality, at once diverse and homogeneous, ever improving as it assimilated many types of men into a unified, superior people. According to this long and widely respected view, the Americans derived some of their very distinctiveness as a nationality from the process of amalgamation."[13]

Contrary to the believers in the melting pot vision, early advocates of cultural pluralism like Horace M. Kallen emphasized a structure of a "fed-eration of nationalities," thereby expressing his belief that ethnic nation-alities neither should nor could be transformed into any generic nationality. But as in the case of federalism, the different views of American ethnicity all took both the unifying and the disunifying factors, both the fusion and the fragmentation, into consideration; their differences were only a matter of shifted emphasis. In discussing the various ways of articulating the na-tional self-understanding that characterized the period up to 1924—the melting pot, the Americanization movement, Anglo-Saxon racialism, and cultural pluralism—Philip Gleason points out:

> The four perspectives can be most usefully distinguished according to whether their inherent tendency is toward unity or multiplicity, whether they place great-er stress on the *unum* or the *pluribus* in the national motto. The melting pot and cultural pluralism aspire to encompass both, but the former is assimilationist in

---

[12] See also Nathan Glazer and David P. Moynihan, *Beyond the Melting Pot: The Ne-groes, Puerto Ricans, Jews, Italians, and Irish of New York City* (Cambridge, Mass: MIT Press, 1968).

[13] Higham, *Strangers in the Land: Patterns of American Nativism 1860-1925* (New York: Atheneum, 1974) 21.

tendency and assigns priority to unity, while the latter is anti-assimilationist and ... looks to the preservation of a multiplicity of distinct ethnic nationalities.[14]

In America religion has also developed, according to historians, a biformity of concurrent diversity and national unison. Higham has argued, for instance, that in the 19th century there existed two levels of religious ideology; apart from the growing number of denominations, there developed a "pan-Protestant ideology that claimed to be civic and universal. Pledged to leave private beliefs undisturbed, it was vague enough so that increasing numbers of Jews and Catholics could embrace it."[15] That the tension between religious multiplicity and cohesion is no less today is supported by the assessment that the United States now hosts more than eight hundred Protestant-Catholic-Jewish denominations and approximately six hundred alternative religions. Parallel to this proliferation of sects and denominations, the consolidating power of Civil Religion has grown considerably. Robert N. Bellah and other scholars have shown how Civil Religion combines a worship of an all-inclusive, non-sectarian God with a belief in the United States as a chosen land and a faith in the American Way of Life.[16] Most Americans do not experience a contradiction between this "civil faith" and the faith of the church they belong to; they succeed in embracing this biformity, these expressions of fusion and fragmentation, without much hesitation or, even, awareness.

Capitalism and democracy, with their corollary in the private sphere of individualism and public commitment, have been seen as strongly linked with and overlapping the biformities discussed so far. Both of these pairs, it has been argued, express a coexisting belief in separateness and unity, self-interest and cooperation. McClosky and Zaller view capitalism and democracy as "the American Ethos" whose twin components "contribute to serve as the authoritative values of the nation's political structure." These opposite forces are distinctive of an American identity, they claim, stating that "the tension that exists between capitalist and democratic values is a definitive feature of American life that has helped to shape the

---

[14] Gleason, "American Identity and Americanization," in Stephan Thernstrom, ed., *Harvard Encyclopedia of American Ethnic Groups* (Cambridge, Mass.: Harvard UP, 1980) 46.

[15] John Higham, "Hanging Together: Divergent Unities in American History," *Journal of American History* 61:1 (June 1974): 13-24.

[16] Bellah, "Civil Religion in America," in *Beyond Belief: Essays on Religion in a Post-Traditional World* (New York: Harper & Row, 1970) 169-89. See also John F. Wilson, *Public Religion in American Culture* (Philadelphia: Temple UP, 1979).

ideological divisions of the nation's politics."[17] In its emphasis on private ownership, self-interest, competition, and individualism, the capitalist spirit constitutes an anti-communal force, while the democratic spirit—with its ideals of consent, equal rights, and equal opportunities—strives towards creating cohesion and harmony. The trust of many Americans in synchronous individualism and commitment has also been considered a characteristic expression of their culture. Although Bellah *et al.* in *Habits of the Heart* find that individualism, and not democracy as Tocqueville argued, has been the driving force of America, they nevertheless admit that for "all their doubts about the public sphere, Americans are more engaged in voluntary associations and civic organizations than the citizens of most other industrial nations."[18] This assessment finds its parallel in Jacques Maritain's statement from 1958 that "the feelings and instinct of community are much stronger in this country than in Europe ... the result of which is a tension, perpetually varying in intensity, between the sense of community and the sense of individual freedom." [19]

The Short Story Composite —A Literary Biformity

A literary version of this conjunction of unifying and discontinuous energies is, I would argue, the short story composite. With its structure of autonomous short stories interconnecting into a larger whole, it constitutes what might be called a literary—not deformity, but biformity; it could consequently be characterized as yet another expression of the coexistence of unity and diversity, fusion and fragmentation, that informs American culture.

Because of the doubleness of its nature, the short story composite has caused critics definitional problems. As my first chapter made clear, many terms have been employed to characterize this narrative, the most common of which are the *short story cycle* and the *short story sequence*. Most critics of the short story composite have so far devoted their efforts to creating unity and coherence in this narrative mode, attempting, as it may seem, to turn them into novels. Their studies highlight the closural strategies of these works, thereby, in my opinion, distorting this narrative's nature of biformity and doubleness. One might thus say that these critics have served,

---

[17] Herbert McClosky and John Zaller, *The American Ethos: Public Attitudes toward Capitalism and Democracy* (Cambridge, Mass.: Harvard UP, 1984) 1-2.

[18] Robert N. Bellah *et al.*, *Habits of the Heart: Individualism and Commitment in American Life* (Berkeley: U of California P, 1985) 163.

[19] Quoted in Kammen, 112.

in the literary field, the same role as federalists, advocates of the melting pot, and consensus historians did in theirs.

The short story composite is not primarily striving for what Smith calls "appropriate cessation," but is built on the *tension* between the concurrent separateness and interconnectedness of the stories. Let me therefore again draw attention to the oppositional structure of the composite, on the one hand to some of the literary devices and strategies that work in favor of coherence and closure and, on the other, to those, of equal strength and significance, that cause indeterminacy and an open form.

It is important to remember that the short story composite manifests itself in structures characterized by great variety. The closural force, for instance, varies significantly from one composite to another. Certain composites, like *The Pastures of Heaven*, *The Unvanquished*, and Naylor's *The Women of Brewster Place*, are comparatively tightly held together, whereas others, like *In Our Time*, *Go Down, Moses*, and *Lost in the Funhouse*, exhibit a comparatively high degree of fragmentedness. The intratextual links between the stories are thus stronger and more explicit in some composites than in others.

Among the many narrative elements unifying the separate stories one may mention setting, focalization, character, chronology, theme, myth, metaphor, and tone. A strong centripetal force is the retrospective patterning that its structure encourages. Setting creates coherence in *Winesburg, Ohio*, Godwin's *Mr. Bedford and the Muses*, Selby, Jr.'s *Last Exit to Brooklyn*; recurring characters connect the stories of *The Golden Apples*, Jayne Anne Phillips' *Machine Dreams*, *In Our Time*; the stories of *The Unvanquished* are held together primarily by the use of Bayard Sartoris as focalizer throughout the book and by the step-by-step chronology adhered to. These totalizing elements are no different from strategies employed by the novel or the short story.

While certain narrative strategies of the short story composite thus strive for a sense of completeness and interconnection, equally deliberate strategies privilege indeterminacy and discontinuity. Most short story composites are, as we have seen, characterized by numerous such anti-closural forces, such as the fact that the short story composite often skirts final resolution of plot; resists a sense of coherence; favors multiplicity; and is characterized by what might be called potentiality.

The Americanness of the Short Story Composite

To claim American exclusivity for the short story composite would of course be absurd. It is obvious that this narrative form existed before there was an American culture; it is equally apparent that this fictional mode is being employed by writers from numerous other countries. But just as Kammen has argued that the Americans can be called a "people of paradox" on the basis that American culture is *more* paradoxical than that of other countries, I would argue that the short story composite can be seen as a specifically American mode of narrative on account of, on the one hand, its formulation in literary form of biformal cultural values, by many held to be characteristic of America, and, on the other, as a result of this, its being a kind of fiction more frequently produced in the United States than in other Western countries. American writers did not invent this form, contrary to what Anderson suggested;[20] they merely adopted it because they sensed that it was conducive to their culture of biformities. We should probably extend the geographical area in which there is a high frequency of short story composites to include also Canada, thereby making this kind of narrative a North American phenomenon. It is a striking feature in Canadian literature, particularly after 1945, that writers like Munro, Hood, Laurence, Percy, Gaston, Huggan and Hodgins have employed narrative structures identifiable as those of the composite.[21]

For now limiting the discussion to U.S. fiction, one is struck by the large number of such narratives that have been produced during this century. Several new short story composites appear every year at what seems an accelerating pace. In her annotated list of 20th-century short story composites, Susan Garland Mann identifies some 120 items, 92 of which are American.[22] The remaining 31 composites listed were written by authors from Italy, England, Canada, Australia, the Soviet Union, France, Ireland, Spain, Czechoslovakia, and Poland. The enormous disproportion between American and non-American short story composites may partially be explained by Mann's special interest and expertise in American literature. Mann does not pretend to present either a representative or an exhaustive list. Nor do Dunn and Morris who present an annotated list of 215 "composite novels," four fifths of which originate in the United States.[23] In my own readings I have found numerous composites not listed by Mann or Dunn/Morris, most of which, again, are American. Like these critics, however, I also have a greater knowledge of American literature than of that

---

[20] Anderson said of the narrative form he employed in *Winesburg, Ohio*: "I invented it. It was mine." Quoted in Schevill, 96.

[21] Alice Munro, *Lives of Girls and Women* and *Who Do You Think You Are?*; Hugh Hood, *Around the Mountain*; Margaret Laurence, *A Bird in the House*; H.R. Percy, *Flotsam*; Bill Gaston, *Deep Cove Stories*; Isabel Huggan, *The Elizabeth Stories*; Jack Hodgins, *Spit Delaney's Island* and *The Barclay Family Theatre*.

[22] Mann, *The Short Story Cycle*, 187-208.

[23] Dunn and Morris, *The Composite Novel*, 159-82.

from other countries, with the possible exception of Sweden. In 20th-century Swedish fiction I have been able to distinguish only two authors who have employed the composite form: Eyvind Johnson and Ivar Lo Johansson.[24] As a contrast, in the United States a great number of the major writers of this century have written at least one short story composite each: Wharton, Anderson, Cather, Faulkner, Hemingway, Fitzgerald, Steinbeck, Wilder, Welty, Malamud, Barth, Coover, Doctorow, Gass, Updike, Erdrich, Godwin, Naylor, LeGuin, Kingston. In Sweden, then, few writers—major or minor—have adopted this narrative structure; as a consequence no short story composite tradition like that of America has developed. Whether this rather infrequent use of the composite form is an effect of Sweden being less of a paradoxical culture, one that is—or at least has been—characterized by comparative homogeneity, is of course impossible to say.

When it comes to the frequency of the short story composite in other Western countries, I suspect—though admitting incomplete information—that the situation is more or less like that of Sweden: there are short story composites scattered throughout the century, but not enough of them to form a specific narrative tradition. This seems to be true of British literature, with which I have some familiarity. Mann lists only two British authors, Angela Carter and James Herriot, and I have come across five more composites: Clive Sinclair's *Bibliosexuality*, B. S. Johnson's *The Unfortunates* (1969), George MacKay Brown's *Greenvoe* (1972) and *Witch and Other Stories*, and William McIlvanney's *Walking Wounded* (1989). As I am convinced that a methodical investigation would turn up several more Swedish examples of the composite, I am certain that additional British ones may be found. But I am equally sure that a similar investigation would make us aware of even further items of short story composites in American literature. And my impression—for at bottom it is an impression—still remains that an unusually large portion of the fiction produced in the United States employs the form of the short story composite.

If my suggestion is correct—that the short story composite is a narrative more common in the U.S. than elsewhere—the reason for this is not only that it reflects a culture of biformities; one might see at least three additional contributing factors. First, the United States enjoys a strong short story tradition, much more so than, for instance, Sweden.[25] Secondly, the

---

24 Johnson, *Livsdagen lång;* Lo Johansson, *Statarna* (1936-37), *Jordproletärerna* (1941), *Martyrerna* (1968), *Kar-riäristerna* (1969), *Girigbukarna* (1969), *Vällustingarna* (1970), *Lögnhalsarna* (1971), *Vishetslärarna* (1972).

25 See, for instance, Andrew Levy, *The Culture and Commerce of the American Short Story* (Cambridge: Cambridge UP, 1993).

creative writing programs at American universities, a specifically American phenomenon, privilege short fiction. Thirdly, in spite of this strong position of short fiction, the novel is still maintaining its hegemony; it is still considered more prestigious to have a novel published than a collection of stories. When a young writer, for instance, has completed a series of short stories, she knows that if she can connect them into a larger whole, into something that resembles a novel, she will stand a much greater chance of getting published. These three factors combine then, together with the one of biformity, to produce each year in the United States an unusual number of short story composites, and the last of these factors also helps explain why numerous composites—like Erdrich's *Love Medicine*, Kenney's *In Another Country*, and Naylor's *The Women of Brewster Place*—are defined by publishers as novels.

Two American Short Story Composites

I have chosen to illustrate some of the narrative aspects discussed above by focusing on two American short story composites, Harvey Swados' *On the Line* (1957) and Whitney Otto's *How to Make an American Quilt* (1991). Neither of these two can be said to belong with the major composites— books like *Winesburg, Ohio, In Our Time, Go Down, Moses, The Golden Apples*—and as a consequence they have received little critical attention. I consider them to be representatives rather of the large number of minor American composites that are seldom analyzed as composites, some of which are Randall Jarrell's *Pictures from an Institution*, John Horne Burns' *The Gallery*, Elizabeth Spencer's *Marilee*, Hubert Selby, Jr.'s *Last Exit to Brooklyn*, Cornelia Nixon's *Now You See It*, and Lee Smith's *The Devil's Dream*.

Both Swados' and Otto's book are characterized by a, for short story composites, comparatively strong sense of unity and coherence; in a continuum from fusion to fragmentation they would be placed closer to fusion. They do not possess the degree of rupture and disunity that distinguish such works as *In Our Time*, Doctorow's *Lives of the Poets*, Coover's *A Night at the Movies*, and Barth's *Lost in the Funhouse*, but fall rather into the *Winesburg, Ohio*-category, in which individual fates interconnect around a center.

I could have chosen any American short story composite for my discussion and not restricted myself, as I now do, to the works of two white mainstream writers—the composite's open form seems equally suitable for minority writing[26]—but I fell for the temptation to discuss Swados' and Otto's works because, apart from being examples of a specifically American art form, they explicitly point up their Americanness. Where Swados sets out to depict a cross section of an American male world, Otto creates a microcosm of American women. And even more importantly, both these texts are based on specifically American phenomena which at the same time function as both thematic and structural metaphors. As setting for his linked stories Swados chooses the assembly line in an automobile factory, where the parts become a whole, and in a similar way Otto employs the concept of the quilt as an image for human relations and the fused fragmentation of her narrative. Both the assembly line and the quilt could thus be seen as representations of the American culture of biformities.

Harvey Swados' *On the Line* [27] portrays in eight stories the lives of ten men on the assembly line of an upstate New York car factory. The social, racial, and ethnic background of these men vary; they are of different age, and their ambitions and goals differ considerably. It is obvious that Swados has taken pains to make a representative selection of male America. In writing the book, he said in an interview, he "suddenly understood what was happening to the American people, many millions of them, through an analogy of the lives of a few people."[28] Swados' ambition to write an American composite becomes apparent in the opening lines of the story about Pop, an immigrant with a "polysyllabic, unpronounceable last name":

> At bomber bases and in baseball clubhouses, at firehouse pinochle tables and in logging camps, in coal mines and among sand hogs, in the fo'c'sles of freighters and among the loading gangs at their piers, wherever Americans work, play, or fight, always there is one man known as Pop. (71)

These men are joined—one might even say chained together—in the assembly line, competing with each other, dependent on each other, in the dirty, debasing, disabling work they are set to perform. As time goes by, however diverse their background and ambition, they share the experience of having their dreams come to nothing. The assembly line spares no one;

---

[26] As examples of the latter one may mention Gloria Naylor, *The Women of Brewster Place,* Maxine Hong Kingston, *The Woman Warrior*, Amy Tan, *The Joy Luck Club*, Louise Erdrich, *Love Medicine*, Sandra Cisneros, *The House on Mango Street,* and Jamaica Kincaid, *Annie John*.

[27] Swados, *On the Line* (Boston: Little, Brown and Company, 1957).

[28] Swados interviewed by Herbert Feinstein, "Contemporary American Fiction: Harvey Swados and Leslie Fiedler," *Wisconsin Studies in Contemporary Literature* 2:1 (Winter 1961): 86.

it drains them and enslaves them. The only man who likes the work is Harold, the alcoholic, who, in contrast to the hell he formerly inhabited, finds the assembly line to be a life line; because the work makes him so completely exhausted he is no longer tempted to drink. This factory world is described by Charles Shapiro in the following manner:

> Swados has chosen to dramatize a steady tension between the dehumanizing effect of the line and the dreams of the workers who try, at first, to preserve their first enthusiasms ... as the assembly belt rolls on. The factory must destroy the individuality of each man, and as this cruel process is exposed, we come to accept the line as well as despair of it. The little tragedies, placed together, become a damning indictment.[29]

Mass production, here epitomized in the assembly line, mechanizes man and fragments his sense of community. The "mindless monotony" (8) of the work dulls the perception of Leroy, the mulatto who dreams of a career as singer; Kevin, the Irish immigrant—"chained to the drudgery, the monotony, the grinding labor"—is fooled into believing that buying an object, an automobile, will fulfill his dream. The moment when he cannot find his car in the parking lot among hundreds of automobiles, looking exactly alike, acts as an eye-opener; he realizes his enslavement and returns to Ireland (40-42). Orrin, the industrious, loyal worker who is set aside after being injured, learns what it means to be "stupified" (132), and Joe, the "vanishing American," suspects that life on the line is "deliberately designed to lower your own self-esteem." (66)

Work on the line becomes a metaphor of modern man's compartmentalized existence. The noise, the dust, the inhuman pace allow for only short snatches of conversation (31). Working side by side, the men remain separated from each other; Walter does not even know the name of the man next to him (59). The human voice—as illustrated by Leroy's singing—is muted by "air hammers, pneumatic drills, hissing flow guns that could throw three feet of spitting blue-red flame, warning horns of swaying trucks carrying spare parts down the aisles, and the grinding clank of the assembly line itself" (11) The men, hooked up together, are ultimately lonely, isolated components.

The assembly line thus becomes, in Swados' book, an image of Western capitalist culture, an indictment ultimately of the American way of life. And simultaneously the line constitutes an analogy to the structure of the

---

[29] Charles Shapiro, "Harvey Swados: Private Stories and Public Fiction," in Harry T. Moore, ed., *Contemporary American Novelists* (Carbondale: Southern Illinois UP, 1964) 189.

book: a series of separate stations at which new parts or working opera-
tions are added, accumulating until the product is finished.

This sense of united separation is thus manifested in the book's structure, in the way the stories are autonomous but also hooking into each
other. The unifying elements are those of setting, theme, and recurring
characters and events, and the stories are interconnected in a way that si-
mulates the assembly line. Although there are variations, the general structural pattern is the following: each story is devoted to one character, and
two thirds of the way into the story, Swados introduces a new character
from the assembly line, usually the man standing next to the protagonist;
this character will then be the protagonist of the next story. In the first third
of the new story, references are made to the protagonist of the preceding
story, after which he drops out, and somewhat later a new character appears who will be the protagonist of the following story. To take one example, Kevin, the protagonist of the second story, "Fawn, With a Bit of
Green," was introduced to us in the preceding story about Leroy (12-13).
Now, in the first part of Kevin's story, two incidents of the preceding
story—one being the accident that ruins Leroy's voice—are retold from
Kevin's point of view.[30] Some ten pages later into Kevin's story young
Walter appears who will take over the action in the next story. This relay
structure is not as mechanically executed as it may seem from my
schematization, but it does emphasize and bring out the monotonous
movement of the assembly line.

As in all short story composites, the disunifying elements are what characterize the genre: the interstices between the stories, the multivocality, the
lack of a single coherent plot, the lack of final resolution. There is little
sense of cyclicality in this composite; the stories follow sequentially, and
at the end of the book there is no attempt at creating a sense of closure to
the whole work. Several of the stories are open-ended (69, 137-38, 165-
66), as is the entire book. The pattern of connectives in Swados' composite
may well benefit from being analyzed by means of Wittgenstein's family
resemblance concept, discussed in the previous chapter.

Whitney Otto's *How to Make an American Quilt* dramatizes the lives of
eight women belonging to a quilting circle in the small town of Grasse
outside Bakersfield, California. Like Swados, Otto deliberately includes in
the group characters of diverse background, as the narrator puts it, "eight

---

30 In this structure we see an example of the "double" existence of the stories that I
have discussed in previous chapters. In each story of *On the Line* there is information
that is "redundant" to the composite but vital to the autonomous story (25, 29, 52, 106,
109, 140, 173, 176).

women of varying ages, weight, coloring, and cultural orientation."[31] Toward the end of the book, in a comment on the fact that two of the members of the circle, Anna and Marianna, are black, the text says: "It was this recognition of their differences that allowed the group to survive, not pretending to transcend them. The impulse to unify and separate, rend and join, is powerful and constant." (232) Otto thus aims at portraying one representative segment of American culture, its coexistence of diversity and a sense of community.

In the way Swados uses the assembly line, Otto has adopted the quilt as an American metaphor of both theme and structure. The patches put together in a design come to constitute an analogy to American pluralism and history and to human relations in general and marriage in particular. It also serves as an analogue to the narrative structure of interconnected stories.

Otto depicts the history of American women as a quilt composed of historical events and sees quilting as women's particular comment on that history (9-14). She also draws attention to the famous Names Quilt that covers nine acres and bears nine thousand names, a quilt "representing those Americans who have died youthful deaths from an incurable disease. This quilt is eclectic in its beauty (consider that America is the great melting pot and no two deceased are alike), staggering in its implication of waste" (144).

The thematic focus of the composite, however, is not so much history as the everyday life of American women, in particular their relations to lovers, husbands, children, and friends. And also here the quilt becomes the grid through which these relations are examined. In many of the stories the expectations of men and women to find "the perfect marriage or the ideal lover union" are thwarted, and Otto points out that such a complete fusion of souls is "as uncommon as any wondrous thing" (50). Nor is such symbiosis desirable. This longed-for, idealized unity of exchanged souls, "transferred from one to the other as a great gift and act of faith," is a healthy basis neither for a relationship, nor for a quilt: "But the body grows lonely for its old soul ... and longs to have it returned. A quilt, though stitched together, will always be separate, individual parts." (87)

Forgetting that lovers are "separate, individual parts" usually leads, in Otto's stories, to stagnation and death. Sophia marries Preston and after a few years of marriage they have seriously restricted each other (75-76). In another story, suitably called "String of Pearls," Constance is married to a travelling salesman, Howell, who spends long periods away from home. Their relationship is working well; Constance loves Howell partly because

---

[31] Otto, *How to Make an American Quilt* (New York: Ballantine Books, 1991) 7.

he lets her be (100). They have struck a balance between unity and separateness.[32] When Howell decides to quit travelling and stay home, they get on each other's nerves (105) and Constance feels that this "constant state of togetherness" is wearing on her (107). Em Reed, another member of the quilting circle, is married to the failed painter Dean. Em makes the mistake of viewing marriage "as combined halves that make a whole" (128), of demanding to become one with her husband, an attitude which leads to a lack of respect for the other as well as for oneself and to confusion as how to resolve this dependency. Em thinks: "She did not know; they were already too much part of each other to know." The quilting circle and the quilt are presented as models for human relations: The members of the group meet regularly, sharing their past, their sufferings, their longings, without being engulfed, without giving up their separate identities. And the result of the group's activity, the quilt, embodies fusion and discreteness, constituting a biformity in cloth.[33]

Helen Fiddyment Levy has pointed to quilting as a model for certain fictional works, not only composites, by Cather, Welty, Porter, and Glasgow.[34] Elaine Showalter discusses in an interesting historical overview the development of quilting as a metaphor of women's culture and writing. Among other things, she shows how "the patchwork quilt came to replace the melting-pot as a central metaphor of American cultural identity."[35] To my knowledge, however, no author has more deliberately than Otto employed the quilt as a paradigm for the structure of a narrative text. *How to Make an American Quilt* consists of seven stories and seven interchapters called "Instructions." These fourteen texts are framed by a "Prologue" and an epilogue called "The Crazy Quilt." The textual frame corresponds to the border of the quilt, the interchapters to the sashes that keep the quilt patches or blocks apart, and the stories of the composite to the patches themselves. The interchapters, apart from giving instructions on quilting, also draw explicit parallels to the themes dramatized in the stories. Taken together these narrative strategies—frame, interchapters, interlocking stor-

---

[32] Otto seems to regard the same balance of closeness and separateness as an ideal also for friendship, as in the relationship between Constance and Marianna.

[33] Otto's cycle presents other analogous metaphors of fusion and fragmentation, like Preston's statement that "the sun was formed from broken stars" (65) or the image of grafting bushes that dominates the end of the book, where Marianna feels that the "fusion of the bushes can only give the illusion of oneness, but can never truly be one." (228, 215)

[34] Levy, *Fiction of the Home Place: Jewett, Cather, Glasgow, Porter, Welty, and Naylor* (Jackson: UP of Mississippi, 1992) 27-30.

[35] Showalter, "Common Threads," in *Sister's Choice: Tradition and Change in American Women's Writing* (Oxford: Clarendon Press, 1991) 169.

ies—serve to establish coherence and closure together with such other totalizing devices as the setting of the town, the quilting circle, and the recurring characters.

But these narrative connectives are, if not negated, at least balanced by numerous disjunctive elements such as the gaps between the stories, the multiplicity of protagonists and plots, the shifting focalization, and the fragmented, even contradictory, chronology. No one single protagonist is allowed a hegemonic position; the eight women make up a collective of individuals. While the prologue and epilogue, and presumably also the interchapters, are told by a first-person narrator, the granddaughter of one of the quilters, the seven stories are narrated in the third person singular with the respective protagonist as focalizer. As an analogy to these manifestations of indeterminacy and open form, Otto suggests a particular quilt design, the Crazy Quilt, to which she returns throughout the composite (8, 49, 79, 124, 233-36). In contrast to the more unitary theme quilt, the Crazy Quilt is comprised of "remnants of material in numerous textures, colors." Its blocks cannot really be called squares, "since the stitched-together pieces are of all sizes and shapes" (8), and, characterized by "its lack of order, its randomness, its shrouded personal meanings," it is a quilt that "requires many hands, many meanings juxtaposed with each other" (49). A few of the women in the circle are made uncomfortable by the Crazy Quilt: Sophia does not enjoy its "freedom of color and pattern" (79), and Em feels that the making of such a quilt is too personal and revealing a project (124). In the coda, entitled "The Crazy Quilt," the narrator also points out that this design has simultaneously divided and joined the women of the quilting circle (236).

To return to my original supposition—that there is a correspondence between the American cultural pattern of biformity and the short story composite—obviously not only fiction writers have constructed America as a quilt. In his by now well-known speech at the 1988 Democratic convention in Atlanta, Jesse Jackson told an enthusiastic audience of how his grandmother, who had not been able to afford a blanket, had sewn patches together into a quilt, "a thing of beauty and power and culture." He went on to make the analogy to the diversity of American culture, speaking of the legitimate rights of numerous marginalized groups—farmers, workers, women, students, blacks, hispanics, gays and lesbians—portraying them as inhibiting patches of the quilt that makes up the United States, reiterating after discussing each group: "But your patch is not big enough!"

The formation of an American identity must be viewed as a continuous, never-ending process. And as analysts of American culture over time have mapped increasingly larger social and cultural areas, in which various structures of biformity could be detected, it would seem only natural that a literary scholar like myself would come along to draw attention to yet another area, the short story composite—a narrative mode through which this coexistence of fusion and fragmentation could suitably manifest itself—thereby making myself a participant in the ongoing construction of an American identity.

Six:
The Fringe Story—Or, How to Integrate the Resisting Text

In most novels the individual sections/chapters are of approximately equal thematic and/or structural significance. In general, no chapter is overshadowing the others, and no chapter is so marginalized as to seem unintegrated; there exists, so to speak, a balance between the various segments of the narrative. Not so in the short story composite. Many composites display a variability so seemingly capricious that it challenges the narrative conventions concerning a text's symmetry. Some composites are so dominated by one story that the others appear dwarfed; such stories may be termed "anchor stories." Many composites contain stories so poorly integrated that they do not seem to belong at all; these I call "fringe stories" and will be studied in this chapter.

Before turning to the fringe story, however, let me briefly discuss the "anchor story." Quite a few composites contain one story that from sheer length seems to assume a hegemonic position in the text, such as "The Dead" in *Dubliners*, "Big Two-Hearted River" in *In Our Time,* the title stories of Faulkner's and Doctorow's composites, "Knight's Gambit" and "Lives of the Poet." In most cases, such as the ones mentioned above, anchor stories are placed at the end of the composite. But on occasion they are situated in the middle of the book, as is "The Bear" in *Go Down, Moses* and "The Strike" in Selby's *Last Exit to Brooklyn*. Never, it seems, are anchor stories placed at the beginning of a composite. Because of its significance and length[1] the anchor story has been viewed as a novella[2] or a "miniature novel," as Nabokov called "The Country Husband" in Cheever's *The Housebreaker of Shady Hill*.[3] It has generally been seen as *the* kernel story of the volume. To take one example, "The Bear," according to Brooks, for most readers "overshad-

---

[1] On the basis of length alone a story does not qualify as an anchor story. Though "Godliness" is much longer than any other story of *Winesburg, Ohio*, it remains marginal in the composite.

[2] Frederick Karl on "Knight's Gambit" in *William Faulkner. An American Writer*, 766.

[3] See Kennedy, ed., *Modern American Short Story Sequences*, 145.

ows everything else in the book,"[4] and Sundquist holds that "it is nearly as difficult to imagine *Go Down, Moses* without its bear as it is to imagine *Moby-Dick* without its whale."[5] The dominant position of the anchor story challenges novelistic conventions concerning the symmetrical text and is one of the many features that distinguishes the short story composite from other forms of narrative. This disruptive function it shares with the "fringe story."

Because of its marginality, the fringe story has been a critical stumbling-block. It has often been, I feel, the victim of the overcommitment of critics to tuck in all the loose ends. The fringe story thereby becomes an interesting focal point if we want to study the process of gestalt formation within literary criticism. In this process of creating coherence and homogeneity at any cost, three different critical strategies seem to emerge: the fringe story is either 1. rejected/ignored so that unity may be established in the rest of the composite, or 2. "forced" into submission by means of various, more or less ingenious attempts at thematic and/or structural integration, or 3. elevated into a paradigmatic position where it is said to express the "essence" of the whole composite.

The fringe story is to me a true stumbling-block. It is the aporia of the short story composite which reveals the composite's indeterminate, discontinuous nature. These stories are, I hold, deliberate contraventions of narrative coherence and unity; they are the very sign, though not the only one, of the disruption that characterizes this mode of writing. I am not thereby implying that there are *no* links between the fringe story and the rest of the composite, only that it is intended to be only tangentially connected and that most critical attempts at totalization have been too ambitious and have neutralized texts that should be allowed to remain marginal.

Kernels, Satellites, and Fringe Stories

In narrative, according to Barthes, there are two subclasses of the functional unit: *cardinal* functions (or *nuclei*), which constitute the "real hinge points" of the narrative, and *catalyzers*, which are of a complementary nature, filling in "the narrative space separating the hinge functions."[6] In relation to the nucleus, the catalyzer is an expansion; while an expansion can be deleted, a nucleus cannot. Chatman translates, as

---

4 Cleanth Brooks, *William Faulkner: The Yoknapatawpha Country*, 244.

5 Eric J. Sundquist, *Faulkner: The Divided House* (Baltimore: Johns Hopkins UP, 1983) 133.

6 Roland Barthes, "Introduction to the Structural Analysis of Narratives," *A Barthes Reader*, ed. by Susan Sontag (New York: Hill and Wang, 1982) 265.

we saw in a previous chapter, Barthes' terms into *kernels* and *satellites*. A kernel is then the major event, which "advances the plot by raising and satisfying questions."[7] While the kernels are nodes in the narrative structure and cannot be deleted without destroying the narrative logic, the satellite can be logically deleted, although such deletion will naturally lead to an aesthetically impoverished text. The function of the satellite is that of "filling in, elaborating, completing the kernel."(54) Rimmon-Kenan argues that the satellites/catalysts "expand, amplify, maintain or delay" the kernels.[8]

This distinction into kernel and satellite events can be amplified, at a higher level, to explain the relations among stories of many short story composites. A short story composite often consists of a few central or nuclear stories and other stories of less significance to the logic of the plot, stories which may be regarded as satellites. In Chapter Four I mentioned as an example Welty's *The Golden Apples*, in which I consider "Shower of Gold," "June Recital," and "The Wanderers" to be kernel stories without which the composite would suffer considerably. The other four stories may be seen as satellites and either one could be taken out, or be replaced by another, new story, without great damage to the plot of the composite as a whole.

One kind of story operates, however, as an extreme satellite story. At first glance it seems not to have any intratextual links at all with the other stories—whether through narrator, characters, or setting. The reader experiences this kind of story as marginalized, and for this reason it may be termed a *fringe story*. One could give many examples of such fringe stories. A few are: "The Revolutionist" in Hemingway's *In Our Time*, "Etta Mae Johnson" in Naylor's *The Women of Brewster Place*, "Lulu's Boys" in Erdrich's *Love Medicine*, "The Water Works" in Doctorow's *Lives of the Poets*, "Music from Spain" in Welty's *The Golden Apples,* and "The Baby Makes Three" in Selby's *Last Exit to Brooklyn*. I will here focus my discussion on three well-known fringe stories which have caused great critical confusion: Anderson's "Godliness" from *Winesburg, Ohio*, Hemingway's "My Old Man" from *In Our Time*, and Faulkner's "Pantaloon in Black" from *Go Down, Moses*.

---

[7] Seymour Chatman, *Story and Discourse: Narrative Structure in Fiction and Film* (Ithaca: Cornell UP, 1978) 53.

[8] Shlomith Rimmon-Kenan, *Narrative Fiction: Contemporary Poetics* (London: Routledge, 1983) 16.

Anderson's "Godliness"

In the prologue to *Winesburg, Ohio*, "The Book of the Grotesque," the old author says about the characters we are about to meet that "the moment one of the people took one of the truths to himself, called it his truth, and tried to live by it, he became a grotesque and the truth he embraced became a falsehood."[9] This, to me, may be taken as an admonition from Anderson to the reader/critic not to make the same mistake and reduce the many truths s/he will encounter in the composite into a single truth, but instead to acknowledge the multiplicity and variability of his work. He presumably hoped that readers would assume the same open attitude he himself later expressed when he characterized his book as possessing a "new looseness" and added that his "stories were obviously written by one who did not know the answers."[10]

Most critics, it seems to me, have not heeded Anderson's advice. Numerous critical attempts — some excessive, others more level-headed — have been made to find paradigms that would neatly include all the stories, that would establish an organic unity to the composite.

A number of critics have noticed that Anderson's themes in the book concern incompleteness, isolation, and lack of communication. Edwin Fussell believes that "Anderson is indisputably the man who writes about discontinuity among persons and about the behaviors and feelings that spring from that discontinuity."[11] Others have pointed to the book's inconsistencies in chronology and the age of the characters,[12] factors which also contribute to the sense of disruption. In spite of these insights scholars have been slow to accept the form of the book as one well suited to its theme; they have felt a need to seek a unity that Anderson apparently did not believe in.

Various types of totalizing patterns have been suggested. The text has been seen as depicting a cross-section of a small American town at the end of the 19th century — too limited a view, I believe, since numerous aspects of ordinary town life are missing. It has been presented as a study in "human isolation," and one critic has argued that the first three

---

9 Sherwood Anderson, *Winesburg, Ohio*. Introduction by Malcolm Cowley (New York: Viking Press, 1960) 25.

10 Sherwood Anderson, *Memoirs*, quoted from The Viking Critical Library edition of *Winesburg, Ohio*, ed. by John H. Ferres (New York: Viking Press, 1966) 14.

11 Edwin Fussell, "*Winesburg, Ohio*: Art and Isolation," in the Viking Critical Library edition of *Winesburg, Ohio*, 384.

12 Forrest L. Ingram, *Representative Short Story Cycles of the Twentieth Century* (The Hague: Mouton, 1971) 167-68.

stories illustrate three human needs which people are unable to communicate: emotions, thoughts, and love. This inability is elaborated on in the middle stories until the last two stories come "to a tentative solution to the problem of human isolation."[13] The theme of grotesqueness has also been proposed as unifying all the stories,[14] and so has the theme of the characters' "transcendental yearnings" that will never be fulfilled.[15] Maybe the most common way of reading this text, however, is to highlight its characteristics as *Bildungsroman*. The central plot then becomes the initiation of George Willard, and the characters, "the grotesques," that he meets contribute to his growing awareness and maturity.[16]

The intratextual aspects of the book have received considerable attention, the connective devices that make it into more than a collection of stories. Scholars have discussed the unifying functions of repeated symbols, words, and phrases; of repeated locales like streets, the newspaper, the New Willard House; of recurring characters like Helen White, Kate Swift, Seth Richmond, and, in particular, George Willard, whose name appears in 19 of the 21 stories. Other elements creating coherence have been suggested: the fact that all but five stories take place in the evening,[17] and that they all are plotless, consisting rather of "revelations" or "epiphanies": the characters are caught "at an essential moment in time that reveals a series of brief, intuitive, but true glimpses of the human heart. Each story reveals the essence of the central character's life as Anderson knows it."[18]

To return to my earlier discussion about kernel stories and satellite stories, *Winesburg, Ohio* is characterized, on the one hand, by stories that are more central, stories where the intratextual links are comparatively strong, and, on the other, by more marginal ones, like "Paper Pills," where George Willard is not even mentioned, and "Adventure," and "The Untold Lie," which could be deleted without seriously dis-

---

[13] David D. Anderson, *Sherwood Anderson: An Introduction and Interpretation* (New York: Holt, Rinehart and Winston, 1967) 41-49.

[14] Ray Lewis White, Winesburg, Ohio: *An Exploration* (Boston: Twayne Publishers, 1990) 56-94.

[15] Ralph Ciancio, "'The Sweetness of the Twisted Apples': Unity of Vision in *Winesburg, Ohio*," *PMLA* 87:5 (October 1972): 994-1006.

[16] See, e.g., Walter B. Rideout, "The Simplicity of *Winesburg, Ohio*," in the Viking Critical Library edition of *Winesburg, Ohio*, 294-99; Rex Burbank, *Sherwood Anderson* (New York: Twayne Publishers, 1964) 66-77; Ray Lewis White, Winesburg, Ohio: *An Exploration*, 35-55; Dunn and Morris, *The Composite Novel*, 52-53.

[17] Rideout, "The Simplicity of *Winesburg, Ohio*," 292.

[18] David D. Anderson, *Sherwood Anderson*, 38.

rupting the plot of the book. White finds the two latter stories to be "almost completely separable from the other stories."[19]

Lorch sees the problem that such marginality causes to the unity of the book:

> Two closely related difficulties must be overcome if we are to find structural unity in *Winesburg, Ohio*. The first is the manner in which the book goes beyond the figure of George Willard, and the second is the way in which the stories in which he does not appear fit into its structural patterns.[20]

Lorch manages to find the unity he is looking for by assigning to the main characters of satellite stories such as "The Book of the Grotesque" and "Paper Pills" the function of foils, embodying the ideals against which George and the other characters are measured, and by pronouncing "Adventure" and "The Untold Lie" to be variations on the "basic characters and actions."

Finally, Lorch comes to the stumbling-block, "perhaps the ultimate test of the book's unity," that is "Godliness," a story which has caused also other critics much worry. In most respects "Godliness" is radically different from the other stories of the composite. Consisting of four parts, it is four times longer than the others. The other stories of the composite express a key moment in a character's life, while "Godliness" covers the events of three generations. And while the character George Willard is present in virtually all the other stories, he is absent here. The other stories take place in Winesburg; the action of "Godliness" is situated on a farm outside of town. If the primary unifying theme of the book is that of human isolation or grotesqueness, this story deviates also thematically from the rest. The themes of "Godliness" are rather those of hubris and the Weberian thesis of the Protestant ethic and the spirit of capitalism. Also, the tone is different. While most of the stories in the composite are lyrical and meditative, "Godliness" resorts to a heavy-handed preaching and editorializing that reminds the reader of the weaker moments in Dreiser's writings. In the words of Burbank, the story about Jesse Bentley "violates the symbolic structure of the book, for the narrative of Jesse Bentley's change from prophet to capitalist conforms so much to the idea it dramatizes that it lapses into direct statement and contrived allegory. ... When his grandson David fells him with a slingshot, the parallel

---

[19] White, Winesburg, Ohio: *An Exploration*, 86.
[20] Thomas M. Lorch, "The Choreographic Structure of *Winesburg, Ohio*," *CLA Journal* 12:1 (September 1968): 62-63.

with David and Goliath approaches incredibility."[21] The character of Jesse differs widely, according to Dewey, from the grotesques in the book:

> Where they are retiring, he is assertive; where they seem frozen and static, he is a dynamo; where they are lost in self-pity, he crows of his many accomplishments; where they bottle themselves up into tiny chambers, he sees a vision that encompasses hundreds of acres; where they nurse quiet anxieties to escape Winesburg, he thrusts his roots deeply; where they seem confused and plagued with doubt, he subscribes to a clear, theological order; where they seem curiously infertile, he begats with Biblical intensity.[22]

It seems thus obvious that "Godliness" is hardly at all integrated into the composite.

Three different critical reactions to such a fringe story as "Godliness" can be observed: one which rejects or ignores the story because it mars the wholeness; one which seeks to find some basis for integration, and one that essentializes the story. As an example of the first, one may mention Howe's contention that "*Winesburg* seems remarkably of a piece. The only stories that do not fit into its pattern are the four-part narrative of Jesse Bentley, a failure in any case, and possibly 'The Untold Lie'."[23] Others, like Phillips, point to the interlockings between stories, but "forget" to include "Godliness" in their discussion.[24]

Ingram is a representative of the integrationist position. He asks: "What function do such stories as the four parts of 'Godliness' serve in the collection?"[25], but provides no compelling answer. Having difficulties acknowledging the discreteness of the story, he unconvincingly attempts to establish a harmonious whole. He states, for instance, that "the themes and motifs of the 'Godliness' stories are perfectly consonant with those coursing through the rest of the cycle" (194), a statement which may certainly be questioned. In a similar vein Mann asks whether "Godliness" "enhance[s] or damage[s] the overall unity of the book? ... Does

---

21 Burbank, 76. For a similar view of the story see Jarvis A. Thurston, "Technique in *Winesburg, Ohio*," in The Viking Critical Library edition of *Winesburg, Ohio*, 341.

22 Joseph Dewey, "No God in the Sky and No God in Myself: 'Godliness' and Anderson's *Winesburg*," *Modern Fiction Studies* 35:2 (Summer 1989): 251.

23 Irving Howe, *Sherwood Anderson* (n.p.: William Sloane Associates, 1951) 106.

24 William L. Phillips, "How Sherwood Anderson Wrote *Winesburg, Ohio*," in Ray Lewis White, ed., *The Achievement of Sherwood Anderson: Essays and Criticism* (Chapel Hill: U of North Carolina P, 1966) 62-84.

25 Ingram, *Representative Short Story Cycles of the Twentieth Century*, 165.

the independence of 'Godliness' overwhelm its importance as a part of *Winesburg*?" And she answers: "I would say no since the characters, events, and themes developed here echo what happens in the rest of the book."[26] The echo may be there, but it certainly is not very loud.

Other critics try to be more precise than Ingram and Mann in their arguments on why "Godliness" is an integrated text. Laughlin holds the story to be "outstanding precisely because it is brilliantly in step with the other stories in the frame, and with a larger context as well. Especially by its style, symbols and characters it is integrally attached to the Winesburg grotesques." Jesse Bentley, his daughter Louise, and his grandson David take up positions among the other grotesques.[27] Conversely, Lorch finds grounds for integrating "Godliness" into the composite in the fact that Jesse is the *opposite* of the grotesques, personifying rather the destructive forces of convention in the community that make victims of the grotesques.[28] Dewey, who so clear-sightedly noticed the discrepancy between Jesse and the grotesques, prefers as a consequence another road of integration. He links the characters of "Godliness" rather to the theme of George Willard's growth to maturity, arguing that Jesse, Louise, and David are precursors to George in a development from religious fanaticism to the mission of the artist: "George reshapes that feverish frenetic search for spiritual communion to produce his knowing sophistication."[29]

The third critical strategy of integration, of pronouncing a story paradigmatic, may be represented by O'Neill, who attempts to merge "Godliness" with the whole by arguing that the story itself has an integrative function, "underlining and simplifying for us an element of crucial importance in most of *Winesburg*." The story of Jesse thus becomes the essence of the composite, and Jesse himself has "emblematic significance" for the rest of the book. The story, according to O'Neill, "reveals in a more thorough and straightforward way the nature of the fanatical, the obsessive and the lonely, as well as other key psychological forces at work throughout the book." The characters of Jesse, Louise, and David focus and reinforce our overall impressions of *Winesburg*, "for each is seen to be an amplified and dramatically simplified version of the es-

---

[26] Mann, *The Short Story Cycle: A Genre Companion and Reference Guide*, 61.

[27] Rosemary M. Laughlin, "Godliness and the American Dream in *Winesburg, Ohio*," *Twentieth Century Literature* 13:2 (July 1967): 97.

[28] Lorch, "The Choreographic Structure of *Winesburg, Ohio*," 64-65.

[29] Dewey, "No God in the Sky and No God in Myself: 'Godliness' and Anderson's *Winesburg, Ohio*," 258.

sential types to which Anderson returns over and over again in *Wines-burg*."[30]

Most of the readings presented above refuse to acknowledge not only the disruptive structure of *Winesburg, Ohio* as a composite but in particular the marginal position of "Godliness." I am not denying that the story may share echoes with other stories, but I feel strongly that the "looseness" of Anderson's composite and the fringe position of "Godliness" should be allowed to remain as they were obviously intended and not be subsumed under the centripetal forces of critical organicism.

Hemingway's "My Old Man"

In some ways, Hemingway's *In Our Time* is a more open work than *Winesburg, Ohio*; Hemingway was no doubt inspired by Anderson's work, but managed to make the narrative structure more indeterminate and discontinuous. The structure consists of stories interspersed with interchapters, or vignettes. The intratextual links are, however, relatively few compared to those of *Winesburg*. There are few explicit connectives between the interchapters and the stories and even in the relation between the stories there is considerable fragmentation. Several of the stories are devoted to Nick Adams, who then becomes the single most unifying element of the book, but there are quite a number of stories and interchapters which do not have Nick as protagonist.

The disconnected structure of this short story "cluster," as I would call it, lends itself well to an analysis in terms of kernel, satellite, and fringe stories. The stories about Nick dominate *In Our Time*: he is mentioned in seven stories and one interchapter. The first five stories and the last form a frame which privileges the figure of Nick. He may furthermore be the unnamed protagonist of "A Very Short Story" and a few of the interchapters, like "Chapter VII," "Chapter XI," and "Chapter XIII." The Nick-stories and -vignettes thus form a core in the book; they are the kernel narratives. Apart from these the book contains six stories and a number of interchapters not explicitly connected to the Nick-stories; these might then be termed satellite narratives. While some of these satellites may be linked to the kernel narratives, there are two stories which fit less well into the designs or patterns made up by critics, namely "The Revolutionist" and "My Old Man." Using the terminology I suggested earlier, these stories may be considered fringe stories.

Many critics have tried to integrate the disconnected stories and interchapters into a design with as few loose ends as possible to disturb the

---

30 John O'Neill, "Anderson Writ Large: 'Godliness' in *Winesburg, Ohio*," *Twentieth Century Literature* 23 (1967): 67-83.

harmony. Few have been as radical as Philip Young, who did away with all the non-Nick stories, added an introductory piece, "Three Shots," and a conclusion "On Writing," which Hemingway had excised from *In Our Time*, and several stories not originally in the book, changed the order of two stories—because he felt the chronology was wrong—and finally published this construct as *The Nick Adams Stories*.

Other scholars have claimed that all the stories can be read as part of the education of Nick Adams. In such a version, Krebs in "Soldier's Home" is in reality Nick and the unhappy couple in "Cat in the Rain" are Nick and Helen. And the non-Nick stories are said to have, as Burhans puts it, "a central character like him in all but name."[31]

As I pointed out in Chapter One, a slightly different use of Nick as the totalizing paradigm is proposed by Moddelmog. Basing her argument on the nine excised pages mentioned above, now called "On Writing," she argues that Nick must be considered the author of the stories preceding "Big Two-Hearted River" and she continues: "In a classic psychoanalytic paradox, the closer the matter is to Nick the writer, the further away Nick the character is likely to be. The non-Nick stories can thus hold the key to Nick's innermost secrets and fears."[32] The obvious danger of such a construction of conformity is that it takes the critic away from the actual text toward an "ideal text."

But if such integrationist strategies were valid, the protagonists—to take just one example—of "A Very Short Story" and "Soldier's Home" should have had similar experiences, be of a similar nature, and express similar emotional reactions to war. The unnamed protagonist of "A Very Short Story" is wounded in Italy, has an affair in the hospital with a nurse, goes back to the front, leaves for America after the armistice to get a job, lives in Chicago and seems fairly well adjusted, is rejected by the nurse but finds comfort in other girls and contracts gonorrhea. Krebs in "Soldier's Home" is stationed in Germany, he gets back to his small home town in Oklahoma "years after the war was over,"[33] carrying with him a deep psychological wound. As Leigh states: "His disintegration

---

31 Clinton S. Burhans, Jr., "The Complex Unity of *In Our Time*," in Jackson J. Benson, ed., *The Short Stories of Ernest Hemingway: Critical Essays* (Durham, N.C.: Duke UP, 1975) 17. See also Jackson J. Benson, "Patterns of Connection and Their Development in Hemingway's *In Our Time*," in Michael S. Reynolds, ed., *Critical Essays on Ernest Hemingway's* In Our Time (Boston: G. K. Hall & Co, 1983) 108.

32 Debra A. Moddelmog, "The Unifying Consciousness of a Divided Conscience: Nick Adams as Author of *In Our Time*," *American Literature* 60:4 (December 1988): 591-610.

33 Ernest Hemingway, *In Our Time* (New York: Charles Scribner's Sons, 1958) 89.

during the war leaves him barely able to function."[34] He is not interested either in a job or in girls; he suffers from an alienation that completely paralyzes him. As the characters and experiences of the anonymous hero of "A Very Short Story" and Krebs have little in common, the question remains: *Which* of them is representative of the education of Nick Adams? One way of solving the problem is to claim, as Wood has done, that *In Our Time* is unified by a "composite personality," consisting of Nick and all the other characters put together into a "drifting and disillusioned member of the lost generation."[35]

Apart from treating *In Our Time* as a *Bildungsroman*, critics have chosen to foreground other connective devices such as theme, primarily the interwoven themes of initiation and the quest for a code of life. In Chapter One I gave examples of how the theme of seeing and perception has been held forth as "the central unifying force in *In Our Time*,"[36] and how Grimes broadens this view of the book—which he declares to be a "novel"—by claiming that it is unified by the movement from "looking at" to "living in" the times.[37] Hemingway's use of a network of imagery has also been seen as creating coherence. Hasbany's reading might serve as an illustration of this approach:

> So Hemingway assaults us with image superimposed on image until a new totality of insight is created from the thirty-two pieces of work he has assembled and superpositioned on each other. It is a creation of an image of a time, an image of an agonized humanity, grimacing at the reality of being in our time, and yet also the image of naiveté and hope in the figures of the revolutionary

---

[34] David J. Leigh, "*In Our Time*: The Interchapters as Structural Guides to a Psychological Pattern," *Studies in Short Fiction* 12:1 (1975): 2.

[35] Carl Wood, "*In Our Time*: Hemingway's Fragmentary Novel," *Neuphilologische Mitteilungen* 74.4 (1973): 722. Winn also sees the unity of *In Our Time* as consisting in the creation of such a composite personality, a "figure living 'in our time'." See Harbour Winn, "Hemingway's *In Our Time*: 'Pretty Good Unity'," *The Hemingway Review* 9:2 (Spring 1990): 139. The same argument, that the book coheres through a "collective protagonist," is forwarded by Dunn and Morris in *The Composite Novel*, 64-65.

[36] Benson, "Patterns of Connection and Their Development in Ernest Hemingway's *In Our Time*," 106.

[37] Larry E. Grimes, "*In Our Time*: An Experiment in the Novel," in *The Religious Design of Hemingway's Early Fiction* (Ann Arbor: UMI Research Press, 1985) 41.

and of the Greek king, who despite his house imprisonment, wants to go to America.[38]

Several scholars have ventured to structure the interchapters and stories into groupings and categories in order to minimize the disunity of the work. Mann surveys three such attempts, by Leigh, Silverman, and Slabey, at subdividing the stories into groups and putting labels on them. It turns out, not surprisingly, that there is little agreement not only on how to divide them but also on which labels to attach.[39]

In these pursuits of totalization, two stories have caused critics severe headaches: "The Revolutionist" and "My Old Man." Contrary to all the other stories, these two are written in the first person singular. Neither the protagonist nor the narrator of "The Revolutionist" seems to fit into the progress of Nick's education, and the same is true of Joe Butler and his father in "My Old Man." The suggestion that the latter story actually would make more sense among the early Nick stories,[40] that Hemingway has made a mistake in the chronology, is not really convincing, since Joe bears no resemblance to Nick as a boy.

Several critics have felt that "My Old Man" is distinct in some way from the rest of the stories. Some have argued that it is too Andersonian and consequently an apprentice piece. An early reviewer who rejected all stories as not really "stories," excepted "My Old Man" which he found beautifully executed.[41] Fitzgerald expressed exactly the opposite view when he showed great admiration for all of *In Our Time* except "My Old Man," finding it the book's single false note.[42] Benson also points to the story's discreteness: "'My Old Man' is ... significantly, the least organically related, in style and manner, to the collection as a whole."[43]

Critics who have concerned themselves with the structure of *In Our Time* as a short story composite have either "forgotten" to include "My Old Man" in a larger design or have unenthusiastically submitted often

---

[38] Richard Hasbany, "The Shock of Vision: An Imagist Reading of *In Our Time*," in Linda W. Wagner, ed., *Ernest Hemingway. Five Decades of Criticism* (n.p.: Michigan State UP, 1974) 239.

[39] Mann, *The Short Story Cycle*, 78-79.

[40] Burhans, "The Complex Unity of *In Our Time*," 27.

[41] A review by Hershel Bricknell, referred to by Carlos Baker in *Ernest Hemingway: A Life Story* (New York: Charles Scribner's Sons, 1969) 158-59.

[42] Fitzgerald, "How to Waste Material: A Note on My Generation," *Bookman* 63 (May 1926): 262-65.

[43] Benson, "Patterns of Connection and Their Development in Hemingway's *In Our Time*," 104; see also Mann, *The Short Story Cycle*, 76.

overly ingenious attempts at integration. Joe Butler reminds us of Nick, one critic claims, since they both share similar experiences, personality traits, and family or social backgrounds,[44] a characterization which bears little resemblance to the actual text. It has further been held that the story echoes the theme of initiation and disillusionment from the other stories,[45] which is fair enough, but which does not really link it very closely to the rest of the stories, since such themes as initiation may be found in most American short stories of this century. Wagner suggests yet another connection, though to me a rather feeble one: that in the last two stories "Hemingway broadens his interest in romantic love to include different kinds of love"—in "My Old Man" one man's responsibility for another.[46] Slabey finds ground for integration in the theme of fatherhood; Joe's affection for his jockey father recalls Nick's attitude towards his father, and the lesson Nick has learned, about to become a father himself, is that if "love and marriage do not always take precedence over male companionship, fatherhood does."[47] Winchell contends, in line with Slabey's argument, that "what makes the stories an integrated whole is a common attitude toward domestic life," and that "My Old Man," by showing the bonding of father and son, "conforms quite predictably to the Hemingway doctrine that the strongest loyalties are those that unite men with other men."[48]

The integrationist strategy of turning the fringe story into a paradigmatic one does not seem to have been applied in the case of "My Old Man." To my knowledge no critic has endeavored to argue that the story about Joe and his father functions as a metaphor for the whole composite, which may be seen as proof of its utter marginality. "My Old Man" cannot, and should not, in my view, be refused its fringe position even if it thereby constitutes a challenge to our sense of wholeness. We need to acknowledge that *In Our Time* is not a harmonized work; much of the excitement we experience in reading it stems from the undeniable tension that exists between the connectable and the unconnectable, between its closure and openness.

---

[44] Mann, *The Short Story Cycle*, 75.

[45] Burhans, "The Complex Unity of *In Our Time*," 27.

[46] Linda W. Wagner, "Juxtaposition in Hemingway's *In Our Time*," *Studies in Short Fiction* 12:3 (1975): 252.

[47] Robert M. Slabey, "The Structure of Hemingway's *In Our Time*," *Moderna Språk* 60:3 (1966): 272-85.

[48] Mark Royden Winchell, "Fishing the Swamp: 'Big Two-Hearted River' and the Unity of *In Our Time*," *South Carolina Review* 18:2 (Spring 1986): 24-25.

Faulkner's "Pantaloon in Black"

Even though he is not a protagonist of the story proper, the first three paragraphs of "Was," and thus also of *Go Down, Moses*, are devoted to Isaac McCaslin, pointing up from the start the central role that Uncle Ike will play in the book. The McCaslin family and the McCaslin plantation, many critics would claim, become the dominating unifying element of the composite.[49] The stories in which Ike serves as focalizer and character naturally come to form a tri-partite nucleus of the book: "The Old People," "The Bear," and "Delta Autumn" thus constitute the kernel stories, with "The Bear" as the innermost center of the nucleus.[50]

The four remaining stories can be regarded as satellite stories. Three of these are fairly loosely related to the kernel stories. "Was" and "The Fire and the Hearth" may be seen as making up the background to the Ike-stories, "Go Down, Moses" as showing the effects of actions of the kernel stories. Many of the connective devices unifying the Ike-stories are missing, however, in these stories. The tone is different, the wilderness theme is missing, the character of Ike is absent, and part of "Go Down, Moses" takes place in a different location. The fourth satellite story, "Pantaloon in Black," is very tenuously linked to the other six. Its only connection are two short references to the preceding story, "The Fire and the Hearth." It could thus well be characterized as a fringe story.

Many paradigms have been suggested to increase the cohesion of *Go Down, Moses*, to make the satellite stories look like kernels, to give equal weight to all the stories and a roundness and sense of "appropriate cessation" to the composite. Apart from situating all the stories under the

---

[49] For readings which put the McCaslin family at the center, see, for instance, Cleanth Brooks, *William Faulkner: The Yoknapatawpha Country* (New Haven: Yale UP, 1963) 244; Lyall H. Powers, *Faulkner's Yoknapatawpha Comedy* (Ann Arbor: U of Michigan P, 1980) 162; Lawrance Thompson, *William Faulkner: An Introduction and Interpretation* (New York: Barnes & Noble, 1963) 82-98; Hans H. Skei, *William Faulkner: The Novelist as Short Story Writer. A Study of William Faulkner's Short Fiction* (Oslo: Universitetsforlaget, 1985) 233-43; Stanley Sultan, "Call Me Ishmael: The Hagiography of Isaac McCaslin," *Texas Studies in Literature and Language* 3:1 (1961): 50; Stanley Tick, "The Unity of *Go Down, Moses*," *Twentieth Century Literature* 8:2 (July 1962): 65-73.

[50] Walter Brylowski considers, for instance, the three stories to "constitute a single coherent work" and the four others to be "rather loosely related stories added for the book length Faulkner often mentioned as necessary to insure the purchaser his value on the dollar." See *Faulkner's Olympian Laugh: Myth in the Novels* (Detroit: Wayne State UP, 1968) 153.

roof of the McCaslin plantation, critics have proposed various themes to bridge dangerous gaps and avoid a threatening narrative chaos. Such propositions of amalgamation are, for instance, those of bondage vs. freedom,[51] the ritual hunt,[52] the journey, black and white relations, wilderness,[53] and initiation.[54]

Structural gestalt formations are also commonly proposed. Typically, they treat the stories about Ike McCaslin as kernels, regarding the three first stories of the volume as one unit, preparing the reader for the nuclear stories. Critics do not agree, however, what constitutes the unit. Sultan sees the initial stories as preparing for the Ike-stories in that, in a three-step fashion, they provide comic, epic, and tragic aspects of the Carothers McCaslin legacy.[55] Powers similarly considers these stories to present Isaac's heritage: "This first section of three stories presents quite clearly enough those sins of disrespect for and hence exploitation of the land and of human beings which are regularly the basic concern of Faulkner's fiction."[56] Schleifer proposes that the first three stories are unified by way of the theme of initiation of courtship, while the next three find coherence through the initiation of the hunt.[57] Reed chooses to form a different gestalt. He makes "Was" the wellspring of the ensuing stories: "every cause that has an effect in the book and every pattern that develops through the other stories can be found there."[58] Thornton finds that Faulkner achieves an "impressive novelistic unity" by means of "latent juxtaposition," a technique of establishing a network or web of juxtaposable elements such as cages, beds, and cots.[59]

---

[51] Thompson, *William Faulkner*, 81-85; Weldon Thornton, "Structure and Theme in Faulkner's *Go Down, Moses*," in Leland H Cox, ed., *William Faulkner: Critical Collection* (Detroit: Gale Research Company, 1982) 328-68.

[52] Olga Vickery, *The Novels of William Faulkner* (Baton Rouge: Louisiana State UP, 1961). See also Eric J. Sundquist, *Faulkner: The House Divided*, 134, 140.

[53] For a survey see Mann, *The Short Story Cycle*, 121-26; see also Michael Millgate, *William Faulkner* (London: Oliver and Boyd, 1961) 75.

[54] Ronald Schleifer, "Faulkner's Storied Novel: *Go Down, Moses* and the Translation of Time," *Modern Fiction Studies* 28:1 (Spring 1982): 109-27.

[55] Sultan, "Call Me Ishmael: The Hagiography of Isaac McCaslin," 51-55.

[56] Powers, *Faulkner's Yoknapatawpha Comedy*, 168.

[57] Schleifer, "Faulkner's Storied Novel," 124.

[58] Joseph W. Reed, Jr., *Faulkner's Narrative* (New Haven: Yale UP, 1973) 186-87.

[59] Thornton, "Structure and Theme in Faulkner's *Go Down, Moses*," 331, 334.

Latimer argues that the composite's unity rather emerges from the fact that it reenacts the basic pattern and content of Attic comedy.[60]

All critical attempts at integration notwithstanding, "Pantaloon in Black" still remains only marginally related to the other stories. Its discreteness shatters coherence and closure, making it clearly a fringe story. "Pantaloon in Black" is timeless: it can only with difficulty be placed in the book's chronology. Rider, the black protagonist, cannot be inserted into the McCaslin geneaology, nor is he related or connected with any other character in the book, as far as we know; the text fails to mention any family relationships. There are no references in the story to events or story lines of preceding stories. Only two references, mentioned in passing, link "Pantaloon in Black" to the preceding story "The Fire and the Hearth." Rider rents his house from Carothers Edmonds and, as Uncle Lucas Beauchamp did forty-five years earlier, on his wedding night he builds a fire on his hearth. The other stories in the composite contain references and establish connectives to more than one other story; to give just one example, the poker game in "Was" is referred to once in "The Fire and the Hearth" and "Delta Autumn" and twice in "The Bear." No such intratextual links occur in "Pantaloon in Black." No succeeding story refers back to "Pantaloon," unless the opening sentence of "The Bear" is meant as such an explicit link: "There was a man and a dog too this time."

As Creighton and others have shown, Faulkner revised most of the stories quite extensively while forming the composite of *Go Down, Moses*. Two stories received less revision, "Pantaloon in Black" and "Go Down, Moses."[61] Since Faulkner paid so much attention to revising the stories, it seems quite clear that he intended these two—particularly "Pantaloon" which displays even fewer connective devices than "Go Down, Moses"—to remain marginally integrated. "Pantaloon in Black" could quite easily have been much more closely linked to the other stories, if Faulkner had so wished. Faulkner stated, for instance, that Rider was "one of the McCaslin Negroes,"[62] information which easily could have been included in the story. In addition, Beck suggests that it would

60 Kathleen Latimer, "Comedy as Order in *Go Down, Moses*," *Perspectives on Contemporary Literature* 10 (1984): 3.

61 Joanne V. Creighton, *William Faulkner's Craft of Revision* (Detroit: Wayne State UP, 1977) 115, 146. See also James Early, *The Making of Go Down, Moses* (Dallas: Southern Methodist UP, 1972) 97, and Marvin Klotz, "Procrustean Revision in Faulkner's *Go Down, Moses*," *American Literature* 37:1 (March 1965): 13.

62 Malcolm Cowley, *The Faulkner-Cowley File: Letters and Memoirs 1944-1962* (New York: Viking Press, 1966) 113.

have been easy for Faulkner to bring Roth Edmonds into the story "to provide the added dimension of his awareness of them, and thus to tie 'Pantaloon in Black' more closely to the other narratives in *Go Down, Moses*."[63] The fact that he refrained from such linkings strengthens my conviction that the story must be read as being deliberately disruptive, creating a rupture not expected to be healed by the reader.

All critics have recognized the rift caused by "Pantaloon in Black," but most of them have not been willing to accept this discontinuity as a natural part of the short story composite. Reactions to the story have varied from dismissing it on the basis of its apartness, to emphasizing thematic similarities to the other stories, to, conversely, accentuating its function of counterpoint and contrast, to constructing for it an emblematic function.

Some critics have found no reason to include "Pantaloon in Black" in their discussions of *Go Down, Moses*. They have acknowledged the autonomy of the story, seen its marginal position, but have refused to accept it as an integral part of the open work that constitutes the short story composite. They have dismissed it as disfiguring the harmony of the totality. Trilling and Tick both find coherence in *Go Down, Moses* only on the condition that "Pantaloon in Black" be excluded; Tick sets the story aside as being "non-essential" and "irrelevant."[64] Brooks does not consider the story to be a "necessary part" of the composite, and Reed states that if it "has any place at all in this book," it is by means of contrast.[65] Limon forwards an argument with which I sympathize but which I sense must be modulated. He declares "Pantaloon in Black" to be the "anomaly" of *Go Down, Moses*, a book which is "either a collection of stories or a novel, depending on the success one has in integrating 'Pantaloon in Black' into it." Limon argues that the story cannot be integrated but that it "reveals *Go Down, Moses* to be a collection of stories and not a novel," and that, as a consequence, it should be read as "purposely unintegrated."[66] To me Limon's position is too absolutist. The stories of *Go Down, Moses* are not *un*integrated, as Limon claims, only much less integrated than the chapters of a novel. Nor is "Pantaloon in Black" completely unintegrated, as we have seen, but it is only

---

63 Warren Beck, *Faulkner* (Madison: U of Wisconsin P, 1976) 374.

64 Lionel Trilling, Review of *Go Down, Moses* in *The Nation* 154 (30 May, 1942): 632; Tick, "The Unity of *Go Down, Moses*," 69.

65 Brooks, *William Faulkner: The Yoknapatawpha Country*, 257; Reed, Jr., *Faulkner's Narrative*, 190-91.

66 John Limon, "The Integration of Faulkner's *Go Down, Moses*," *Critical Inquiry* 12:2 (Winter 1986): 422-23, 437.

marginally connected with the rest of the book. Limon's contention that the only choice we have in defining *Go Down, Moses* is between a novel and a collection of stories shows his unwillingness to see the short story composite as a genre in itself and also reveals what I have pointed to many times in this book, namely that such established genres as the novel and the short story tend to exclude all other forms of fictional narrative.

Others see "Pantaloon in Black" as a transitional story that prepares the reader for the McCaslin stories, a world "where the wilderness can be gnawed at till its destruction is achieved."[67] It shows the effects of slavery and segregation on both blacks and the master class, exposing a society that has become accustomed to regarding human beings—and wilderness—as commodity.[68] The story is also unified with the rest of the composite, according to others, through its love motif—"the Negro's capacities and the white's inabilities to love"[69]—and through its emphasis on the importance of the community of the family, the fire on the hearth.[70] Toolan considers *Go Down, Moses* to be a novel unified by "a network of motifs and verbal and situational echoes" such as "having to be a negro; the power of the heart; blood; types of housing; and bringing/coming/going home."[71] Toolan's main interest lies in showing how the motif of "breathing" links "Pantaloon in Black" to the rest of the composite, an undertaking in which he succeeds less well in my opinion. Thornton is on the right track, it seems to me, when he states that "it is almost as if Faulkner had included it in order to frustrate our attempts to find unity in the volume." But unfortunately he quickly withdraws from such an apparently threatening proposition: "But in fact this story is wonderfully unified with the rest of the novel." The wonderfully unifying elements are, according to Thornton, the love between Rider and Mannie which sheds light on the love of previous couples; the theme of

---

67 Skei, *William Faulkner: The Novelist as Short-Story Writer*, 247. See also Thompson, *William Faulkner*, 85; Warren Akin IV, "'The Normal Human Feelings': An Interpretation of Faulkner's 'Pantaloon in Black'," *Studies in Short Fiction* 15 (1978): 397-404; Sundquist, *Faulkner: A House Divided*, 143.

68 Richard P. Adams, *Faulkner: Myth and Motion* (Princeton, N.J.: Princeton UP, 1968) 145; Early, *The Making of Go Down, Moses*, 11.

69 John L. Cleman, "'Pantaloon in Black': Its Place in *Go Down, Moses*," *Tennessee Studies in Literature* 22 (1977): 172.

70 Donald R. Noble, "Faulkner's 'Pantaloon in Black': An Aristotelian Reading," *Ball State University Forum* 14:3 (Summer 1973): 18.

71 Michael Toolan, "'Pantaloon in Black' in *Go Down, Moses*: The Function of the 'Breathing' Motif," *Journal of the Short Story in English* 2 (January 1984): 155-65.

freedom; the juxtaposition of objects and motifs such as cages, cots, mounds of dirt, and scenes of eating; and the foiling of the story against "Go Down, Moses."[72]

The function of "Pantaloon in Black" has also been seen as one of foreshadowing, to prepare the reader for Ike's decision to relinquish the land, presented in the fourth section of "The Bear." Taylor writes that "although the commissary scene takes place before Rider's birth, we must assume that Rider's portrait is inserted to illustrate the kind of experience Isaac has had."[73] Another example of foreshadowing is suggested by Kuyk who sees the death of Rider as prefiguring the "ritual suicide" of the Bear and of Sam Fathers.[74] Forkner in his turn considers Rider's fate to foreshadow Samuel Worsham Beauchamp's execution in "Go Down, Moses."[75]

In certain instances the wish to unify *Go Down, Moses* has led to excessive inferential walks: critics have so desired for "Pantaloon in Black" to fit into the composite that they have seen in the story what is simply not there. Vickery, for instance, finds that the main unifying element in the book is the ritual hunt and that the "grim, relentless tracking down of Rider" makes "Pantaloon in Black" conform to the surrounding stories.[76] But as also other critics have pointed out, Rider is never hunted or tracked down; after the killing, he is found sleeping on his own porch and does not resist being arrested. Cleman makes another mistake when he claims that Rider illustrates the "re-enslavement" of blacks, thereby linking the story to "Was."[77] Other critics have more correctly, I think, emphasized Rider's heroic stature and that "American life, which promises little to men of his race, seems to offer Rider much."[78] Rider is a leader of men, he is economically independent, and he determines his own fate when he decides to commit suicide by kill-

---

[72] Thornton, "Structure and Theme in Faulkner's *Go Down, Moses*," 345-47.

[73] Walter Taylor, "Faulkner's Pantaloon: The Negro Anomaly at the Heart of *Go Down, Moses*," *American Literature* 44 (1972): 437.

[74] Dirk Kuyk, *Threads Cable-strong: William Faulkner's* Go Down, Moses (Lewisburg: Bucknell UP, 1983) 73.

[75] Ben Forkner, "The Titular Voice in Faulkner's 'Pantaloon in Black'," *Journal of the Short Story in English* 1 (March 1983): 40.

[76] Vickery, *The Novels of William Faulkner*, 125.

[77] Cleman, "'Pantaloon in Black': Its Place in *Go Down, Moses*," 175-76.

[78] Taylor, "Faulkner's Pantaloon: The Negro Anomaly at the Heart of *Go Down, Moses*," 434-35; see also Noble, "Faulkner's 'Pantaloon in Black': An Aristotelian Reading," 17.

ing Birdsong.[79] And when Dunn and Morris write that "[i]n Faulkner's story-texts the protagonists, all male and all related through Anglo- and African-American branchings on the McCaslin tree, (e)merge as the single embodiment of a family composite," they invest Rider with a status he quite clearly does not possess.[80]

Still other critics consider the function of the story to be one of contrast, a counterpoint to the surrounding stories, primarily to "The Fire and the Hearth." Rider's distance from whites is seen as contrasting evocatively with Lucas' "almost Machiavellian manipulation of human relationships."[81] Rider and his wife are regarded as foils to Lucas and Molly suggesting "that the primitive world, to which Lucas reaches back in time, has, in this community, survived into the 1940s."[82] Hochberg believes that all the stories are united through the "basic relationships of black and white to the land," but since in "Pantaloon in Black" Rider has no relationship to the land, the only way Hochberg can make the story fit is to declare that it serves as a counterpoint to that of Lucas Beauchamp.[83] Creighton echoes this line of argument when she declares the story's tone to be contrapuntal:

> Although the story is not as essential as the others in the volume because it deals with peripheral characters and adds no new vital information to the developing composite, yet it contributes to a changed tone; the humor is lessened through repeated instances of confrontation and misunderstanding between the races.[84]

The discreteness of "Pantaloon in Black" has also encouraged critics to essentialize it. Volpe argues, to take one example, that if *Go Down, Moses* may be said to have a climax "this story serves the climactic function. The preceding stories are preludes to it; the four stories that follow are thematically derived from the basic recognition of the equal humanity of the Negro."[85] Stoneback holds that the story is a "prose-po-

---

[79] See Eberhard Alsen, "An Existential Reading of Faulkner's 'Pantaloon in Black'," *Studies in Short Fiction* 14:2 (Spring 1977): 172, 178.

[80] Dunn and Morris, *The Composite Novel*, 73.

[81] Reed, *Faulkner's Narrative*, 190.

[82] Brooks, *The Yoknapatawpha Country*, 256-57.

[83] Mark R. Hochberg, "The Unity of *Go Down, Moses*," *Tennessee Studies in Literature* 21 (1976): 58-60.

[84] Creighton, *William Faulkner's Craft of Revision*, 115.

[85] Edmond L. Volpe, *A Reader's Guide to William Faulkner* (New York: Octagon Books, 1974) 235.

em" which has no direct narrative or dramatic relation to the rest of the book but "exists as a poetic image which serves to crystallize and to u-niversalize certain fundamental aspects of the McCaslin family story."[86] In a similar way, but with a different rationale, Cleman sees the story as emblematic. The love motif implied in "Was" and more strongly suggested in "The Fire and the Hearth" is here "isolated" and "generalized"; the absence of the McCaslins and the story's timelessness provide a "culmination."[87]

The variety and the contradictory nature of the many readings of "Pantaloon in Black" are to me evidence of the critical confusion concerning the unity of Faulkner's composite. I agree with Donaldson when she says that "the reading of *Go Down, Moses* might profit more by emphasizing the underlying discontinuity of the tales than pointing to their continuity."[88] As a consequence we must acknowledge that "Pantaloon in Black" constitutes a considerable breach in the thematic and structural coherence of the composite, that this narrative riptide was an intended strategy on Faulkner's part, that it thwarts the reader's deeply rooted expectations of closure and unity, that it constitutes a narrative feature shared by many short story composites and therefore may be considered a genre characteristic, and, finally, that the reader who dismisses it or too ingeniously integrates it is doing violence to the open work called *Go Down, Moses*.

The Fringe Story as Aperture
As may be deduced from my discussion above, stories such as "Godliness," "Pantaloon in Black," and "My Old Man" are not, in my view, failures or aberrations; instead they constitute essential generic components of the short story composite. A rejection or subordination of such satellite stories means a misrepresentation of a genre that does not seek traditional harmony, coherence, or closure.

From a thematic and an intratextual point of view, stories such as those discussed above are fringe stories, marginalized by their lack of links to the other stories. I consequently find most of the totalizing readings referred to above to be attempts to neutralize what is distinctive of the genre of the short story composite, attempts to, often subconsciously,

---

[86] H. R. Stoneback, "Faulkner's Blues: 'Pantaloon in Black'," *Modern Fiction Studies* 21 (1975): 242.

[87] Cleman, "'Pantaloon in Black': Its Place in *Go Down, Moses*," 172.

[88] Susan Donaldson, "Contending Narratives: *Go Down, Moses* and the Short Story Cycle," in Evans Harrington and Ann J. Abadie, eds., *Faulkner and the Short Story* (Jackson: UP of Mississippi, 1992) 129.

impose on it conventions associated with the novel. It would, of course, be tempting to explain the separateness of the fringe story by ascribing to it, as some critics do, the status of being representative of the whole, of constituting a synthesis or emblem, but, having studied a number of these stories, I am convinced that such an essentialist assumption is ungrounded; they remain thematically marginal.

Structurally, however, fringe stories cannot be considered marginal. On the contrary, they are what might be called "aporetic," since they constitute aporias, final impasses, which so frustrate our expectations of closure, coherence, and unity, and which so undermine conventional novelistic presuppositions, that we are forced to acknowledge the disrupted structure specific to the genre of the short story composite. Stories such as "Godliness," "My Old Man," and "Pantaloon in Black" thus constitute openings, apertures, eye-openers, which make us realize, to turn back to Anderson's phrasing, the "new looseness" of this form of writing, reflecting the basically disruptive, "flowing" nature of life and the fact that most of us do not "know the answers."

Seven:
Subverting Social and Narrative Convention:
Eudora Welty's *The Golden Apples*

Eudora Welty intended the name of Morgana, the stage on which *The Golden Apples* is set, to carry connotations of *fata morgana* to show that the citizens of that town "were living absorbed in illusions."[1] One such illusion, willingly embraced by many of the townspeople, is that they live in a well-ordered world. The protagonists of the stories in *The Golden Apples* strenuously strive to establish a continuity and a well-organized pattern on which to base their lives. Disorder and breach of convention may exert an alluring attraction on Morgana's population, but more than that such disruptions are threats with which they must come to terms. Thus Welty's short story composite dramatizes the tension between order and disorder.

Many critics have been aware of the theme of the illusory, self-imposed order. What few of them seem to have noticed, however, is the fact that the form and structure of the book closely support this theme. Though much critical attention has been given to the unifying elements of its form, less has been written on the fragmented, discontinuous structure of the book and how this deliberately underlines and reinforces one of the central ideas of the work. I will here focus on the tension between the unifying and the discontinuous elements which makes *The Golden Apples* such an exciting book.

Morgana's Self-imposed Order
To make the irregular orderly, to explain away the anomalous, to form patterns out of the desultory, and to simplify complexity are fundamental human strategies of survival. In order to come to grips with the terror of chaos, the majority of humankind needs to categorize, compartmentalize, and conventionalize their experience. In this respect the citizens of Morgana are representative members of the human race. Louis D. Rubin, Jr. summarizes their predicament well:

---

[1] Jan Nordby Gretlund, "An Interview with Eudora Welty," in Peggy W. Prenshaw, ed., *Conversations with Eudora Welty* (Jackson: UP of Mississippi, 1984) 214.

Places like Morgana—human communities—exist to ward off and mask, through ritual and social complexity, an awareness of the finally unanswerable and inexplicable nature of existence in time and eternity. They are founded on the agreement—it is an unacknowledged compact between its members—not to admit to the existence of chaos and violence that cannot be controlled, explained, scaled down to manageable proportion. Life must, in Morgana's scheme of things, work out, exhibit order, be sufficient to human needs.[2]

The people of Morgana choose different means of ordering their reality, all with the purpose of making life livable: they try to understand the exotic and unsymmetric, making them fit their conformist pattern; they dramatize, often in the form of legend and myth, the disorderly and transcendent; they reject and ostracize those who breach the code of convention.

The majority of Morgana's citizens are people like Cassie, who cannot "see herself do an unknown thing,"[3] or the women on their way to the Rook party "drowning out something" (280) and "hurrying together in a duck-like line" (281). If there is anything that unsettles them it is, as is the case for Mr. Morrison, "for people not to be on the inside what their outward semblances led you to suppose" (327). These good citizens feel a need to incorporate everything into their conventional view, to place others "in their hour or their street or the name of their mothers' people" (325). They subscribe to the official truths of the community. So does Perdita Mayo, one of the group, proclaim, for instance, that "the whole world knows" that Jinny has been unfaithful to Ran (381, 390), whereas there are strong indications that it is equally possible that Ran "ailed first" (385).

When the orderly people encounter people and events which clash with their own world view, they strive to understand them and thereby defuse the threat they constitute. In "Moon Lake," Nina and Jinny are fascinated and disturbed by the boldness and the disorder of Easter. The orphan, who has started her breasts and flaunts a jackknife, who for no obvious reason bites Mr. Nesbitt's "collection hand" (347), is intriguing but a threat to the daughters of conformist Morgana. Easter has even had the audacity to name herself, an act Jinny and Nina have no sympathy for. Jinny, who has been named for her maternal grandmother, proclaims

---

[2] Louis D. Rubin, Jr., "Art and Artistry in Morgana, Mississippi," in *A Gallery of Southerners* (Baton Rouge: Louisiana State UP, 1982) 62.

[3] Eudora Welty, *The Golden Apples,* in *The Collected Stories of Eudora Welty* (New York: Harcourt Brace Javanovich, 1980) 316. Further references will be given within parenthesis in the text.

that Easter is "just not a real name" (357), and Nina objects to the irregular spelling, crying: "Spell it right and it's real!" (357) Nina is drawn to what Easter represents, "the other way to live" (361), and she wants, like the orphan, to be a child of the night living her life with an open, welcoming hand (361). But she is already molded by the small town code; Nina's hand falls asleep and is "helpless to the tearing teeth" of the "wild beasts" of Morgana's conventions (362). When Easter eludes Nina's and her friends' comprehension, and when they cannot join Easter's world, they dismiss her. Easter's near-death by drowning makes them "tired," and Little Sister Spights wishes her to "go ahead and die and get it over with" (371).

An alternative to explaining away and dismissing the disruptive is to transform it into legend and myth. Eudora Welty once said about "Why I Live at the P.O." that in a little place like that the "only entertainment people have is dramatizing the family situation, which they do fully knowing what they are doing."[4] This longing to dramatize is applicable also to the inhabitants of the small-town community of Morgana. The weaving of yarns and the forming of legends are a form of entertainment, but they are also a way of incorporating the discordant elements into the adopted social code.

The people around whom the tales are spun are the "misbehavers." Rumors circle around outsiders like Miss Eckhart, who is said to have been sweet on Mr Sissum. There is no evidence for this, but people are nevertheless convinced: "How did they know she was sweet on Mr. Sissum? But they did" (297). The town also wants to believe, once again without proof, that Miss Eckhart in her misery intended to throw herself upon Mr. Sissum's coffin; only Cassie realizes that maybe she "simply wanted to see" (299). After her "foreign" behavior in the cemetery interpreted as crying—"for they decided it must have been crying she did"—some ladies stop their children from taking further piano lessons. The gossips have managed to neutralize the possible threat Miss Eckhart represents.

King MacLain is a threat to social and moral norms. His irrational and immoral behavior must be tamed, and so it is mythologized. As readers we are given few facts about MacLain; our knowledge of him is based on hearsay and rumor. He is made up by a community which has the double need for drama and ordering. He is assigned the role of the vicarious rebel who lives out Morgana's hidden desires so that its peace can be upheld. Gradually he grows into a mythical figure, a hero in a folk-

---

4 "Eudora Welty," in Charles Ruas, *Conversations with American Writers* (New York: Knopf, 1985) 10.

tale, and Welty deliberately associates him with various classical myths. Vande Kieft comments on this social process of ordering by stating that it serves to "make something known and fixed out of this event, a story or a legend; to take the sting, the surprise, the comedy or tragedy, out of the glorious, pathetic, baffling humanity around them."[5]

Like a folktale hero, King MacLain is expected to turn up in unexpected places and at unexpected times. He is believed to have gone to California. He is "seen" getting a haircut in Texas and taking part in the inauguration of Governor Vardaman in Jackson. He is reported to return occasionally to Morgana, but the evidence comes from gullible townspeople. King is said to have illegitimate children everywhere, and his reputation as irresistible ladies' man makes women like Mattie Will in "Sir Rabbit" imagine being seduced by him in the woods, an illustration by Welty of how folktales like those about the Neck or female wood spirits come into existence.[6]

Phenomena that can neither be made to comply nor be mythologized are rejected by Morgana's citizens. When Cassie and Virgie tell their parents about Mr. Voight exposing himself, they are not believed (295). Miss Eckhart is excommunicated because she is a foreigner, a Yankee, a passionate artist, and because she goes on living in the community after having been sexually assaulted by a black man. People wished she would then have moved away, so that "they wouldn't always have to remember that a terrible thing once happened to her" (301). She reminds them of passions and threats they would rather forget. Not only Miss Eckhart suffers in the town's ordering process. Virgie, Loch, and Eugene do not fit the pattern and either leave or live in an inner exile.

Eudora Welty makes it quite clear that the self-imposed order of Morgana is a superficial and brittle one. It is an attempt at self-deception, a voluntary blinding of the self to the confusion and disarray underneath. It is also a denial of life-giving forces like art and passion. It is in the end a futile denial of man's loneliness and a pretense at a sense of community.

---

5 Ruth M. Vande Kieft, *Eudora Welty* (New York: Twaine Publishers, 1962) 119-20.

6 Patricia S. Yaeger and Merrill Maguire Skaggs both correctly identify "Sir Rabbit" as a fantasy or a daydream. See Yaeger, "'Because a Fire Was in My Head': Eudora Welty and the Dialogic Imagination," in Albert J. Devlin, ed., *Welty. A Life in Literature* (Jackson: UP of Mississippi, 1987) 147, and Skaggs, "Morgana's Apples and Pears," in Prenshaw, ed., *Eudora Welty. Critical Essays* (Jackson: UP of Mississippi, 1983) 233.

Unifying the Short Story Composite

Most critics of short story composites might be described as well-behaved citizens of Morgana. Their first impulse has been to establish order and unity in this form of loosely structured fiction. In this respect, the scholars who have devoted themselves to *The Golden Apples* are, in general, no exception. Welty's book does not quite fit the conventions of either the novel or the short story collection, and so, since the novel is considered a superior form of writing, critics have felt an urge to make a novel out of Welty's book by pointing to all the structural and thematic links which they feel create a unified whole. A few critics even call the book a novel.[7] McHaney points out that *The Golden Apples* is a book that "manages to create a complex unified impression in the manner of the novel"; it is not, however, a "full-fledged novel," but a composite of stories.[8] His use of "full-fledged" reveals his priorities; he would have liked to be able to give it the stamp of approval as novel, but has to be satisfied with the fact that it is written in the "manner" of one. In trying to make *The Golden Apples* fit the conventions of the traditional novel, these critics neglect the specificity of the short story composite as a genre. So as not to disturb the self-imposed order, all the disruptive elements that fall by the wayside are ignored.

These attempts at unification have taken various expressions. The unities of place, chronological time, and reappearing characters have rightfully been pointed to. Themes like "fascination"[9] and "wandering"[10] have been suggested as bridges between the anomalies and complexities of the stories. Mythical patterns have been common features in the same ordering process. Greek and Celtic myths have often been applied to the book in order to lessen its impression of openness and to

---

[7] See, for instance, Yaeger, "'Because a Fire Was in My Head': Eudora Welty and the Dialogic Imagination," 152, 167, and Louis Rubin, Jr., "The Golden Apples of the Sun," in *The Faraway Country : Writers of the Modern South* (Seattle: U of Washington P, 1963) 133, 153.

[8] Thomas L. McHaney, "Eudora Welty and the Multitudinous Golden Apples," *Mississippi Quarterly* 26 (Fall 1973): 589.

[9] Danièle Pitavy-Souques, "Technique as Myth: The Structure of *The Golden Apples*," in Peggy W. Prenshaw, ed., *Eudora Welty: Thirteen Essays* (Jackson: UP of Mississippi, 1983) 151.

[10] Julia Demmin and Daniel Curley, "Golden Apples and Silver Apples," in Prenshaw, ed., *Eudora Welty: Thirteen Essays*, 142.

tighten its loose form.[11] The geometrical circle, cyclicality, and music have also been used as means of imposing unity on the book.[12]

The citizens of Morgana are gullible; they want to believe what they are told. In a similar fashion many critics have been overly trustful of the narrators and focalizers in *The Golden Apples*. As I will try to show below, the possible unreliability of witnesses and narrators like Mrs. Rainey, Old Plez, Cassie, and Loch is used by Welty to call into question the order these people create. But a number of critics have taken for granted that King McLain pays a return visit in "Shower of Gold"; that the old woman in "June Recital" without any doubt is Miss Eckhart, even though so many things speak against it; that King McLain actually forcibly seduces Mattie Will in "Sir Rabbit." In all these instances Welty has left so much unsaid or told through untrustworthy narrators that the first impression of verisimilitude is soon challenged and a strategy of disruption and subversion is revealed.

Discontinuity and Multiplicity

Despite the claims of certain critics, *The Golden Apples* is not a novel. To shed light on its structure one may refer to two metaphors emanating from the book itself. Assembling and connecting the stories of *The Golden Apples*, Welty in a felicitous simile likens herself to Miss Eckhart arranging her June recital. The June recital consists of several "texts" delivered by shifting focalizers, interspersed with breaks and silences. There are in both recital and composite a progression and a unifying context, though the contributions within the frame are separate and distinct.[13] Another way of looking at the structure of the book is to compare it to Welty's picture of Loch blowing the horn in "Moon Lake": "Off in the thick of the woods came a fairy sound, followed by a tremulous silence, a holding apart of the air. ... There was another fairy sound, and the pried-apart, gentle silence" (358). Welty's composite

---

11 Wendell V. Harris, "The Thematic Unity of Welty's *The Golden Apples*," *Texas Studies in Literature and Language* 6 (1964/65): 92-95; H. C. Morris, "Zeus and the Golden Apples: Eudora Welty," *Perspective* 5 (Autumn 1952): 190-199; Ruth M. Vande Kieft, "The Search for the Golden Apples," in *Eudora Welty,* 111-149; Demmin and Curley, "Golden Apples and Silver Apples," in Prenshaw, ed., *Eudora Welty: Thirteen Essays,* 130-145.

12 McHaney, "Eudora Welty and the Multitudinous Golden Apples," 611; Thomas L. McHaney, "Falling into Cycles: *The Golden Apples*," in Dawn Trouard, ed., *Eudora Welty: Eye of the Storyteller* (Kent, Ohio: Kent State UP, 1989) 173-89; Skaggs, "Morgana's Apples and Pears," 221.

13 Welty, *One Writer's Beginnings* (Cambridge, Mass.: Harvard UP, 1984) 101.

could be seen as a series of fairy sounds, the stories, each followed by a "tremulous" silence, a "pried-apart, gentle silence," the gaps and voids, the hiatuses between the stories, which whisper of the unmentionable and the uncertain.

Eudora Welty herself has denied that *The Golden Apples* is a novel,[14] repeatedly emphasizing its short story character. The first stories were written without any intention of letting them connect. It only dawned on her fairly late that the characters were related "by the strongest ties— identities, kinships, relationships, or affinities already known or remembered or foreshadowed."[15] In the rewriting process, however, she retained the loose structure; later she even included *The Golden Apples* in *The Collected Stories,* which shows that she saw the book's short story quality as more significant. In addition, Welty has described herself as primarily a short story writer, whose novels have happened "by accident."[16] She also claims to be in favor of a literature which is "very seldom neat, is given to sprawling and escaping from bounds, is capable of contradicting itself, and is not impervious to humor." This almost sounds like a definition of the short story composite. Within the larger unifying frame of *The Golden Apples*—the homogenuous elements of place, recurring figures, sustained themes, myths, and symbols—we face a world characterized by fragmentation and heterogeneity. The stories are separate with time gaps in-between. Even though there is a general chronological development, we are not entirely sure how much time has elapsed from one story to another. This separateness also characterizes the inner structure of stories such as "Moon Lake," where the fragments/ sections are not connected by direct links. One story, "Music from Spain," is less integrated than the others, a fringe story; its setting is different, and its mood is more dreamlike. These incongruities, gaps, and silences point up the fragmented nature of the world depicted.

The Golden Apples lacks a main protagonist, a main theme, and a climax, the absence of which contribute to the reader's impression of a multi-faceted structure. Skaggs describes this lack of unity in the following manner: "the book does not focus on any one or any group of characters, does not unfold a single story line, does not explore an identifiable problem, theme, or set of social concerns, does not even use a sin-

---

[14] Charles T. Bunting, "'The Interior World': An Interview with Eudora Welty," *The Southern Review* 8:2 (1972): 715.

[15] Welty, *One Writer's Beginnings,* 98-99.

[16] Jean Todd Freeman, "Eudora Welty," in Richard Layman, ed., *Conversations with Writers II* (Detroit: Gale Research Company, 1978) 285.

gle setting."[17] To Skaggs' characterization could be added that Welty's use of multiple narrators or focalizers, also within one story, adds to the reader's impression of divergence and disconnectedness.

"Shower of Gold"

In order to reveal the fragility of man's constructed order, Welty employs a technique of subversion and dubiety, leaving, for instance, the reader without sufficient information, thereby deliberately creating gaps in the story. She introduces extraneous material, details of apparent trivia, which are not organically integrated and which may lead the reader off on a tangent. She makes use of a fractured, warped chronology. She includes opaque "symbols" which are left dangling; she plants narrative seeds which are never brought to fruition. She speaks through untrustworthy narrators and focalizers. She presents fragments of myth which do not substantially add to a larger, consistent pattern. It would be easy to give examples of Welty's disruptive technique from all the stories of the book, but I will here limit myself to focusing mainly on the first two, "Shower of Gold" and "June Recital," drawing attention to narrative elements which fragment the smooth surface order.

At first sight—which is where many critics have stopped—"Shower of Gold" tells the story of King MacLain's return to his home and of how, more or less on the threshold, he changes his mind and leaves in haste. As we penetrate the story, however, we realize that it has passed through several minds whose motives and perceptivity may be questioned.[18] The story is told by Mrs. Rainey, who has gotten it from members of the church, who in their turn have been told by Mrs. Stark who cajoled or scared it out of Old Plez. The narration is thus at least thrice removed from the source of action. Mrs. Rainey is now telling it, with embellishments of her own, to an anonymous passer-by. About the rumors of King MacLain she says at one point "that's people's careless way of using their eyes" (268). The story told in "Shower of Gold" is yet another example of such carelessness.

If we start with the narrator, Mrs. Rainey, it seems that she herself does not really believe in the story. Early in her narration she says:

---

17 Skaggs, "Morgana's Apples and Pears," 220.

18 Danièle Pitavy-Souques is also concerned with the function of the narrator as part observer, part *romancière*, assuming the point of view of other focalizers and inventing new information. Pitavy-Souques draws attention to some of the ambiguities discussed here. "'Shower of Gold' ou les ambiguités de la narration," *Delta* 5 (November 1977): 63-81.

Well, what happened turned out to happen on Hallowe'en. Only last week—
and seems already like something that couldn't happen at all.
    My baby girl, Virgie, swallowed a button that same day—later on—and that
happened, it seems like still, but not this. (268-269)

She continues to call what happened "only a kind of *near* thing" (269).
    The original eyewitness to the event is the Negro Old Plez, and Mrs.
Rainey does not seem quite convinced of Old Plez' reliability. She
makes comments concerning his telling like "allowing for all human
mistakes" (271), and she emphasizes his trustworthiness, maybe a bit too
much, to convince the visitor (and herself) of his story being true. After
all, Mrs. Rainey knows that the witness is both old and a "nigger."
    Mrs. Rainey also seems to be affected by the storytelling situation—
that of chance encounter—and appears to be given to dramatization. The
temptation to add colorful details, particularly in a story about the
town's romantic legendary hero, is of course strong. When she gets to
the point where King is about to knock on the door, Mrs. Rainey extra-
polates, saying: "and then puts his present behind his coat. Of course he
had something there in a box for her" (271). Old Plez, as far as we know,
did not notice such a box.
    It is repeatedly pointed out that the person who witnesses the stranger
approaching Snowdie's home is old. Not only is he called Old Plez, but
his age is emphasized in phrases like "And the oak leaves scuttling and
scattering, blowing against *old* Plez and brushing on him, the *old* man"
(273, emphasis added). It is also made clear that he is superstitious
enough to believe that the stranger might have been a ghost (273). We
are also informed that Plez was alone on the street that particular evening; there is nobody to corroborate his story. In addition, one gets the
impression that this is a Negro willing to tell whites whatever they want
to hear. First he tells Snowdie that he has not seen anybody near her
house (273). Later "Mrs. Stark got hold of Plez and got the truth out of
him" (273). But maybe he "fabricated" (273) as much to Mrs. Stark as
he did to Snowdie. Mrs. Stark is a strong-willed woman, a member of
Morgana's aristocracy. She "hates men" (267) and feels a strong urge to
protect Snowdie (267). It would please her to make King appear a cow-
ard who runs away. So, it would not be unlikely for Plez to supply her
with a suitable version of the story.
    Plez' rendition of what happened suffers from numerous contradic-
tions and inadequacies. Clearly he never did identify the stranger as
King. Plez was not even close enough to see what color of the skin the
man had. All he can say is that the stranger in front of him had "a white

man's walk" (270), implying that he never saw the face.[19] Later, from
his position at the Presbyterian church, Plez *assumes*, not being able to
see it, that King/the stranger looks through the blinds. Even though he
never was close enough to see the man's skin, he volunteers the
information that "he had on fine tennis shoes" (271).

This construing of facts continues in the part dealing with King's
reaction to the noisy trick-or-treat of the twins. First Plez holds that King
runs away "down the yard and over the ditch," plowing into "the rough
toward the Big Black" behind the MacLain house (272). Plez claims
King then "passed right by him." But Plez, we remember, was stationed
by the Presbyterian church, which is not located at the back of the Mac-
Lain house. Later Plez hesitates and cannot "swear to the direction"
(274). One of the twins, Eugene Hudson, tells Mrs. Rainey that King left
"through the gate" (272). In the next story, "June Recital," we are informed that the ditch is located *behind* the MacLain house (277). So,
either King left through the gate and passed right by Plez or left over the
ditch behind the house disappearing into the woods. Obviously, somebody is fabricating here. Welty deliberately presents us with contradictory information, which makes us question the entire event of King's
return. The unreliable narrator and witnesses thus make "Shower of
Gold" another example of "people's careless way of using their eyes"
and their tongues.

"June Recital"

In "June Recital" Welty tells the story of how Miss Eckhart, representing disruption and outlandishness, is ousted from the community so as
not to disturb its complacency. By adopting a discontinuous narrative
strategy, Welty skillfully underlines this theme. The pattern here is much
more complex than in "Shower of Gold," and Welty continues to an
even more subtle degree subversively to question the surface action. She
presents focalizers, Loch and Cassie, who cannot be trusted;[20] she introduces contradictory facts and she distorts chronology.

Section I is told through the consciousness of Loch, a fourteen-year-
old, feverish boy living in a dream world (276-277, 279). His fantasies
are in particular connected with the neighbor house, once belonging to
the MacLains. From his bed he suddenly hears a little piano tune, com-

---

[19] Mrs. Rainey and Snowdie later thought "it was just a nigger that was going by"
(271); maybe that is exactly who it was.

[20] Danièle Pitavy-Souques presents a perceptive discussion of the different *regards*
of Loch and Cassie in "Watchers and Watching: Point of View in Eudora Welty's
'June Recital'," *The Southern Review* 19:3 (July 1983): 483-509.

ing from the vacant, next-door house (280). In a short while, an old lady appears, "round and unsteady-looking" and with a "countriness" over her (281).

Many critics have not questioned the identity of this woman,[21] assuming that she is Miss Eckhart returning to her old room in the MacLain house. She *could* possibly be Miss Eckhart, in the same way that the stranger in "Shower of Gold" *could* be King, but there is no proof that she is. The only person to identify the old woman as Miss Eckhart is Cassie, and she does so solely on the basis of the woman's white ankles (324). All the time being behind her, Cassie never sees the old woman's face. Nobody else recognizes her. Loch was Miss Eckhart's neighbor while she lived in the MacLain house. He is fourteen at the time of the story, and was twelve when Miss Eckhart was forced to move. He should be able to remember what she looked like. But not once, while studying her closely through the window, does he see any likeness to Miss Eckhart. Fatty Bowles, the grocer, supplied Miss Eckhart and her mother with food for years (305), and his daughter took piano lessons from her (313). Old Man Moody lives close enough to the MacLain house to have his wife's chickens out in the yard (322). Still neither of these men recognizes the old woman, even though they meet her face to face (320). Nor does Mr. Voight/ MacLain (another uncertain identity) (322). When the old woman leaves the house, she meets her star pupil, Virgie Rainey. A mere two years have elapsed since Virgie stopped taking lessons, and yet she does not recognize the old woman as Miss Eckhart (325-326). This refusal to acknowledge each other, Corcoran explains, "springs from the proud, almost despairing desire to preserve some kind of selfhood."[22] To me it seems as if Corcoran's explanation "springs from ... the almost despairing desire" to preserve textual coherence. Wall holds that Morganans, by denying Miss Eckhart's old identity and by giving her a new identity as a madwoman, have set Virgie free so that she "*can* pass without speaking on the sidewalk."[23] But Virgie's lack of interest can also be explained by the

---

[21] See, for instance, Pitavy-Souques, "Watchers and Watching," 490-91; Carol S. Manning, *With Ears Opening Like Morning Glories: Eudora Welty and the Love of Storytelling* (Westport, CT: Greenwood Press, 1985) 15; Yaeger, " 'Because a Fire Was in My Head'," 159; McHaney, "Eudora Welty and the Multitudinous Golden Apples," 598.

[22] Neil Corcoran, "The Face that Was in the Poem: Art and 'Human Truth' in 'June Recital'," *Delta* 5 (November 1977): 27-28.

[23] Carey Wall, "'June Recital': Virgie Rainey Saved," in Trouard, ed., *Eudora Welty: Eye of the Storyteller*, 24.

simple fact that, maybe, the old woman is *not* Miss Eckhart. This impression is corroborated by the additional fact that not a single woman in the Rook Party manages to recognize her even though she passes right through the group (326).

Numerous other inconsistencies and contradictions contribute to undermining our view of the progress of events. The playing of the piano tune, "Für Elise," is a case in point. The first two times Loch hears it (280) the old woman has not yet arrived. At this point the tune is not identified as "Für Elise." It may have been Virgie playing it the first times; she is already in the house, properly identified by Loch. The third time he hears the tune, he sees and hears the old woman playing it (285) with one finger. But would Miss Eckhart, the piano teacher, have played it that way, with one finger?

In Section II, taking place simultaneously with Section I but depicted from Cassie's point of view, the tune appears four times (285, 286, 287, 302). The fourth time seems to correspond with the third time in Section I: "*Für Elise*. It came again, but in a labored, foolish way. Was it a man, using one finger?" (302). Again, it seems unlikely that Miss Eckhart would play the tune in such a way.

What also intrigues one is how it is even possible for Loch and Cassie to hear the tune the third and fourth times. By then the old woman has not only closed the window but also stuffed the cracks with paper and hung a quilt over the front window, thereby making the room "tight as a box" (283-284). Loch may still have heard the tune, since he is close by in the tree, but it is doubtful, indeed, if Cassie could have heard it in her bedroom inside the house next-door.

The two first sections also contain other irregularities. In Section II there is a dialogue between Loch and Cassie (287), which does not correspond to anything in Section I. If the conversation takes place after the second time Loch hears the tune (280), it is not recorded in this section. If it takes place after the third time he hears the tune (285), he is out in the tree, and could not possibly have had the conversation. One may wonder whether Welty here simply is careless; knowing her meticulous care with details, one is rather inclined to see it as inconsistencies deliberately introduced.

The age and appearance of the woman are also troublesome for the reader and speak against her being Miss Eckhart. It is true that, after having moved, Miss Eckhart "got older and weaker" (307), but is it really credible that she in the short time of less than two years has turned into this old white-haired (317), "unsteady-looking" (281) woman with an air of "countriness" (281) around her? Would Morgana's chief representative of culture undergo such a drastic change in such a short time? This is yet another detail which makes it difficult to accept the old woman as Miss Eckhart.

All these disruptive details may not mean much individually, but taken together they fragment our view of Miss Eckhart's return. The old woman may be the music teacher, but, then again, she may not be. Eudora Welty thereby draws attention to the indeterminacy and openendedness of the text—and of life itself.

Expectations Thwarted

Gretlund has drawn attention to Welty's frequent use of "apparent trivia,"[24] which partly serve to create verisimilitude but which also may carry crucial information. "This is, of course," Gretlund writes, "perfectly true to life, where the important events are not pointed out, and their importance is perhaps only realized later." The importance of many "trivial" details introduced by Welty, often remains unclear. She may draw attention to objects in a way that the reader will be tempted to see them as symbolic, but she often chooses not to indicate of what they are symbolic. She also includes information that is difficult to understand because it is given without a context. She further employs elements of myth, some of which seem to have only a marginal relation to the themes of the stories. Such narrative elements have been termed "false advance mentions" or "snares," that is, a "kind of deliberate evasion of the truth."[25] The narrative competence of the reader is thus manipulated and teased without being satisfied. From incomplete, often contradictory information the reader is provoked to draw incorrect conclusions.[26] All of these forms of "trivia" have the function of disintegration, of pointing to the fact that life is not as well-ordered and easily understood as human beings (and traditional novels) want to portray it.

---

[24] Jan Nordby Gretlund, "The Terrible and the Marvellous: Eudora Welty's Chekhov," in Trouard, ed., *Eudora Welty: Eye of the Storyteller*, 109. For further discussions of such "futile" notations, see Roland Barthes, "The Reality Effect," in *The Rustle of Language* (New York: Hill and Wang, 1986) 141-48, and Martin Price, "The Irrelevant Detail and the Emergence of Form," in J. Hillis Miller, ed., *Aspects of Narrative* (New York: Columbia UP, 1971) 69-91.

[25] Roland Barthes, *S/Z* (New York: Hill and Wang, 1974) 75; Gérard Genette, *Narrative Discourse: An Essay in Method* (Ithaca, N.Y.: Cornell UP, 1980) 77. Shlomith Rimmon-Kenan calls this narrative device "false preparation" in *Narrative Fiction: Contemporary Poetics* (London: Routledge, 1983) 48.

[26] See Umberto Eco, *The Role of the Reader: Explorations in the Semiotics of Texts* (Bloomington: Indiana UP, 1984) 206-10.

In *The Golden Apples*, Welty in particular highlights trees, flowers, fruits, cats, and butterflies. It may be that some of these carry a message vital to the understanding of the stories, but certainly not all, and Welty does not distinguish between them. Most of them, it seems to me, never fulfill the symbolic promise invested in them. They serve as a secret code to which we are never given the key.

The highlighting of pecans, magnolias, figs, mimosas, chinaberries, and cereus serves to create an atmosphere of sensuousness, which expresses a mood rebellious to the Puritan morality of Morgana. But apart from that general function it is difficult to determine their individual symbolic value. The fig tree, for instance, of "June Recital" is given such prominence that we expect it to carry a more specific meaning.[27] In the beginning of the story, Loch examines through the telescope the "distant figs: like marbles yesterday, wine-balls today." He thinks: "Getting those would not be the same as stealing. On the other side of fury at confinement a sweet self-indulgence could visit him in his bed" (277). Loch is waiting for the sailor to take the figs (278). "They were rusty old fig trees but the figs were the little sweet blue. When they cracked open their pink and golden flesh would show, their inside flowers, and golden bubbles of juice would hang, to touch your tongue to first" (278). The erotic language is obviously there to reflect Loch's youthful desire aroused by the activities of Virgie and the sailor.

The fig tree is part of Loch's fantasy world. "The big fig tree was many times a magic tree with golden fruit that shone in and among its branches like a cloud of lightning bugs—a tree twinkling all over, burning, on and off, on and off. The sweet golden juice to come—in his dream he put his tongue out, and then his mother would be putting that spoon in his mouth" (279). Now the fig tree has a different function from expressing Loch's erotic urge; it takes on mythological proportions to him, becoming a tree of life.

Towards the end of "June Recital," Cassie rushes out improperly dressed to prevent the arrest of what she believes is Miss Eckhart. In an astonishing reversal of this dramatic moment, Loch interrupts her, saying "Back yonder ... I can show you how ripe the figs are" (324). Instead of running after the woman, Cassie obeys her brother and they go to the fig tree to have a look at it. This puzzling scene, so out of context, brings again the fig tree into relief. But what is the accumulated significance of the tree and its fruit?

---

[27] The pecan tree plays a similar role in "Shower of Gold" and "June Recital" (272-273, 317).

Does it help us to look at mythology? The fig tree has been central to Greek, Roman, Jewish, Christian, Buddhist, and Timorian beliefs; however, in each religion it connotes different things. What does the fig tree "symbolize" in *The Golden Apples*? Does it signify Bacchanalian revelry or the forbidden fruit of the Garden of Eden, as Jewish legends teach? Does it evoke the wisdom Buddha found under the tree or the sense of brotherhood connected with the fig in the religious rites of Timor?

One might apply some of these meanings to Welty's book. One could argue, I am sure, concerning the last fig scene (324), that we here see a reversal of the Jewish legend of the tree of knowledge and its forbidden fruit. Loch/Adam tempts Cassie/Eve to eat the forbidden fruit which will open their eyes to what is just happening around them. Immediately after Welty writes: "The Morrisons [Cassie and Loch] had nowhere to go." They are, because of their sin, turned out of the Garden; they are homeless. But what would such a reading add to our overall understanding of the book? It is my conviction that the fig tree in *The Golden Apples* may work as an evocative emblem of a general mythological nature, but it does not carry a specific meaning, organic to Welty's short story composite. To my understanding the fig tree cannot be seen as a coherent symbol which significantly contributes to our comprehension of the composite.

A similar accentuation is given to cats in *The Golden Apples*, both in "Moon Lake" and "Music from Spain." In the earlier story, the cat called Cat appears at regular intervals with its "mask-like" face. It is spotlighted on four different occasions (351, 352, 353, 359), but if it carries a secret message this is not easily decoded. In "Music from Spain," the incident of a cat gazing at something—a bird or a snake?—is pointed up in such a fashion that the reader expects it to be emblematic of the main action in the story:

> In the foreground was a cat. In the deep grass she held a motionless and time-honored pose.
> Her head was tree-quarters turned toward them where they stood. It seemed to have womanly eyebrows. Her gaze came out of her face with the whole of animal comprehension; whether it was menace or alarm in the full-open eyes, her face made a burning-glass of looking. Her eyes seemed after so long a time to be holding her herself in their power. She crouched rigid with the devotion and intensity of her vision, and if she had caught fire there, still she could not, Eugene felt, have stirred out of the seizure. She would have been consumed twice over before she disregarded either what she was looking at or her own frenzy (416).

But to my understanding this passage does not carry such emblematic overtones. The cat does not symbolize anything. Eugene, and we, may imagine that and try to construe an orderly pattern, but to Welty, I suspect, this is another example of her disruptive technique. The same is true, I feel, for the butterflies appearing in the same story (400, 404). The butterfly tattoo on the inside of the Spaniard's wrist and the Negro woman's birthmarks in the form of a butterfly may be seen by Eugene as parts of a pattern he is trying to unravel in his quest, but again these "symbols" are so opaque that they deliberately obscure rather than elucidate the meaning of the story.

Eudora Welty creates gaps in *The Golden Apples* both by leaving information out and by inserting extraneous information. Central to the form of the short story composite is discontinuity, and Welty's suggestive narrative technique is built on "secret" codes and "private" details. The absence of linear continuity, narrational univocality, and dominating protagonists makes for a fragmented picture. And the introduction of phrases and statements which are essentially private, and deprived of context, underlines that fragmentariness. We become observers watching scenes from life we cannot fully comprehend.

The individual stories of *The Golden Apples* appear in chronological order, but Welty never makes explicit how much time has elapsed from one story to the next. Through internal evidence it is, however, possible to reconstruct a time scheme, which I will attempt to do further below. Due to the breaks in continuity we meet characters at different points of their lives. We notice that they have changed or developed, but the cause of their change is not apparent. The MacLain twins are initially "both King all over again" (267), but later on, in "The Whole World Knows" and "Music from Spain," they appear to have developed in different directions. We do not know the reason why Eugene left Morgana for San Francisco[28] ; nor is it clear why he now gives the impression of being almost the opposite of Ran.

The same lack of information characterizes our picture of the Morrisons. Loch's personality is consistently drawn—imaginative, unconventional, lonely—but the pieces we get are few, and we have difficulties understanding why he turned out so different from Cassie. In the description of Loch's development, Welty removes him further and further from us. In "June Recital" he is one of the focalizers, and we see him up

---

[28] Obviously, Eugene may have left in search of his father, who is believed to have gone west, but that does not explain why Eugene leaves, and not Ran, who is also involved in such a search for his father, as is evident from "The Whole World Knows."

close. In "Moon Lake" he is on the fringes, depicted by other, more central characters. In "The Wanderers," finally, he is reported, in passing, as having moved to New York. Mrs. Morrison also defies closer analysis. Why is she so cool and unhappy (287)? Why does she hate Miss Eckhart and the MacLain house with such fierceness (288, 295)? Why does she disappear so mysteriously time and again (298, 299)? Why does she ultimately kill herself (449)? By refusing to supply the answers to these questions, Welty gives the impression of a refracted, uncertain world.

Welty also includes in her narrative numerous comments and statements which, at least to me, are not easily accounted for. In "Shower of Gold" we are informed that the blinds are down in the MacLain house and Mrs. Rainey comments: "We shut the West out of Snowdie's eyes of course" (270). In "The Whole World Knows" Miss Perdita is upset that Ran has moved back into the old MacLain house, "sleeping in that little hot upstairs room with a western exposure" (381). What role does the West play to mother and son? Why do they have to be protected against it? Is it simply the fact that the Big Black runs west of town (451), the river on whose bank King left his straw hat? Or is it that the husband and father is rumored to have gone west?

Miss Moody says to Ran in "Moon Lake": "Oh, Ran. How could you? Oh, Ran" (370), an emotional outburst that is as sudden as it is unwarranted. Somewhat later in the same story it is Mrs. Stark's turn to assail Ran: "Why don't you go home—now!" (371) These utterances seem completely out of context. If "Moon Lake" and "The Whole World Knows" had taken place simultaneously, these admonitions could have been comments on Ran's abandoning Jinny, but this is not so since there is a gap of about ten years between the two stories. We are again left with a puzzle.

Welty once stated that "a shadowing of Greek figures" serves a function in *The Golden Apples*, "gods and heroes that wander in various guises, at various times, in and out, emblems of the characters' heady dreams."[29] Mythology thus becomes a unifying factor in the composite, but at the same time Welty makes clear that the figures are disguised and emblematic and that they appear irregularly. The inclusion of such mythological figures is certainly very deliberate, but they seem to be intended as glimmers from the past, not as clues to a systematic reading of the book. No consistent analogies can thus be established between the plot and the myths of Zeus, Aengus, Perseus, or Morgan Le Fay, notwithstanding various attempts in that direction. Curiously, however, no-

---

[29] Welty, *One Writer's Beginnings*, 99.

body seems to have noticed that Loch's position in the tree, hanging upside down from his knees, resembles that of the Hanged Man (285, 315) in the tarot cards, thus also incorporating the Fisher King (King MacLain) into the story. This multiplicity of myths will be further discussed in the next chapter.

Welty's use of symbols, trivial details, and insufficient information thus serves the double purpose of creating verisimilitude and suggesting various possible ways of interpreting that world, thereby "igniting" our imagination.

Chronological Disruption

The stories of *The Golden Apples* are printed more or less in chronological order. The progress of time, however, is vague; the reader is invited to construct his or her own chronology. In this process, the reader runs into inconsistencies which again contribute to undermining and fragmenting Welty's fictional world.

When do the different stories take place, and how old are the characters in the individual stories? Let us try to establish a chronology for the book and choose as a starting-point one of the more precise dates alluded to. In "June Recital" we are told that Mrs. Rainey is burying her son, dead in the war (326, 450). America entered the war in 1917; the story presumably takes place around 1918. We are further told in that story that both Cassie and Virgie are sixteen (278); they were consequently born around 1902. In "Shower of Gold" Virgie is a baby (269); that story thus takes place around 1903. The twins, Ran and Eugene Mac-Lain, are children around five, which would place their birth at approximately 1898. This dating is supported by the fact that "Moon Lake," in which story Ran is twenty-three (369), seems to take place around 1921. This date can be arrived at by means of Harold Bell Wright's *The Re-creation of Brian Kent* which has been in the camp for a couple of years (349, 351); Wright's book was a bestseller in 1919 and 1920. In "Moon Lake" Loch, who was around fourteen in "June Recital," would then be seventeen, which fits well the description of him. Jinny Stark and Nina Carmichael are around fourteen in "Moon Lake," being a few years younger than Virgie and Cassie, as is evident from "June Recital."

The first section of "Sir Rabbit" may be situated when the twins are teenagers, i.e. around 1914-15, the second part only a few years later, since Mattie is still a girl-wife (335). Jinny is twenty-five (381) in "The Whole World Knows"; that makes Ran about thirty-four and places the story around 1932. In "Music from Spain," Eugene is in his forties (393). We meet in that story a man who has been discharged from the army (398), indicating that the time of action is approximately 1943-46, which would make Eugene at least forty-five. "The Wanderers," finally, takes place around 1949. Eugene has returned to Morgana, has died from consumption, and has been buried for awhile. In the last story, consequently, Ran is fifty or more, Virgie and Cassie around forty-six, and Jinny and Nina fortyish.

In trying to establish this chronology, one stumbles on what seems to be incongruities, presumably subversively incorporated into the text by Welty as disruptive elements. For instance, in "The Wanderers" we are informed that Miss Snowdie is "nearly seventy" (432). If Ran is fifty or more, she must have been nineteen or less when the twins were born, which does not seem strange. The difficulty arises rather when we notice in "Shower of Gold" that Snowdie had been married to King for several years before the twins arrived. During the first years of their marriage, King left twice, the first time "for a good spell," the second time for three years (264); at least five years, then, elapsed from the time they were married to the time the twins were born. That would make Snowdie fourteen at the time of the wedding, which is hardly credible, but not impossible. However, Snowdie's chronology becomes even less credible when we read that, prior to her marriage, she had received a "nice education" and had started teaching school (265). Taken together these details do not quite add up.[30]

Other possible disruptions in chronology appear in "The Wanderers." Virgie in that story should be around forty-six; it is, however, indicated that she is under thirty-five (436). Jinny should be around forty-two but said to be in her thirties (444). Nina, also forty-two, is pregnant and Jinny has small children. Little Sister Spights is two in "June Recital" (285), making her about thirty-two in "The Wanderers," but she is nevertheless described there as belonging to the "young courting people" who sit in the back rows at the funeral holding hands (428, 445, 446). In the same story it is pointed out that people found Loch "too good" and "too young" when he went to war (449), a surprising statement. At the end of World War I, the time of "June Recital," Loch is about fourteen, so he surely did not take part in that war. In 1941, when America entered World War II, he may have joined, but he would hardly have qualified as being "too young" at the age of thirty-seven.

---

[30] What may also be an anomaly is the way the MacLain house is depicted at various points in the book. In "June Recital," the house is abandoned by Miss Francine and is more or less delapidated. In "The Whole World Knows," Miss Francine has evidently moved back, now keeping house for Ran MacLain (375, 381, 383).

Deceptive Closure
Reading the concluding story, "The Wanderers," one initially wonders if Eudora Welty is giving in to the pressure of convention, metaphorically becoming an orderly citizen of Morgana. On the surface, this story seems to be a typical case of closure: almost all of the characters of the preceding stories are predictably made to reappear at Katie Rainey's funeral. Resolutions are produced, themes and myths are re-emphasized. The circular structure is underlined; the frame of the book is the centrality of Mrs. Rainey in the first as well as the last story. Vande Kieft sums it up in the following manner:

> As an epilogue, it provides the denouement of several careers followed, lends perspective to the meaning and interrelations of these life histories, and gives a sense of mutability. It also provides a fully detailed portrait of the Morgana community by showing it engaged in a major tribal ritual, that of the funeral; furthermore, it re-capitulates and makes concluding statements of the major themes of the book.[31]

"The Wanderers" thus appears to be intended to unify what has earlier been disrupted, to tie most of the loose ends into a nice knot, to create the order that has so far been missing. In that sense, the last story seems to counteract much of the thematics and narrative strategies of *The Golden Apples*. The ending of the book may thus give a first impression of pat conventionality.

As so often when dealing with the art of Eudora Welty, however, one soon has reason to modify this initial impression. Like the earlier stories, the surface text of "The Wanderers" is undercut by Welty's technique of dubiety. It is true that the last story answers a number of questions, but simultaneously it gives birth to new questions which are left unresolved. It does create closure but it is a closure that is curiously open-ended.

I have already pointed to several instances of anomalous chronology in "The Wanderers," and there are other similar disruptive phenomena in the story. New facts and people are introduced which negate the trend toward unification. Mr. Mabry, Dr. Williams, Old Man Rainey, and Brother Dampeer, not mentioned earlier, are allowed to demand our attention.

There are a number of similar "mysteries" which have not been introduced earlier and which are not resolved. We are, for instance, told that

---

[31] Vande Kieft, *Eudora Welty*, 138.

Jinny looks at "the burns and scars on Virgie's hands ... making them stigmata of something at odds in her womanhood" (444). When did Virgie get these burns and scars, and what does the last comment imply? Other questions crop up as we read. Was Mrs. Rainey pregnant—"with more than they guessed" (431)—when she married Fate Rainey? Pregnant by whom? King MacLain? Why does Missie Spights look at Virgie "with eyes wide in a kind of wonder and belligerance" (434)? What secret is hidden in that look? Do Virgie and Ran love each other and maybe have a clandestine affair (445, 446, 450, 455)? Is this the reason Virgie hates Maideen (450), the girl who killed herself for Ran? There may be solutions to some of these enigmas in other parts of Welty's rich weave, but I have not been able to discover them.

In the same way as in the preceding stories, Welty in "The Wanderers" highlights plants suggesting that they have a "symbolic" dimension. The night-blooming cactus brought by the old woman in the middle of the night may be seen as an emblem of the transience of life, but why she appears at this point and what this incident is meant to point up is not clear. The big chinaberry tree in the MacLain yard is also emphasized (437, 451, 456), but in this case there is, apart from its vague emblematic quality, an additional complexity. The chinaberry described as having "branches spread winglike" (451) was cut down years earlier (437).

In this story of closure, Welty also includes absurd elements which easily detract from the attempt at amalgamation: the jarring conversation between Mr. Nesbitt and Virgie (433-434), so out of place at the funeral; the weird act of Mrs. Flewellyn "who had caught the last breath of her husband in a toy balloon, by his wish, and had it at home still—most of it, until a Negro stole it" (435); and Jinny MacLain staring at the corpse with live lizards dangling from her ears (447). With such examples Welty with magnificent humor breaks the mood of denouement and completion.

Of particular interest in "The Wanderers," however, is the way Welty lets the theme counteract the form. In the preceding stories the theme of Morgana's self-imposed order was undercut by Welty's subversive narrative strategies. In "The Wanderers" she conversely lets the form, a story of closure, be fairly conventional (at least on the surface), while the theme tells the story of the old order coming apart. She thereby maintains the fascinating tension between homogenizing and disrupting narrative elements.

The modern world has finally come to sleepy Morgana. Morgan's Woods is being cut down (428). The MacLain road now "goes the wrong way"; though still the same, "only now the wrong people went by on it. They were all riding trucks, very fast or heavily loaded, and carrying blades and chains, to chop and haul the big trees to mill. They were not eaters of muscadines, and did not stop to pass words on the season and what grew. And the vines had dried" (435). The MacLain house is now a ruin (437), and the Morrison house has been "cut up for road workers and timber people" (457). The old order of Morgana is gone, and the old citizens, though still dreaming, have lost the meaning of their vision; they are "still watching and waiting for something they didn't really know about any longer, wouldn't recognize to see it coming in the road" (429).

Many of the citizens representing the old order are now dead or set aside. Mrs. Morrison has killed herself (449). Though still living in his house, Mr. Morrison is confined to an upstairs corner room with the shade down, looking at the world through his telescope (457), presumably the very same that Loch used to create his dream world in "June Recital." Eugene MacLain is dead (458), as are Mrs. Rainey, Miss Eckhart, and Old Plez.

The most striking example of how the old social construction is coming apart is the shattering of the myth of King MacLain. The superhuman stature of Snowdie's runaway husband, created by romantic Morganans, is revealed as a sham. The portrait of King is shocking in its honesty. We meet an old, senile man incapable of taking care of himself, who makes hideous faces and sticks his tongue out "wagging like a child's" (438-439, 446, 447). In no way can he continue to play the dramatic role of vicarious trespasser of convention. By depicting the real King MacLain, Welty shatters permanently the illusion of the well-ordered Morgana.

Eight:
A Multiplicity of Myths: *The Golden Apples*

Eudora Welty's *The Golden Apples* is a short story composite, consisting of seven autonomous, yet interlocking stories. Numerous attempts have been made to unify the book, most of which have overlooked the deliberately discontinuous structure of Welty's work. Multiplicity is as we have seen a central generic characteristic of the short story composite. Most composites—there are always exceptions to be found—present multiple plots, themes, protagonists, and focalizations; no one theme or point of view is allowed to hegemonize the work. This multivoiced chorus also includes metaphors and myths. Eudora Welty's *The Golden Apples*,[1] is a text richly reverberating with multiple narrators, themes, focalizations, and fragments of myth. The latter consist primarily of classical myths—Graeco-Roman, Celtic, and Germanic myths—but also yet other mythical elements which so far have eluded Welty criticism.

The Golden Apples is characterized by a profusion of allusions to fragments from numerous myths. No single myth is allowed to assume a totalizing significance; no single culture is privileged. At the end of the book, the reader has been exposed to many strands of myth, but when he looks back at all the individual parts, like surveying the pieces of a jigsaw puzzle, turning them around this way and that, trying them in various positions, he must acknowledge that they are not complementary. The echoes from different ancient cultures simply do not make up a unified pattern. To use another metaphor, Welty refrains from presenting a weave of myth that creates a coherence through which the book may be interpreted; it is rather a quilt of numerous myth patches.

Eudora Welty's general attitude toward literature is one that discourages both didactic and allegorical stances, as evidenced in, for instance, the following quote from "Must the Novelist Crusade?":

> Great fiction, we very much fear, abounds in what makes for confusion; it generates it, being on a scale which copies life, which it confronts. It is very seldom neat, is given to sprawling and escaping from bounds, is capable of con-

---

[1] Welty, *The Golden Apples,* in *The Collected Stories of Eudora Welty* (New York: Harcourt Brace Jovanovich, 1980).

tradicting itself, and is not impervious to humor. There is absolutely everything in great fiction but a clear answer.[2]

Welty cautions critics not to seek simplistic answers or too much neatness when considering her own use of mythology. In one interview she warned against reading her work too literally, pointing out that her inclusion of myth is not to be seen as an attempt at creating allegory.[3] Discussing *The Golden Apples* she once claimed that she there drew "[f]reely on myths—all kinds of myths, Greek, Norwegian, anything," just because she felt they "do permeate life and endure in our imagination," and she gave the example of the golden apples which she used "in several different senses." She also confessed that she had suffered from "people," presumably critics, who found "one-to-one symbolism" in the book,[4] and elsewhere she said that "anyone who attributes my stories to myths very specifically and thoroughly is overshooting it. I would rather suggest things."[5] In the Freeman interview, referred to above, Welty also said: "In *The Golden Apples* I used mythology, but the stories weren't meant to illustrate a myth. I just used mythology, just as I used Mississippi locations and names" (304). Welty later stated that "a shadowing of Greek figures" serves as a tie between the stories of *The Golden Apples*, "gods and heroes that wander in various guises, at various times, in and out, emblems of the characters' heady dreams."[6] However, her choice of words—"shadowing," "various," "guises," "in and out," "emblems"—makes it clear that these mythological figures and events in no way function as a model or pattern on which to base a systematic reading of the composite. The inclusion of these mythological elements is certainly very deliberate, but they seem to be intended as glimmers from the past, not as clues to a methodical analysis of the text. No consistent analogies can thus be established between the plot and the myths of Zeus, Aengus, Perseus, or Morgan Le Fay, notwithstanding various critical attempts in that direction.

---

[2] Welty, *The Eye of the Story: Selected Essays and Reviews* (New York: Vintage Books, 1979) 149.

[3] Jean Todd Freeman, "Eudora Welty," in Richard Layman, ed., *Conversations with Writers II* (Detroit: Gale Research, 1978) 303-04.

[4] Scot Haller, "Creators on Creating: Eudora Welty," *Saturday Review* (June 1981): 46.

[5] Jan Nordby Gretlund, "An Interview with Eudora Welty," in Peggy W. Prenshaw, ed., *Conversations with Eudora Welty* (Jackson: UP of Mississippi, 1984) 224.

[6] Eudora Welty, *One Writer's Beginnings* (Cambridge, Mass.: Harvard UP, 1984) 99.

Critical Profusion

Most Welty critics have recognized the abundance of mythological allusion in *The Golden Apples* and have exerted great imaginative power in making sense of these components and/or of making them subservient to the plot. These critics, however, have not come to an agreement either on the function of myth in Welty's composite, or on the meaning of individual myths for a reading of various story lines.

Critics have seen Welty's use of myth in at least three different ways. Holding that the inclusion of mythical elements adds richness to the text, one small group of scholars contend that it is futile, as Pitavy-Souques puts it, to decode "the characters and events of the book according to a strict mythological system."[7] Few critics go as far as Morris who claims that *The Golden Apples* is an unsuccessful experiment since it "breaks down most seriously" in its attempts to "fuse previously separate myths into an artistic whole,"[8] but many agree with Demmin and Curley that neither any one of the classic myths "nor any combination of them in their classic form gives anything like a satisfactory shape to the book as a whole":

> We must be aware, however, that Welty's handling of myth is very tricky. She turns it on and she turns it off. There is nothing like a systematic development of the whole story, nothing approaching the rigidity of allegory. Rather the myth remains something in the background, a note to be struck in some complex harmony of her own. She uses it. She abandons it. She extemporizes on it. She invents new elements. The reader must be very watchful not to be led to carry the parallel of the myth too far or on the other hand to forget the pervasive effect of its undertone.[9]

Even when more consistent outlines of mythical patterns seem to emerge, these critics raise a warning against a totalizing reading. Discussing the presence of Celtic myth in "Sir Rabbit," Kendig, for instance, reminds us that Welty "repeatedly disrupts the mythic pattern and so discourages easy parallels. Like the elusive King MacLain, these

---

[7] Danièle Pitavy-Souques, "Technique as Myth: The Structure of *The Golden Apples*," in Peggy W. Prenshaw, ed., *Eudora Welty: Thirteen Essays* (Jackson, Miss.; UP of Mississippi, 1983) 148.

[8] Harry C. Morris, "Eudora Welty's Use of Mythology," *Shenandoah* 6:2 (Spring 1955): 34-40.

[9] Julia Demmin and Daniel Curley, "Golden Apples and Silver Apples," in Prenshaw, ed., *Eudora Welty: Thirteen Essays*, 130.

Celtic motifs tease us as they flash and vanish through the story, so that we can never claim easy frame stability."[10] I agree with these critics who view the mythical components as a non-complementary and discontinuous narrative device. I do not, however, share Morris' view that Welty fails to join the various myths into an "artistic whole," but am convinced that Welty deliberately wants the mythical fragments to remain discrete and unfusable echoes from ancient times.

Another group of critics tend to see Welty's use of mythical characters and events as parallel to the plot of *The Golden Apples* and as a code for reading the text; to these critics myth assumes a strong closural function. Numerous more or less totalizing interpretations based on Graeco-Roman and Celtic myths have been suggested. Primarily the Zeus cycle and the Wandering Aengus legend have been employed as models for unifying the seven stories of Welty's work. In "Eudora Welty and the Multitudinous Golden Apples," for instance, McHaney takes Morris to task for the "erroneous" conclusion that Welty fails to fuse the myths, for not seeing "the unifying force of the mythology." In this essay, McHaney rather aims to show "how the form of the book, which is an almost symphonic orchestration of closely related parallels between old myth and modern reality, structures, and thus properly reveals, the several meanings of the golden apples."[11] And in a much later article, "Falling into Cycles," McHaney argues that in Welty's fiction "the mythological past and the personal past are linked," that the prevalence of things cyclical in *The Golden Apples* brings Eliot's and Joyce's "mythical method" to mind, narrative strategies which contribute to the fact that the cyclical pattern in the end "presents one woman's vision of a true dance of the elements, a union of all that humankind may hope and see and know."[12] Many other critics, like Vande Kieft, Corcoran, and Harris have in a similar fashion underlined the unifying function of mythological analogues.[13] Dunn and Morris claim that the archetypal

---

10 Daun Kendig, "Realities in 'Sir Rabbit': A Frame Analysis," in Dawn Trouard, ed., *Eudora Welty: Eye of the Storyteller* (Kent, Ohio: Kent State UP, 1989) 127.

11 Thomas L. McHaney, "Eudora Welty and the Multitudinous Golden Apples," *Mississippi Quarterly* 26 (Fall 1973): 590-91.

12 McHaney, "Falling into Cycles: *The Golden Apples*," in Trouard, ed., *Eudora Welty: Eye of the Storyteller*, 173-189.

13 Ruth M. Vande Kieft, *Eudora Welty* (New York: Twaine Publishers, 1962); Neil Corcoran, "The Face that Was in the Poem: Art and 'Human Truth' in 'June Recital'," *Delta* 5 (November 1977): 27-34; Wendell V. Harris, "The Thematic Unity of Welty's *The Golden Apples*," *Texas Studies in Literature and Language* 6 (1964/ 65): 92-95.

patterns "are somehow related in a complex mythic tapestry whose interwoven patterns tease the mind and memory."[14] Their use of "somehow" is interesting; to me it gives evidence not so much of the actual existence as of their desire and hope of finding a totalizing mythological pattern.

Yet another critical view of Welty's inclusion of myth can be described as a synthesis of the two discussed above. Several critics reject the idea of close analogies between classical myth and Welty's stories, yet claim that the presence of myth gives rise to new patterns or myths. Demmin and Curley, quoted above as an example of critics who deny the existence of a systematic mythical pattern in *The Golden Apples*, hold that Welty employs the old material "for the creation of her own myth of human wholeness, a myth that will finally transcend not only the ancient myths of the male godhead but also the even more ancient myths of the female mysteries." From "Moon Lake," the middle story, these critics argue, and until the end, the power of Zeus wanes and "the symbols of female power begin to come into prominence."[15] Pugh agrees with Pitavy-Souques that myth in *The Golden Apples* eludes decoding, but goes on to state that Welty "is working inside a mythical frame that absorbs and supercedes disparate mythic events," a frame that consists of "an archetypal Apollonian-Dionysian duality" in which sun and moon are focal points.[16] In her Bakhtinian feminist reading of *The Golden Apples*, Yaeger argues that Welty dissociates mythical characters like Perseus from their mythical origins, expropriating and redefining images from the masculine tradition. Welty's prose, Yaeger says, "is an absorbing excercise in freeing language from previous meaning." Welty "begins to 'free' language systems that have encouraged us to associate gynophobia and heroism."[17]

The lack of critical consensus concerning Welty's use of myth also characterizes the potential correspondence between individual mythical figures and their counterparts in the Morgana world. That critics explore such diverging analogies is to me further evidence of the difficulty of establishing a consistent mythological model of interpretation, and that,

---

[14] Dunn and Morris, *The Composite Novel*, 83.

[15] Demmin and Curley, "Golden Apples and Silver Apples," 130, 132.

[16] Elaine Upton Pugh, "The Duality of Morgana: The Making of Virgie's Vision, the Vision of *The Golden Apples*," *Modern Fiction Studies* 28:3 (Autumn 1982): 435-36.

[17] Patricia S. Yaeger, "'Because a Fire Was in My Head': Eudora Welty and the Dialogic Imagination," in Albert J. Devlin, ed., *Welty: A Life in Literature*, 146, 154, 155.

rather, the classical myths constitute fragmented reminders of a common human past.

While certain citizens of Morgana have been associated with only one mythical origin, a majority of the Morganans have been linked to more than one classical figure. In addition, in a few instances, the same mythical heroes have been employed to serve as models for more than one Morgana character. Analogies have been suggested between Mattie in "Sir Rabbit" and Leda, between Victor Rainey and Mars, Mr. Sissum and Orpheus, Emma in "Music from Spain" and Penelope, and Cassie Morrison and Cassiopeia.[18]

Many Morganans, however, have been connected with several mythical models. Thus King MacLain invites parallels to both Zeus and the Wandering Aengus, and his wife Snowdie has been linked to both Hera and Danaë. In their son Ran critics have found similarities to Pollux and a Celtic deity, and the other twin, Eugene, has been associated with, in turn, a Celtic deity, Odysseus, Perseus, Castor, Hercules, and Theseus. Mrs Morrison has been seen as a latterday version of both the Sibyl and the "glimmering girl" of the Wandering Aengus myth. The mythical ancestors of her son Loch, according to critics, are Aengus, Perseus, Argus, Poseidon, and Odysseus. Miss Eckhart carries within her echoes from Aengus, Perseus, Eurydike (in her love for Mr Sissum), and Circe, and Virgie Rainey's story parallels those of Aengus, Perseus, Venus, and Artemis. The Spaniard in "Music from Spain" has been suggested to echo Atlas, Dionysios, and the Minotaur.

As becomes clear from this enumeration of suggested analogies, certain mythical figures are related to several Welty characters. The Wandering Aengus becomes a symbol for all the "wanderers" in the book: King, Virgie, Loch, and Miss Eckhart. Odysseus, another wanderer, is connected with Loch and Eugene. Perseus (and his relation to the Medusa) is made a near-parallel to the lives and acts of Eugene, Miss Eckhart, Loch, and Virgie. That there is textual evidence for most of the above correspondences shows the richness of Welty's text. This multiplicitous and at times contradictory abundance, however, reveals the futility, as Pitavy-Souques points out, of attempting a decoding of events and characters according to a strict mythological system of parallels. Instead, the multiplicity and polyphony of the myths become part of the short story composite's open, dialogic narrative strategy.

---

[18] I choose, here and below, not to identify the critical sources for all these suggested parallels, since this would make for very tedious reading.

Perseus and the Medusa

Let us select one specific fragment from Graeco-Roman mythology, which assumes a seemingly central position in *The Golden Apples,* in order to investigate whether anything close to a consensus exists concerning this scene.

At the end of "The Wanderers," and consequently at the end of *The Golden Apples*, Welty spotlights one of Miss Eckhart's pictures showing Perseus holding the head of the Medusa. Placed where it is, in the final pages of the text, the description of the picture and its meaning to Miss Eckhart and Virgie has been viewed as one of the central passages of the book:

> Miss Eckhart had had among the pictures from Europe on her walls a certain threatening one. It hung over the dictionary, dark as that book. It showed Perseus with the head of the Medusa. "The same thing as Siegfried and the Dragon," Miss Eckhart had occasionally said, as if explaining second-best. ...
>
> The vaunting was what she remembered, that lifted arm.
>
> Cutting off the Medusa's head was the heroic act, perhaps, that made visible a horror in life, that was at once the horror in love, Virgie thought—the separateness. She might have seen heroism prophetically when she was young and afraid of Miss Eckhart. She might be able to see it now prophetically, but she was never a prophet. Because Virgie saw things in their time, like hearing them—and perhaps because she must believe in the Medusa equally with Perseus—she saw the stroke of the sword in three moments, not one. In the three was the damnation—no, only the secret, unhurting because not caring in itself—beyond the beauty and the sword's stroke and the terror lay their existence in time—far out and endless, a constellation which the heart could read over many a night.
>
> Miss Eckhart, whom Virgie had not, after all, hated—had come near to loving, for she had taken Miss Eckhart's hate, and then her love, extracted them, the thorn and then the overflow—had hung the picture on the wall for herself. She had absorbed the hero and the victim and then, stoutly, could sit down to the piano with all Beethoven ahead of her. With her hate, with her love, and with the small gnawing feelings that ate them, she offered Virgie her Beethoven. She offered, offered, offered—and when Virgie was young, in the strange wisdom of youth that is accepting of more than is given, she had accepted *the* Beethoven, as with the dragon's blood. That was the gift she had touched with her fingers that had drifted and left her.
>
> In Virgie's reach of memory a melody softly lifted, lifted of itself. Every time Perseus struck off the Medusa's head, there was the beat of time, and the melody. Endless the Medusa, and Perseus endless. (459-460)

The emblematic sheen of this passage has made it difficult for critics to avoid commenting on it, but the opaqueness of the text has given rise to a diversity of readings. For instance, Vande Kieft sees the painting as expressing the struggle between good and evil, in which evil is never "pure and unambiguous" and heroism not "a simple matter of the triumph of good over evil."[19] Harris reads the text as concerned with the tension between man's separateness and happiness, between aspiration and fulfillment, and Pitavy-Souques holds that this scene unifies the book both structurally and thematically in that it suggests three organizing principles: "all the short stories have a plot based on fascination, they are all constructed with a mirror-effect, and the theme of separateness runs throughout the volume."[20] Both Rubin and Demmin/Curley read the passage as Virgie's acceptance of herself, as a resolution characterized by integration, harmony, and transcendence.[21] To show the openness of this passage, I would like to suggest yet another reading, emphasizing what I consider neglected aspects of the text.

The *Medusa* is the Queen of Darkness and an emblem of terror, her prime characteristic being her power to turn people who look at her into stone. She was also considered the guardian of city walls.[22] *Perseus* is the son of Zeus and Danaë (cf "Shower of Gold") and represents sun and light. Together with Athena, who was the Medusa's enemy, Perseus was the inventor of the flute.[23] Miss Eckhart compares the Medusa-Perseus story to the one about Siegfried and the Dragon. *Siegfried*, like Perseus, is a sun hero.[24] In the Nibelungenlied, *Regin* is "a wonder smith transformed into a dragon," who represents darkness, thereby being analogous to the Medusa.[25] Regin—as smith also called Mimir— wants to kill Siegfried because of his arrogance, beauty, and strength,

---

[19] Vande Kieft, *Eudora Welty*, 141-43.

[20] Harris, "The Thematic Unity of Welty's *The Golden Apples*," 95; Pitavy-Souques, "Technique as Myth: The Structure of *The Golden Apples*," 155.

[21] Louis D. Rubin, Jr., "Art and Artistry in Morgana, Mississippi," in *A Gallery of Southerners* (Baton Rouge: Louisiana State UP, 1982) 64; Demmin and Curley, "Golden Apples and Silver Apples," 144-45.

[22] See Louis Herbert Gray, ed., *The Mythology of All Races*, Vol. 1 (Boston: Marshall Jones Co., 1916) 33-36; Gertrude Jobes, *Dictionary of Mythology, Folklore, and Symbols*, Vol. 2 (New York: Scarecrow Press, 1962) 1084.

[23] See Gray, ed., *The Mythology of All Races,* Vol. 1, 34; Pierre Grimal, *The Dictionary of Classical Mythology* (Oxford: Blackwell, 1985) 360-62; Jobes, *Dictionary of Mythology, Folklore, and Symbols*, Vol. 2, 1257-58.

[24] Jobes, Vol. 2, 1448.

[25] Jobes, Vol. 2, 1330, 1448.

but instead Siegfried manages to kill the dragon/smith, the guardian of a treasure.

Both Perseus and Siegfried are heroes associated with light and art and beauty, who liberate mankind from darkness and terror, the Medusa and Regin. To the citizens of Morgana the illusion of a well-ordered world of convention has functioned as the Medusa protecting their "city wall" from threatening foreign intruders but simultaneously turning the Morganans to stone. Disruptive forces of strength, beauty, and art, like the qualities of Perseus and Siegfried, finally cause the order of Morgana to become less monolithic, a necessary beheading. Cutting off convention's head is a "heroic act" that to Virgie makes visible "a horror in life, that was at once a horror in love ... the separateness." The inability of social community and human relations to ward off man's ultimate separateness must be exposed. For man to be able to live a full life, the harmonious but deadening order needs to be balanced against a threatening but also potentially life-giving chaos. Virgie feels the need to "believe in the Medusa equally with Perseus," to incorporate into her life both the order and disorder of life. She wants to see both the moment— "the stroke of the sword in three moments"—and the continuity, the full picture. Miss Eckhart similarly realized the need for this balance in absorbing both "the hero and the victim." As a young girl Virgie accepted Miss Eckhart's offering of passionate, rebellious art, thus challenging small-town conventions. She accepted *the* Beethoven "as with the dragon's blood"; like Siegfried, bathing in the Dragon's blood, she believed herself invulnerable.[26] As she grew up, however, Virgie was unable to keep Miss Eckhart's gift of rebellion alive, and conformed to Morgana's complacency. But there comes a moment when she realizes the need to make chaos part of her life; as a consequence, she must leave the community that for so long molded and restricted her.

The Medusa-Perseus painting, according to Harris, suggests "the eternally repeated struggle of the human situation which allows one to aspire toward, but never reach, the golden apples."[27] Certainly, the title of the book alludes to the Hesperidian illusions of harmonious life that we are aspiring towards, but it also refers to the apple of discord, belonging to Eris, the goddess of strife, the apple fought over by Aphrodite, Athena, and Hera, the struggle leading to the Trojan War. It may also refer to the frequent occurence in Celtic mythology of life-giving apples, golden or not, mentioned in such tales as *The Voyage of Bran, The Voy-*

---

[26] Jobes, 1448.

[27] Harris, "The Thematic Unity of Welty's *The Golden Apples*," 95

age of Mael Duin, and *The Voyage of the Hút Corra*.[28] In addition, the title may be seen as underlining a reader's desire to establish the orderly narrative designs and mythological patterns, which in the final analysis turn out to be, if not discordant, at least evasive and beyond our complete reach.

Native American Twin Myth
Most of the Graeco-Roman and Celtic myths referred to above are more or less explicitly present in the text of *The Golden Apples*. The title of the initial story, "Shower of Gold," points directly to the story of Zeus and Danaë. The quotation in "June Recital" from Yeats' "The Wandering Aengus" similarly points the reader in a particular direction. The description of the painting of Perseus and the Medusa in "The Wanderers," and the reference to Siegfried, unequivocally present myths of which the reader can no longer remain unaware.

Other myths, like the Norwegian one Welty herself referred to, are less visible. And myths which might be expected to have found expression in the text because of their closeness to the world of Morgana are conspicuously absent. McHaney has pointed to such an absence of orthodoxical belief:

> Where in Welty is the Christian cycle, the calender of the Judeo-Christian year that one might expect in the doubtless Calvinist world of Morgana? Are we to believe that the observant Welty has overlooked this system? I think not. ... But the church's rituals are essentially invisible, overshadowed by the systems that interest and inspire Welty ... —humankind's potent conceptions of the relations between men and women and the world above, below, and around them. [29]

Not only are church rituals invisible, but explicit references to a Christian typology are missing. Welty avoids making allusions to Old Testament characters who could have functioned as models; nor does she indicate that any one of the Morgana citizens should be seen as a Christ, Mary, or Paul figure. If one compares *The Golden Apples* with texts by, for instance, William Faulkner, the difference is striking. The Judeo-Christian myths so openly visible in *The Sound and the Fury*, *Absalom, Absalom!*, and *A Fable* find no manifest expression in Welty's world. Maybe a closer look at *The Golden Apples*, though, would yield frag-

---

[28] See, for instance, Howard Rollin Patch, *The Other World* (Cambridge, Mass: Harvard UP, 1950) 52-53.
[29] McHaney, "Falling into Cycles: *The Golden Apples*," 184.

ments of implied Christian myths, an investigation I am not at present inclined to undertake.

What to me is of greater fascination at the moment is another mythical world which "should" have made a more visible impact on Welty's composite, namely American Indian mythology, which must have been a substantial component of the Morgana culture. There are few open references to Native American culture or beliefs in *The Golden Apples*, and the ones that do occur are not related to specific myths.[30] Nevertheless, the plot of Welty's stories reveals quite a few similarities to American Indian creation myths, and I would like to suggest the subsurface presence of these myths in order to show that the mythological web spun by Welty is even more multiplicitous than has hitherto been believed. I am aware of course that there are many divergencies and variations in the myths of American Indian tribes, but many tribes seem to share certain creation myths. One such myth concerns the Sun God and his twin sons, a myth often referred to as "Where the Two Came to Their Father," whose events exhibit many parallels to the story lines of *The Golden Apples*.

Many of the Graeco-Roman, Celtic, or Germanic myths echoed in *The Golden Apples* seem related to the creation of the universe, particularly to the Sun and the Moon, light and darkness. In many cultures, the Sun God fathers twins. The Hindu sun god Surya mates with Sanjna who gives birth to the two Aswins, the messengers of dawn. In Celtic mythology the twins Eber and Eremon typify the contest between light and darkness. Zeus gets Castor and Polydeuces together with Leda; the twins become heroes of the Argonaut expedition (in quest, not of the Golden Apples, but of the Golden Fleece). They represent night and day, moon and sun.[31] Zeus also fathers, with Antiope, the twin sons Amphion and Zethus. Other twin brothers from Greek mythology are Cryasor and Pegasus, springing forth from the decapitated Medusa. Cryasor personifies "the fierce power of the sun, born at the moment his mother the moon is slain by Perseus the sun."[32] Pegasus is the steed of Belerophon (sun), and is also bearer of thunder and lightning for Zeus.

Numerous analogies could be suggested between these classical models and events and characters in *The Golden Apples*, particularly King MacLain and his twin sons. In this study I prefer, however, to concentrate on similar elements in Native American myths because I find in Welty closer correspondences to the indigeneous twin myths than to the

---

[30] See *The Golden Apples*, 351, 361, 402.

[31] Another pair of twins, Calais and Zeter, also took part in the same expedition.

[32] Gertrude Jobes, *Dictionary of Mythology, Folklore, and Symbols* , Vol. I, 334.

European counterparts. The additional fact that *The Golden Apples* actually portrays America and not Europe speaks in favor of investigating native rather than foreign myths. My pointing to these analogies with American Indian myth is motivated by a desire to give an additional dimension to the text and does not mean that I consider them to unify Welty's stories.

The myth of the Sun God fathering illegitimate twin boys who at the age of twelve go in search of him is common, with variants, to the Navaho, Hopi, Zuñi, Ojibway, Winnebaga, and Tewa cultures. The similar twin myth of Lodge-Boy and Thrown-Away has been recorded in at least nineteen other tribes.[33] Whether Eudora Welty was aware of these twin myths we do not know. If Natchez culture, which is reflected in her work, had included the Sun God-Twins myth, we could more easily have assumed a knowledge of it on her part. But even if Natchez mythology—of which we know little because of its having been more or less wiped out in the 1730s—was a highly developed form of sun worship, no legend of heavenly twins seeking their father is extant.[34] One Natchez variant of "Lodge-Boy and Thrown-Away" has been recorded, however, in which the twins seem related with a Sun myth, or a creation myth, since, at the end of the story, they go to live, one in the West, the other in the East, making thunder and lightning.[35] Because of the wide distribution of the twin myth, however, Welty may have come across it, maybe in the form of Jeff King's widely acclaimed rendition, *Where the Two Came to Their Father*, which appeared in 1943, a few years prior to the writing of the stories of *The Golden Apples*.[36]

It has been generally accepted that there are echoes of Zeus, the Sun God, in King MacLain. There are, however, equally strong parallels between Welty's rebellious hero and the Native American Sun God. The Sun Father, called Taiowa or Tawa (Hopi), is a roving god who comes and goes as he pleases. His home is located in the east, to which he returns after his travels west. Like the Sun, King "roamed the country end on end" and "might at any time appear and then, over night, disappear"

---

[33] Gladys A. Reichard, "Literary Types and Dissemination of Myths," *Journal of American Folk-lore* 34 (July-September 1921): 272-73.

[34] See Wendell H. Oswalt, *This Land Was Theirs: A Study of the North American Indian* (New York: John Wiley & Sons, 1973) 530-57.

[35] John R. Swanton, "Myths and Tales of the South-eastern Indians," Smithsonian Institution, *Bureau of American Ethnology Bulletin* 88 (Washington, D.C.: U.S. Government Printing Office, 1929): 222-30.

[36] Jeff King, *Where the Two Came to Their Father. A Navaho War Ceremonial*, The Bollingen Series I (New York: Pantheon Books, 1943).

(*TGA* 336). Like King, the Sun has a reputation for having children everywhere; the twins he gets with Changing Woman are only two of many other illegitimate children. The following description from a legend called "The Hopi Boy and the Sun" characterizes well the Sun's promiscuous nature:

> A Mexican was playing with his wife. When the sun saw them, he threw the Mexican aside and cohabited with the woman. "I don't need a wife," he told his son, "because all the women on earth belong to me. If a couple cohabits during the daytime, I interfere as I just did. So I'm the father of all children conceived in the daytime."[37]

Not only has King been suggested as the father of several of Morgana's children–"don't nobody know how many chirren he has" (*TGA* 336, cf 264)—he is also believed to be the seducer, in daytime, of Mattie, in "Sir Rabbit." The white figure moving in the woods is actually portrayed as the sun travelling above the horizon, seen now and then between the trunks of the trees.[38] King is thus depicted as a "white glimmer" who "passed behind another tree" (*TGA* 334) and who "went bobbing on to another tree while he was cajoling, bright as a lantern that swayed in a wind" (336).

King conceiving the twins with Snowdie echoes the Sun Father's visit to Changing Woman:

> Her body was hardly covered, for her gown only hung over her in ragged shreds; she was very lousy and was picking the vermin off and scratching herself. While thus engaged her person was almost wholly exposed, and the sun-rays coming through a crevice in the wall, fell upon her vulva, and she moved with pleasure and then she fell asleep. She told of this occurrence to some elder women, and it came on to rain, and the water began to drip through the roof, and the elder women said to her, "Lie over yonder and let the rain drops fall upon you," and she went over and lay down, spreading her legs apart, and the rain drops fell upon her vulva, and again she moved with pleasure and fell

---

[37] Richard Erdoes and Alfonso Ortiz, eds., *American Indian Myths and Legends* (New York: Pantheon Books, 1984) 149.

[38] In "Sir Rabbit," Welty may also have infused the story with echoes from such American Indian mythological figures as Rabbit, the Trickster, who has a reputation for seducing women in great numbers. See, for instance, legends from Creek and Hitchiti mythology in John R. Swanton, "Myths and Tales of the South-eastern Indians," 2-3, 57. 62-63, 113-14.

asleep. She conceived and gave birth to twins, the first born was Pyüükan-hoya and the other Palünahoya.[39]

Like Danaë, then, she is penetrated by a shower of gold; but unlike the Greek woman, but like Snowdie, she gives birth to twins (the rain drops—or drops from a waterfall in other variants—also emanate from the Sun). In Winnebago myth, the woman is penetrated only by sun rays, no water drops, and gives birth to heavenly twins who seek their father.[40] Changing Woman's alternative names in Navaho mythology are "White Bead Woman,"[41] or "White Shell Woman."[42] In Natchez mythology, the mother of the son of the Sun is called "White Woman."[43] All these names lead one's thoughts to Snowdie, the albino.

The twins of American Indian mythology bear resemblances to Ran and Eugene of *The Golden Apples*. They are precocious, snot-nosed, "foolish and full of mischief"[44] (cf *The Golden Apples*, 271-72, 314). At the age of twelve, the Native American twins—called Uanam Ehkona and Uanam Yáluna in Zuñi mythology, Pöqánghoya and Palöngawhoya among the Hopi —"are consumed with desire" to go in search of their father.[45] Having overcome several obstacles en route, they arrive at the House of the Sun, where they have to undergo tests, one of which is to be placed in a heated flint oven or sweat house, to prove that they are

---

[39] Alexander M. Stephen, "Hopi Tales," *Journal of American Folk-lore* 42 (January-March 1929): 11. For other descriptions of the birth of the twins, see Frank Hamilton Cushing, "Outlines of Zuñi Creation Myths," in *Thirteenth Annual Report of the Bureau of Ethnology 1891-92* (Washington, D.C.: Government Printing Office, 1896) 381; "Changing Woman and the Hero Twins after the Emergence of the People" (Navajo), *The Heath Anthology of American Literature*, Vol. 1 (Lexington, Mass.: D. C. Heath and Co., 1990) 41-42; Washington Matthews, *Navaho Legends: Collected and Translated* (Boston: Houghton Mifflin, 1897) 105-06; "A Gust of Wind" (Ojibway) in Erdoes/Ortiz, eds., *American Indian Myths and Legends*, 150-51; Jeff King, *When the Two Came to Their Father*, 20-21.

[40] Paul Radin, *The Evolution of an American Indian Prose Epic. A Study in Comparative Literature* (Basel: Ethnographical Museum, 1954) 32-34.

[41] Jeff King, *Where the Two Came to Their Father*, 20.

[42] Matthews, *Navaho Legends*, 105.

[43] Peter Farb, *Man's Rise to Civilization as Shown by the Indians of North America from Primeval Times to the Coming of the Industrial State* (New York: Dutton, 1968) 160.

[44] Stephen, "Hopi Tales," 11.

[45] G. M. Mullett, *Spider Woman Stories. Legends of the Hopi Indians* (Tuscon, Arizona: U of Arizona P, 1979) 55.

the sons of the Sun God.[46] In Tewa myth, the twins visit "the house of Sun old man," but they are never tested.[47]

The MacLain twins are also "consumed with desire" to seek their father. Ran formulates his need in the opening sentence of "The Whole World Knows": "Father, I wish I could talk to you, wherever you are right now" (*TGA*, 375). And Eugene's wish to unite with King is presumably the reason he leaves for the West coast, where his father, like the Sun God, is reported to have gone ("Music from Spain"). Contrary to the Indian myth, the quest of the MacLain twins is abortive: they fail to find their father, and as a consequence they cannot obtain the acknowledgement they are so desperately seeking. A scene from *The Golden Apples* illuminates the similarities but also the differences between the two quests. After the Indian twins were tested in the oven they "came bounding and dancing and, just as children do, they hugged Sun round the knees and Sun hugged them close to his bosom, saying, 'For a truth you are my sons. I did this to try you. Now I know. Now glad I am to fondle my children!'"[48] Another variant says that as they came out of the flint oven "quite unharmed, the Twins leaped out, laughing and dancing about his great knees." Tawa, the Sun, then "gathered them to him and acknowledged them as his own sons."[49] When King MacLain returns home in "Shower of Gold" (*if* it is King returning), the twins "sailed out and circled around their father, flying their arms and making their fingers go scary, and those little Buster Brown bobs going in a circle" (*TGA*, 27). To Plez they look like "nigger cannibals in the jungle": "When they got their papa in their ring-around-a-rosy and he couldn't get out, Plez said it was enough to make an onlooker a little uneasy, and he called once or twice on the Lord. And after they went around high, they crouched down and went around low, about his knees" (*TGA*, 272). King MacLain, however, contrary to the Sun God, does not acknowledge his sons, as they so eagerly wish, but runs away across the ditch.

---

[46] See Mullett, *Spider Woman Stories*, 60-61; "Changing Woman and the Hero Twins after the Emergence of the People," in *Heath Anthology*, 45-47; Stephen, "Hopi Tales," 15-19.

[47] Elsie Clews Parsons, *Tewa Tales* (New York: American Folk-lore Society, 1926) 98-102.

[48] Stephen, "Hopi Tales," 15.

[49] Mullett, *Spider Woman Stories*, 60-61.

Mythological Proliferation

The American Indian twin myth dramatizes man's search for harmony and order in nature and his attempt to fuse the duality of his nature. In his commentary on Jeff King's *Where the Two Came to Their Father*, Joseph Campbell writes:

> The two, Sun-child and Water-child, antagonistic yet cooperative, represent a single cosmic force, polarized, split and turned against itself in mutually supplementary portions. The life-supporting sap-power, mysterious in the lunar rhythm of its tides, growing and decaying at a time, counters and tempers the solar fire of the zenith, life-desiccating in its brilliance, yet by whose heat all lives.[50]

The twins represent various complementary forces in the creation of the world. In Zuñi myth, they assist in the deliverance of mankind from the darkness of the underworld to the sunlight of this world, helping them find the "middle" so that they can come to rest.[51] In the lore of many tribes the twins are empowered by their father the Sun to slay the monsters, representing various kinds of fears man has to come to terms with. They cut off the head of Yéitso, "the Great Fear," and the head rolls down Mount Taylor and becomes a huge rock and the blood coagulates into a lava stream.[52] Representing darkness, defeated by the twins of light, Yéitso parallels the Medusa, whose head is cut off by Perseus, the son of Zeus, the legend explicitly referred to in *The Golden Apples*.

If Eudora Welty intends for us to apply such a myth as the Indian twin myth to her stories, she does not expect us to see one-to-one correspondences. She modifies the myth, reinvents it, inverts it. The quest for harmony in *The Golden Apples* is one never fulfilled; at the end of the book men are still "wanderers," restlessly in search of their "middle." Ran and Eugene never "find" their father in the sense that they are acknowledged or confirmed by him as his sons.

In conclusion, one may again stress that in Welty's text the many myths, also the Native American ones, do not function as paradigms by

---

[50] King, *Where the Two Came to Their Father*, 63. See also Frank Waters, *Masked Gods. Navaho and Pueblo Ceremonialism* (New York: Ballantine Books, 1970) 217-18.

[51] Cushing, *Outlines of Zuñi Creation Myths*, 381-84; "Talk Concerning the First Beginning," *Heath Anthology*, Vol. 1, 26-40.

[52] See, for instance, "Changing Woman and the Hero Twins after the Emergence of the People," *Heath Anthology*, Vol. 1, 40-52.

which character or plot can be explained. The American Indian myths of the heavenly twins do not fill a gap left by the Graeco-Roman, Germanic, Celtic and "Norwegian" myths, so that we can say that a more unified picture emerges. The multiplicitous myths in *The Golden Apples* are not complementary; the collage of myth pieces still remains as evasive as the golden apples.

Bibliography

Adams, Richard P. *Faulkner: Myth and Motion*. Princeton: Princeton UP, 1968.

Adams, Robert M. *Strains of Discord: Studies in Literary Openness*. Ithaca, N.Y.: Cornell UP, 1958.

Akin IV, Warren. "'The Normal Human Feelings': An Interpretation of Faulkner's 'Pantaloon in Black'." *Studies in Short Fiction* 15 (1978): 397-404.

Alsen, Eberhard. "An Existential Reading of Faulkner's 'Pantaloon in Black'." *Studies in Short Fiction* 14 (1977): 169-78.

Altman, Robert. "Introduction: Collaborating with Carver." In Raymond Carver, *Short Cuts*. New York: Vintage Books, 1993.

Anderson, David D. *Sherwood Anderson. An Introduction and Interpretation*. New York: Holt, Rinehart and Winston, 1967.

Anderson, Sherwood. *Winesburg, Ohio*.(1919) With an introduction by Malcolm Cowley. New York: Viking Press, 1960.

— . *Winesburg, Ohio*. The Viking Critical Library. Ed. John H. Ferres. New York: Viking Press, 1966.

Appel, Jr., Alfred. *A Season of Dreams. The Fiction of Eudora Welty*. Baton Rouge: Louisiana State UP, 1965.

Babel, Isaak. *The Red Cavalry*. New York: A. A. Knopf, 1929.

Baker, Carlos. *Ernest Hemingway: A Life Story*. New York: Charles Scribner's Sons, 1969.

Bakhtin, Mikhail. *The Dialogic Imagination. Four Essays*. Austin: U of Texas P, 1981.

— . *Problems of Dostoevsky's Poetics*. Ed. and transl. by Caryl Emerson. Minneapolis: U of Minnesota P, 1984.

Bal, Mieke. *Narratology. Introduction to the Theory of Narrative*. Toronto: U of Toronto P, 1985.

Barth, John. *Lost in the Funhouse. Fiction for Print, Tape, Live Voice*. New York: Doubleday, 1968.

Barthes, Roland. "Introduction to the Structural Analysis of Narratives." In *A Barthes Reader*. Ed. by Susan Sontag. New York: Hill and Wang, 1982. 251-95.

— . "The Reality Effect." *The Rustle of Language*. New York: Hill and Wang, 1986. 141-48.

— . *S/Z*. New York: Hill and Wang, 1974.

Beck, Warren. *Faulkner*. Madison: U of Wisconsin P, 1976.

Beegel, Susan F., ed. *Hemingway's Neglected Short Fiction. New Perspectives*. Tuscaloosa: U of Alabama P, 1989.

Bellah, Robert N. "Civil Religion in America." *Beyond Belief: Essays on Religion in a Post-Traditional World*. New York: Harper & Row, 1970. 169-89.

— et al. *Habits of the Heart: Individualism and Commitment in American Life*. Berkeley: U of California P, 1985.

Benson, Jackson J. "Patterns of Connections and their Development in Hemingway's *In Our Time*." In Michael S. Reynolds, ed., *Critical Essays on Ernest Hemingway's* In Our Time. Boston: G. K. Hall & Co, 1983.

— , ed. *The Short Stories of Ernest Hemingway: Critical Essays*. Durham, N.C.: Duke UP, 1975.

Bercovitch, Sacvan. "Fusion and Fragmentation: The American Identity." In Rob Kroes, ed., *The American Identity: Fusion and Fragmentation*. Amsterdam: University of Amsterdam, 1980.

Blotner, Joseph L. *Faulkner. A Biography*. New York: Random House, 1974.

Bradbury, Malcolm, ed. *The Novel Today. Contemporary Writers on Modern Fiction*. London: Fontana, 1977.

Bredahl, A. Carl. "'The Young Thing Within': Divided Narrative and Sherwood Anderson's *Winesburg, Ohio*." *The Midwest Quarterly: A Journal of Contemporary Thought* 27:4 (Summer 1986): 422-37.

Brooks, Cleanth. *William Faulkner: The Yoknapatawpha Country*. New Haven: Yale UP, 1963.

Brooks, Peter. *Reading for the Plot. Design and Intention in Narrative*. Cambridge, Mass.: Harvard UP, 1984.

Bruccoli, Matthew J. *Some Sort of Epic Grandeur: The Life of F. Scott Fitzgerald*. New York: Carroll & Graf Publishers, 1991.

Bryant, J. A. "Seeing Double in *The Golden Apples*." *Sewanee Review* 82:2 (Spring 1974): 300-15.

Brylowski, Walter. *Faulkner's Olympian Laugh: Myth in the Novels*. Detroit: Wayne State UP, 1968.

Bunting, Charles T. "'The Interior World': An Interview with Eudora Welty." *The Southern Review* 8:2 (1972): 711-35.

Burbank, Rex. *Sherwood Anderson*. New York: Twayne Publishers, 1964.

Burhans, Jr., Clinton S. "The Complex Unity of *In Our Time*." In Jackson J. Benson, ed., *The Short Stories of Ernest Hemingway: Critical Essays*. 15-29.

Burns, John Horne. *The Gallery*. New York: Hayler & Brothers Publishers, 1947.

Cage, Richard P. *Order and Design: Henry James' Titled Story Sequences*. New York: Peter Lang, 1988.

Carson, Franklin D. "Recurring Metaphors: An Aspect of Unity in *The Golden Apples*." *Notes on Contemporary Literature* 5:4 (1975): 4-7.

Carver, Raymond. *Cathedral: Stories*. New York: Knopf, 1983.

— . *Short Cuts*. New York: Vintage Books, 1993.

Cary, Richard. *Sarah Orne Jewett*. New Haven: Twayne Publishers, 1962.

Chatman, Seymour. *Story and Discourse. Narrative Structure in Fiction and Film*. Ithaca, N.Y.: Cornell UP, 1978.

Ciancio, Ralph. "The Sweetness of the Twisted Apples: Unity of Vision in *Winesburg, Ohio*." *PMLA* 84:5 (October 1972): 994-1006.

Cisneros, Sandra. *The House on Mango Street*. New York: Vintage, 1991.

Cleman, John L. "'Pantaloon in Black': Its Place in *Go Down, Moses*." *Tennessee Studies in Literature* 22 (1977): 170-81.

Clute, John and Peter Nicholls, eds. *The Encyclopedia of Science Fiction*. London: Orbit, 1993.

Clements, Robert J. and Joseph Gibaldi. *Anatomy of the Novella. The European Tale Collection from Boccaccio and Chaucer to Cervantes*. New York: New York UP, 1977.

Cohn, Dorrit. *Transparent Minds. Narrative Modes for Presenting Consciousness in Fiction*. Princeton: Princeton UP, 1978.

Coover, Robert. *A Night at the Movies, Or, You Must Remember This*. London: Paladin, 1989.

Cope, Jackson I. and Geoffrey Green. *Novel vs. Fiction: The Contemporary Reformation*. Norman, Oklahoma: Pilgrim Books, 1981.

Corcoran, Neil. "The Face that Was in the Poem: Art and 'Human Truth' in 'June Recital'." *Delta* 5 (November 1977): 27-34.

Cowley, Malcolm. *The Faulkner-Cowley File: Letters and Memoirs 1944-1962*. New York: Viking Press, 1966.

— . "Introduction." In Sherwood Anderson, *Winesburg, Ohio*. New York: Viking Press, 1960. 1-15.

Cox, Leland H., ed. *William Faulkner. Critical Collection*. Detroit: Gale Research Company, 1982.

Creighton, Joanne V. "*Dubliners* and *Go Down, Moses*: The Short Story Composite." Diss Univ of Michigan 1969. *DAI* 31:14. 1792-93A.

— . *William Faulkner's Craft of Revision*. Detroit: Wayne State UP, 1977.

Crowley, John W., ed. *New Essays on* Winesburg, Ohio. Cambridge: Cambridge UP, 1990.

Cushing, Frank H. "Outlines of Zuñi Creation Myths." In *Thirteenth Annual Report of the Bureau of Ethnology 1891-92*. Washington, D.C: Government Printing Office, 1896.

Daniel, Robert W. "Eudora Welty: The Sense of Place." In Louis D. Rubin, Jr. and Robert D. Jacobs, eds. *South: Modern Southern Literature and Its Cultural Setting*. Westport, Conn.: Greenwood Press, 1974.

De Man, Paul. *Blindness and Insight: Essays in the Rhetoric of Contemporary Criticism*. Second ed., revised. Minneapolis: U of Minnesota P, 1983.

Demmin, Julia and Daniel Curley. "Golden Apples and Silver Apples." In Prenshaw, ed. *Eudora Welty: Thirteen Essays*. 130-45 .

Devlin, Albert J., ed. *Welty. A Life in Literature*. Jackson, Miss.: UP of Mississippi, 1987.

Dewey, Joseph. "No God in the Sky and No God in Myself: 'Godliness' and Anderson's *Winesburg*." *Modern Fiction Studies* 35:2 (Summer 1989): 251-59.

Doctorow, E. L. *Lives of the Poets. Six Stories and a Novella*. New York: Random House, 1984.

Donaldson, Susan V. "Contending Narratives: *Go Down, Moses* and the Short Story Cycle." In Evans Harrington and Ann J. Abadie, eds. *Faulkner and the Short Story*. Jackson, Miss.: UP of Mississippi, 1992.

— . "Meditations on Nonpresence: Re-visioning the Short Story in Eudora Welty's *The Wide Net*." *Journal of the Short Story in English* 11 (Autumn 1988): 75-91.

— . "Recovering Otherness in *The Golden Apples*." *American Literature* 63:3 (September 1991): 489-506.

Dos Passos, John. *Manhattan Transfer*. (1925) Boston: Houghton Mifflin, 1953.

Dreiser, Theodore. *A Gallery of Women*. New York: Horace Liveright, 1929.

Du Bois, Cora. "The Dominant Value Profile of American Culture." *American Anthropologist* 57:6 (December 1955): 1232-39.

Dunn, Maggie and Ann Morris. *The Composite Novel. The Short Story Cycle in Transition*. New York: Twayne Publishers, 1995.

Early, James. *The Making of Go Down, Moses*. Dallas: Southern Methodist UP, 1972.

Eco, Umberto. *The Open Work*. Cambridge, Mass.: Harvard UP, 1989.

— . *The Role of the Reader. Explorations in the Semiotics of Texts*. Bloomington: Indiana UP, 1984.

Erdoes, Richard and Alfonso Ortiz, eds. *American Indian Myths and Legends*. New York: Pantheon Books, 1984.

Erdrich, Louise. *Love Medicine: A Novel*. New York: Holt, Rinehart, and Winston, 1984.

— . *Love Medicine: A New and Expanded Version*. New York: H. Holt, 1993.

Erikson, Erik H. *Childhood and Society*. (1951). St Albans: Triad/Paladin, 1977.

Evans, Elisabeth. *Eudora Welty*. New York: Frederick Ungar, 1981.

Farb, Peter. *Man's Rise to Civilization as Shown by the Indians of North America from Primeval Times to the Coming of the Industrial State*. New York: Dutton, 1968.

Faulkner, William. *Go Down, Moses*. (1942). New York: Modern Library, 1955.

— . *The Hamlet*. (1940). New York: Random House, 1956.

— . *Knight's Gambit*. New York: Random House, 1949.

— . *The Unvanquished*. (1938). New York: Random House, 1965.

Feinstein, Herbert. "Contemporary American Fiction: Harvey Swados and Leslie Fiedler." *Wisconsin Studies in Contemporary Literature* 2:1 (Winter 1961): 79-88.

Felman, Shoshana. *Jacques Lacan and the Adventure of Insight*. Cambridge, Mass.: Harvard UP, 1987.

Fishelov, David. "Genre Theory and Family Resemblance—Revisited." *Poetics* 20 (1991): 123-38.

Fitzgerald, F. Scott. *The Basil and Josephine Stories*. Ed. with an Introduction by Jackson R. Bryer and John Kuehl. New York: Scribner, 1973.

— . *Flappers and Philosophers*. (1921). New York: Scribner, 1959.

— . "How to Waste Material: A Note on My Generation." *Bookman* 63 (May 1926): 262-65.

— . *The Pat Hobby Stories*. With an Introduction by Arnold Gingrich. New York: Charles Scribner's Sons, 1962.

Flora, Joseph M. *Hemingway's Nick Adams*. Baton Rouge: Louisiana State UP, 1982.

Fogelin, Robert J. *Wittgenstein*. London: Routledge & Kegan Paul, 1987.

Ford, Richard. *Rock Springs. Stories*. New York: Atlantic Monthly Press, 1987.

Forkner, Ben. "The Titular Voice in Faulkner's 'Pantaloon in Black'." *Journal of the Short Story in English* 1 (March 1983): 39-47.

Fowler, Alastair. *Kinds of Literature. An Introduction to the Theory of Genres and Modes*. Cambridge, Mass.: Harvard UP, 1982.

Frederic, Harold. *Stories of York State*. Ed. by Thomas F. O'Donnell. Syracuse, N.Y.: Syracuse UP, 1966.

Freeman, Jean Todd. "Eudora Welty." In Richard Layman, ed. *Conversations with Writers II*. Detroit: Gale Research Company, 1978. 284-316.

Freyer, Tony. "Federalism." In Jack P. Greene, ed. *Encyclopedia of American Political History*. New York: Charles Scribner's Sons, 1984. 546-64.

Friedman, Alan. *The Turn of the Novel*. New York: Oxford UP, 1966.

Fussell, Edwin. "Winesburg, Ohio: Art and Isolation." In Sherwood Anderson, *Winesburg, Ohio*. The Viking Critical Library. New York: Viking Press, 1966.

Genette, Gérard. *Narrative Discourse. An Essay in Method*. Ithaca, N.Y.: Cornell UP, 1980.

Gerlach, John. *Toward the End. Closure and Structure in the American Short Story*. N.p.: U of Alabama P, 1985.

Gilchrist, Ellen. *I Cannot Get Close Enough: Three Novellas*. Boston: Little, Brown, 1990.

Glazer, Nathan and David P. Moynihan. *Beyond the Melting Pot: The Negroes, Puerto Ricans, Jews, Italians, and Irish of New York City*. Cambridge, Mass.: MIT Press, 1968.

Gleason, Philip. "American Identity and Americanization." In Stephan Thernstrom, ed. *Harvard Encyclopedia of American Ethnic Groups*. Cambridge, Mass.: Harvard UP, 1980. 31-58.

Godwin, Gail. *Dream Children*. New York: Knopf, 1976.

— . *Mr. Bedford and the Muses*. New York: Viking Press, 1983.

Good, Graham. "Notes on the Novella." In Charles E. May, ed. *The New Short Story Theories*. Athens, Ohio: Ohio UP, 1994. 147-64.

Goyen, William. *The House of Breath*. New York: Random House, 1950.

Gretlund, Jan Nordby. "An Interview with Eudora Welty." In Peggy W. Prenshaw, ed. *Conversations with Eudora Welty*. 211-29.

— . "The Terrible and the Marvelous: Eudora Welty's Chekov." In Dawn Trouard, ed. *Eudora Welty: Eye of the Storyteller*. 107-18.

Grimes, Larry. *The Religious Design of Hemingway's Early Fiction*. Ann Arbor: UMI Research Press, 1985.

Grimwood, Michael. "Pastoral and Parody: The Making of Faulkner's Anthology Novels." Diss Princeton Univ 1976. *DAI* 37 (1977): 5828A.

Gross, Beverly. "Narrative Time and the Open-ended Novel." *Criticism* 8:4 (Fall 1966): 362-76.

Gwynn, Frederick L. and Joseph L. Blotner, eds. *Faulkner in the University: Class Conferences at the University of Virginia, 1957-1958*. New York: Vintage, 1959.

Haller, Scot. "Creators on Creating: Eudora Welty." *Saturday Review*, June 1981: 42-46.

Harris, Wendell V. "The Thematic Unity of Welty's *The Golden Apples*." *Texas Studies in Literature and Language* 6 (1964/65): 92-95.

Hasbany, Richard. "The Shock of Vision: An Imagist Reading of *In Our Time*." In Wagner, *Ernest Hemingway: Five Decades of Criticism*. 224-40.

Hemingway, Ernest. *In Our Time*. (1925) New York: Charles Scribner's Sons, 1958.

— . *Men Without Women*. (1927) New York: Scribner, 1955.

— . *The Nick Adams Stories*. Ed. by Philip Young. New York: Charles Scribner's Sons, 1972.

Higham, John. "Hanging Together: Divergent Unities in American History." *Journal of American History* 61:1 (June 1974): 5-28.

— . *Strangers in the Land. Patterns of American Nativism 1860-1925*. New York: Atheneum, 1974.

Hinckley, Henry Barrett. "The Frame-Tale." *Modern Language Notes* 49:2 (February 1934): 69-80.

Hirschman, Albert. *Shifting Involvements: Private Interest and Public Action*. Oxford: Basil Blackwell, 1982.

Hochberg, Mark R. "The Unity of *Go Down, Moses*." *Tennessee Studies in Literature* 21 (1976): 58-65.

Hoffman, Frederick J. *The Art of Southern Fiction: A Study of Some Modern Novelists*. Carbondale: Southern Illinois UP, 1967.

Holloway, John. *Narrative and Structure: Exploratory Essays*. Cambridge: Cambridge UP, 1979.

Holquist, Michael. "Stereotyping in Autobiography and Historiography: Colonialism in *The Great Gatsby*." *Poetics Today* 9:2 (1988): 453-72.

Hood, Hugh. *Around the Mountain: Scenes from Montreal Life*. Toronto: Peter Martin Associates, 1967.

Howe, Irving. *Sherwood Anderson*. N.p.: William Sloane Associates, 1951.

— . "Sherwood Anderson's *Winesburg, Ohio*." In Stegner, *The American Novel from James Fenimore Cooper to William Faulkner*. 154-65.

— . *William Faulkner: A Critical Study*. 2nd Rev ed. New York: Vintage, 1962.

Huggan, Isabel. *The Elizabeth Stories*. New York: Viking Press, 1987.

Hughes, Langston. *Simple Speaks His Mind*. New York: Simon and Schuster, 1950.

Ingram, Forrest L. *Representative Short Story Cycles of the Twentieth Century*. The Hague: Mouton, 1971.

Iser, Wolfgang. *The Act of Reading: A Theory of Aesthetic Response*. Baltimore: Johns Hopkins UP, 1978.

— . "Indeterminacy and the Reader's Response in Prose Fiction." In J. Hillis Miller, ed. *Aspects of Narrative. Selected Papers from the English Institute*. New York: Columbia UP, 1971.

— . "The Reading Process: A Phenomenological Approach." *New Literary History* 3:2 (Winter 1972): 279-99.

Jarell, Randall. *Pictures from an Institution*. (1954) London: Faber and Faber, 1987.

Jewett, Sarah Orne. *The Country of the Pointed Firs, and Other Stories*. (1896) New York: Norton, 1982.

Joyce, James. *Dubliners*. (1914) New York: Knopf, 1991.

Kammen, Michael. *People of Paradox*. Ithaca, N.Y.: Cornell UP, 1980.

Karl, Frederick R. *William Faulkner: An American Writer*. New York: Weidenfeld & Nicolson, 1989.

Kendig, Daun. "Realities in 'Sir Rabbit': A Frame Analysis." In Trouard, ed. *Eudora Welty: Eye of the Storyteller*. 119-32.

Kennedy, J. Gerald. "Toward a Poetics of the Short Story Cycle." *Journal of the Short Story in English* 11 (Autumn 1988): 9-25.

— , ed. *Modern American Short Story Sequences: Composite Fictions and Fictive Communities*. New York: Cambridge UP, 1995.

Kenney, Susan. *In Another Country*. New York: Viking Press, 1985.

Kenshur, Oscar. *Open Form and the Shape of Ideas. Literary Structures as Representations of Philosophical Concepts in the Seventeenth and Eighteenth Centuries*. Lewisburg: Bucknell UP, 1986.

Kermode, Frank. *The Sense of an Ending: Studies in the Theory of Fiction*. New York: Oxford UP, 1966.

— . "Sensing Endings." *Nineteenth-Century Fiction* 33:1 (June 1978): 144-58.

Kincaid, Jamaica. *Annie John*. New York: Farrar, Straus, Giroux, 1985.

— . *Lucy*. New York: Farrar, Straus, Giroux, 1990.

King, Jeff. *Where the Two Came to Their Father. A Navaho War Ceremonial*. The Bollingen Series I. New York: Pantheon Books, 1943.

Kingston, Maxine Hong. *The Woman Warrior: A Memoir of a Girlhood among Ghosts*. New York: Knopf, 1976.

Klotz, Marvin. "Procrustean Revision in Faulkner's *Go Down, Moses*." *American Literature* 37:1 (March 1965): 1-16.•

Köhler, Wolfgang. *Gestalt Psychology*. New York: Liveright, 1947.

Komar, Kathleen L. *Pattern and Chaos. Multilinear Novels by Dos Passos, Döblin, Faulkner and Koeppen.* Columbia, S.C.: Camden House, 1983.

Kreyling, Michael. *Eudora Welty's Achievement of Order.* Baton Rouge: Louisiana State UP, 1980.

Krieger, Murray. *A Reopening of Closure: Organicism against Itself.* New York: Columbia UP, 1989.

Kuyk, Jr., Dirk. *Threads Cable-strong: William Faulkner's* Go Down, Moses. Lewisburg: Bucknell UP, 1983.

Lassaigne, Jacques and Robert L. Delevoy. *Flemish Painting. From Bosch to Rubens.* New York: Skira, 1958.

Latimer, Kathleen. "Comedy as Order in *Go Down, Moses.*" *Perspectives on Contemporary Literature* 10 (1984): 1-8.

Laughlin, Rosemary M. "Godliness and the American Dream in *Winesburg, Ohio.*" *Twentieth Century Literature* 13:2 (July 1967): 97-103.

Laurence, Margaret. *A Bird in the House: Stories.* New York: Knopf, 1970.

LeGuin, Ursula. *Orsinian Tales.* New York: Harper & Row, 1976.

— . *Searoad: Chronicles of Klatsand.* New York: Harper Collins Publishers, 1991.

Leigh, David J. "*In Our Time*: The Interchapters as Structural Guides to a Psychological Pattern." *Studies in Short Fiction* 12:1 (1975): 1-8.

Leitch, Thomas M. *What Stories Are. Narrative Theory and Interpretation.* University Park: Pennsylvania State UP, 1986.

Lemmon, Jr., Dallas Marion. "The Rovelle, or the Novel of Interrelated Stories: M. Lermontov, G. Keller, S. Anderson." Diss Indiana Univ 1970. *DAI* 31 (1971): 3510A.

Levy, Andrew. *The Culture and Commerce of the American Short Story.* Cambridge: Cambridge UP, 1993.

Levy, Helen Fiddyment. *Fiction of the Home Place: Jewett, Cather, Glasgow, Porter, Welty, and Naylor.* Jackson: UP of Mississippi, 1992.

Limon, John. "The Integration of Faulkner's *Go Down, Moses.*" *Critical Inquiry* 12:2 (Winter 1986): 422-38.

Lohafer, Susan. *Coming to Terms with the Short Story.* Baton Rouge: Louisiana State UP, 1983.

Lohafer, Susan and Jo Ellyn Clarey, eds. *Short Story Theory at a Crossroads.* Baton Rouge: Louisiana State UP, 1989.

Lorch, Thomas M. "The Choreographic Structure of *Winesburg, Ohio.*" *CLA Journal* 12:1 (September 1968): 56-65.

Lowe, David A. "A Generic Approach to Babel's *Red Cavalry.*" *Modern Fiction Studies* 28:1 (Spring 1982): 69-78.

Lubbers, Klaus. *Typologie der Short Story*. Darmstadt: Wissenschaftliche Buchgesellschaft, 1977.

Lubbock, Percy. *The Craft of Fiction*. London: Jonathan Cape, 1921.

Lundén, Rolf. "The United Stories of America: Fusion and Fragmentation in the American Short Story Cycle." In Kristiaan Versluys, ed. *The Insular Dream: Obsession and Resistance*. Amsterdam: VU UP, 1995. 285-302.

Luscher, Robert M. "The Short Story Sequence: An Open Book." In Lohafer and Clarey, eds. *Short Story Theory at a Crossroads*. 148-67.

McClosky, Herbert and John Zaller. *The American Ethos: Public Attitudes toward Capitalism and Democracy*. Cambridge, Mass.: Harvard UP, 1984.

McDonald, Edward D, ed. *Phoenix: The Postumous Papers of D.H. Lawrence*. London: Heinemann, 1936.

McHaney, Thomas L. "Eudora Welty and the Multitudinous Golden Apples." *Mississippi Quarterly* 26 (Fall 1973): 589-626.

— . "Falling into Cycles: *The Golden Apples*." In Trouard, ed. *Eudora Welty: Eye of the Storyteller*. 173-89.

Mann, Susan Garland. *The Short Story Cycle. A Genre Companion and Reference Guide*. Westport, CT: Greenwood Press, 1989.

Manning, Carol S. *With Ears Opening like Morning Glories: Eudora Welty and the Love of Storytelling*. Westport, CT: Greenwood Press, 1985.

Marcotte, Edward. "Intersticed Prose." *Chicago Review* 26 (1974/75): 31-36.

Martin, Wallace. *Recent Theories of Narrative*. Ithaca, N.Y.: Cornell UP, 1986.

Matthews, John T. *The Play of Faulkner's Language*. Ithaca, N.Y.: Cornell UP, 1982.

Matthews, Washington. *Navaho Legends. Collected and Translated*. New York: Houghton, Mifflin & Co, 1897.

May, Charles E., ed. *The New Short Story Theories*. Athens: Ohio UP, 1994.

Meyer, Leonard B. "The End of the Renaissance? Notes on the Radical Empiricism of the Avant-garde." *Hudson Review* 16: 2 (Summer 1963): 169-86.

Miller, J. Hillis. "The Problematic of Ending in Narrative." *Nineteenth-Century Fiction* 33:1 (June 1978): 3-7.

— . "Stevens' Rock and Criticism as Cure, II." *Georgia Review* 30:2 (Summer 1976): 330-48.

— , ed. *Aspects of Narrative*. New York: Columbia UP, 1971.

Millgate, Michael. *William Faulkner*. London: Oliver and Boyd, 1961.

Moddelmog, Debra A. "The Unifying Consciousness of a Divided Conscience: Nick Adams as Author of *In Our Time*." *American Literature* 60:4 (December 1988): 591-610.

Morris, Harry C. "Eudora Welty's Use of Mythology." *Shenandoah* 6:2 (Spring 1955): 34-40.

— . "Zeus and the Golden Apples: Eudora Welty." *Perspective* 5 (Autumn 1952): 190-99.

Morson, Gary Saul. *Hidden in Plain View: Narrative and Creative Potentials in "War and Peace"*. Stanford, CA: Stanford UP, 1987.

— . *Narrative and Freedom. The Shadows of Time*. New Haven: Yale UP, 1994.

Mortimer, Gail L. *Daughter of the Swan: Love and Knowledge in Eudora Welty's Fiction*. Athens: U of Georgia P, 1994.

Mullett, G.M. *Spider Woman Stories. Legends of the Hopi Indians*. Tuscon, Arizona: U of Arizona P, 1979.

Munro, Alice. *The Beggar Maid: Stories of Flo and Rose*. New York: Knopf, 1979.

— . *Lives of Girls and Women: A Novel*. New York: McGraw-Hill, 1972.

Naylor, Gloria. *The Women of Brewster Place*. New York: Viking Press, 1982.

Nixon, Cornelia. *Now You See It*. New York: Harper Perennial, 1991.

Noble, Donald R. "Faulkner's 'Pantaloon in Black': An Aristotelian Reading." *Ball State University Forum* 14:3 (Summer 1973): 16-19.

O'Brien, Tim. *The Things They Carried*. Boston: Houghton Mifflin, 1990.

O'Connor, Flannery. *Everything that Rises Must Converge*. New York: Farrar, Straus and Giroux, 1965.

— . *A Good Man Is Hard to Find*. New York: Harcourt, Brace Jovanovich, 1955.

O'Neill, John. "Anderson Writ Large: 'Godliness' in *Winesburg, Ohio*." *Twentieth Century Literature* 23 (1977): 67-83.

Orsini, G. N. Giordano. *Organic Unity in Ancient and Later Poetics. The Philosophical Foundations of Literary Criticism*. Carbondale: Southern Illinois UP, 1975.

Oswalt, Wendell H. *This Land Was Theirs: A Study of North American Indians*. New York: John Wiley & Sons, 1973.

Otto, Whitney. *How to Make an American Quilt*. New York: Ballantine Books, 1991.

Parsons, Elsie Clews. *Tewa Tales*. New York: American Folk-lore Society, 1926.

Patch, Howard Rollin. *The Other World*. Cambridge, Mass.: Harvard UP, 1950.

Peckham, Morse. "Art and Disorder." In Richard Kostelanetz, ed. *Esthetics Contemporary*. Buffalo, N.Y.: Prometheus Books, 1978. 95-115.

Pei, Lowry. "Dreaming the Other in *The Golden Apples*." *Modern Fiction Studies* 28:3 (Autumn 1982): 415-33.

Phelan, James, ed. *Reading Narrative: Form, Ethics, Ideology*. Columbus: Ohio State UP, 1989.

Phillips, Jayne Anne. *Machine Dreams*. New York: Dutton, 1984.

Phillips, Jr., Robert L. "A Structural Approach to Myth in the Fiction of Eudora Welty." In Prenshaw, ed., *Eudora Welty: Critical Essays*, 56-67.

Phillips, William L. "How Sherwood Anderson Wrote *Winesburg, Ohio*." In White, ed. *The Achievement of Sherwood Anderson*. 62-84.

Pitavy-Souques, Danièle. "A Blazing Butterfly: The Modernity of Eudora Welty." *Mississippi Quarterly* 39 (1986): 537-60.

— . "'Shower of Gold' ou les ambiguités de la narration." *Delta* 5 (November 1977): 63-81.

— . "Technique as Myth: The Structure of *The Golden Apples*." In Prenshaw, *Eudora Welty: Thirteen Essays*. 146-56.

— . "Watchers and Watching: Point of View in Eudora Welty's 'June Recital'." *Southern Review* 19:3 (July 1983): 483-509.

Porter, Katherine Anne. *Collected Stories*. London: Cape, 1967.

Powers, Lyall H. *Faulkner's Yoknapatawpha Comedy*. Ann Arbor: U of Michigan P, 1980.

Prenshaw, Peggy W., ed. *Conversations with Eudora Welty*. Jackson: UP of Mississippi, 1984.

— , ed. *Eudora Welty: Critical Essays*. Jackson: UP of Mississippi, 1979.

— , ed. *Eudora Welty: Thirteen Essays*. Jackson: UP of Mississippi, 1983.

Price, Martin. "The Irrelevant Detail and the Emergence of Form." In J. Hillis Miller, ed. *Aspects of Narrative*. 69-91.

Prince, Gerald. *A Dictionary of Narratology*. N.p.: Scolar Press, 1988.

— . *Narratology: The Form and Functioning of Narrative*. Berlin: Mouton, 1982.

Pugh, Elaine Upton. "The Duality of Morgana: The Making of Virgie's Vision, the Vision of *The Golden Apples*." *Modern Fiction Studies* 28:3 (Autumn 1982): 435-51.

Radin, Paul. *The Evolution of an American Indian Prose Epic. A Study in Comparative Literature*. Basel: Ethnographical Museum, 1954.

Reed, Jr., Joseph W. *Faulkner's Narrative*. New Haven: Yale UP, 1973.

Reed, III, Pleasant Larus. "The Integrated Short-Story Collection: Studies of a Form of Nineteenth- and Twentieth-Century Fiction." Diss Indiana Univ 1974. *DAI* 35 (1975): 6730A.

Reichard, Gladys A. "Literary Types and Dissemination of Myths." *Journal of American Folk-lore* 34 (July-September 1921): 269-307.

Reid, Ian. *The Short Story*. London: Methuen, 1977.

Richter, David H. *Fable's End. Completeness and Closure in Rhetorical Fiction*. Chicago: UP of Chicago, 1974.

Rideout, Walter B. "The Simplicity of *Winesburg, Ohio*." In Sherwood Anderson, *Winesburg, Ohio*. Viking Critical Library Edition. 294-99.

Rimmon-Kenan, Shlomith. *Narrative Fiction. Contemporary Poetics*. London: Routledge, 1983.

Ruas, Charles. "Eudora Welty." In *Conversations with American Writers*. New York: Knopf, 1985. 3-17.

Rubin, Jr., Louis D. "Art and Artistry in Morgana, Mississippi." In *A Gallery of Southerners*. Baton Rouge: Louisiana State UP, 1982.

— . "The Golden Apples of the Sun." In *The Faraway Country: Writers of the Modern South*. Seattle: U of Washington P, 1963. 131-54.

Saroyan, William. *My Name Is Aram*. New York: Harcourt, Brace and Co, 1940.

Schevill, James. *Sherwood Anderson: His Life and Work*. Denver: U of Denver P, 1951.

Schleifer, Ronald. "Faulkner's Storied Novel: *Go Down, Moses* and the Translation of Time." *Modern Fiction Studies* 28:1 (Spring 1982): 109-27.

Scholes, Robert and Robert Kellogg. *The Nature of Narrative*. New York: Oxford UP, 1968.

Schumann, Hildegard. *Zum Problem des Kritischen Realismus bei John Steinbeck*. Halle: Max Niemeyer Verlag, 1958.

Selby, Jr., Hubert. *Last Exit to Brooklyn*. New York: Grove Press, 1964.

Selden, Raman. *A Reader's Guide to Contemporary Literary Theory*. Brighton: Harvester Press, 1985.

Shapiro, Charles. "Harvey Swados: Private Stories and Public Fiction." In Harry T. Moore, ed. *Contemporary American Novelists*. Carbondale: Southern Illinois UP, 1964.

Shaw, Valerie. *The Short Story. A Critical Introduction*. London: Longman, 1983.

Shklovsky, Viktor. *Theory of Prose*. Elmwood Park, IL: Dalhey Archive Press, 1990.

Showalter, Elaine. *Sister's Choice: Tradition and Change in American Women's Writing*. Oxford: Clarendon Press, 1991.

Silliman, Ron. "From the New Sentence." In Ron Silliman, ed. *In the American Tree*. Orono, Maine: National Poetry Foundation, 1986.

Silverman, Raymond Joel. "The Short Story Composite: Forms, Functions, and Applications." Diss Univ of Michigan 1970. *DAI* 31:12: 6633A.

Sipiora, Phillip. "Ethical Narration in 'My Old Man'." In Beegel, ed. *Hemingway's Neglected Short Fiction. New Perspectives.* 43-60.

Skaggs, Merrill Maguire. "Morgana's Apples and Pears." In Prenshaw, ed. *Eudora Welty: Critical Essays.* 220-41.

Skei, Hans. *William Faulkner: The Novelist as Short Story Writer. A Study of William Faulkner's Short Fiction*. Oslo: Universitetsforlaget, 1985.

Slabey, Robert M. "The Structure of Hemingway's *In Our Time*." *Moderna Språk* 60:3 (1966): 272-85.

Smith, Barbara Herrnstein. "Narrative Versions, Narrative Theories." *Critical Inquiry* 7:1 (Autumn 1980): 213-36.

— . *On the Margins of Discourse: The Relation of Literature to Language*. Chicago: U of Chicago P, 1978.

— . *Poetic Closure: A Study of How Poems End*. Chicago: U of Chicago P, 1968.

Smith, Lee. *The Devil's Dream*. New York: Putnam, 1992.

— . *Oral History*. New York: Ballantine Books, 1984.

Sniderman, Stephen Lee. "The 'Composite' in Twentieth-Century American Literature." Diss Univ of Washington 1970. *DAI* 31: 403A.

Spencer, Elizabeth. *Marilee: Three Stories*. Jackson: UP of Mississippi, 1981.

Stegner, Wallace. *Teaching the Short Story*. Davis, CA: Department of English, University of California, 1965.

— , ed. *The American Novel from James Fenimore Cooper to William Faulkner*. New York: Basic Books, 1965.

Stein, Gertrude. *Three Lives: Stories of the Good Anna, Melanctha, and the Gentle Lena*. (1907) New York: New American Library, 1985.

Steinbeck, John. *The Pastures of Heaven*. New York: Brewer, Warren and Putnam, 1932.

Stephen, Alexander M. "Hopi Tales." *Journal of American Folk-lore* 42 (January-March 1929): 2-72.

Stevick, Philip. *The Chapter in Fiction. Theories of Narrative Division*. Syracuse, N.Y.: Syracuse UP, 1970.

Stoneback, H. R. "Faulkner's Blues: 'Pantaloon in Black'." *Modern Fiction Studies* 21 (1975): 240-45.

Struthers, John Russell. "Intersecting Orbits: A Study of Selected Story Cycles by Hugh Hood, Jack Hodgins, Clark Blaise, and Alice Munro, in Their Literary Contexts." Diss Univ of Western Ontario 1982. *DAI* 43:5A.

Sultan, Stanley. "Call Me Ishmael: The Hagiography of Isaac McCaslin." *Texas Studies in Literature and Language* 3:1 (1961): 50-66.

Sundquist, Eric J. *Faulkner: The House Divided.* Baltimore: Johns Hopkins UP, 1983.

Swados, Harvey. *On the Line.* Boston: Little, Brown and Company, 1957.

Swanton, John R. "Myths and Tales of the Southeastern Indians." Smithsonian Institution. *Bureau of American Ethnology Bulletin* 88 (1929): 222-30.

Swiggart, Peter. *The Art of Faulkner's Novels.* Austin: U of Texas P, 1962.

Tan, Amy. *The Joy Luck Club.* New York: Putnam's, 1989.

Taylor, Walter. "Faulkner's Pantaloon: The Negro Anomaly at the Heart of *Go Down, Moses.*" *American Literature* 44 (1972): 430-44.

Thomashevsky, Boris. "Thematics." In Lee Lemon and Marion Reis, eds. *Russian Formalist Criticism: Four Essays.* Lincoln: U of Nebraska P, 1965. 61-95.

Thompson, Lawrence. *William Faulkner: An Introduction and Interpretation.* New York: Barnes & Noble, 1963.

Thornton, Weldon. "Structure and Theme in Faulkner's *Go Down, Moses.*" In Leland H. Cox, ed. *William Faulkner: Critical Collection.* 328-68.

Thurston, Jarvis A. "Technique in *Winesburg, Ohio.*" In Sherwood Anderson, *Winesburg, Ohio,* Viking Critical Library Edition. 331-44.

Tick, Stanley. "The Unity of *Go Down, Moses.*" *Twentieth Century Literature* 8:2 (July 1962): 65-73.

Todorov, Tzvetan. *The Poetics of Prose.* Ithaca, N.Y.: Cornell UP, 1977.

Toolan, Michael. "'Pantaloon in Black' in *Go Down, Moses*: The Function of the 'Breathing' Motif." *Journal of the Short Story in English* 2 (January 1984): 155-65.

Torgovnick, Marianna. *Closure in the Novel.* Princeton: Princeton UP, 1981.

Trilling, Lionel. Review of *Go Down, Moses. The Nation* 154 (May 30, 1942): 632.

Trouard, Dawn, ed. *Eudora Welty: Eye of the Storyteller.* Kent, Ohio: Kent State UP, 1989.

Tyler, Anne. *Dinner at the Homesick Restaurant.* New York: Berkeley Books, 1983.

Vande Kieft, Ruth M. *Eudora Welty.* New York: Twayne Publishers, 1962.

Vickery, Olga. *The Novels of William Faulkner: A Critical Interpretation.* Baton Rouge: Louisiana State UP, 1964.

Volpe, Edmond L. *A Reader's Guide to William Faulkner.* New York: Octagon Books, 1974.

Waggoner, Hyatt H. *William Faulkner: From Jefferson to the World.* N.p.: U of Kentucky P, 1959.

Wagner, Linda W. "Juxtaposition in Hemingway's *In Our Time.*" *Studies in Short Fiction* 12:3 (1975): 243-52.

— , ed. *Ernest Hemingway. Five Decades of Criticism.* N.p.: Michigan State UP, 1974.

Wall, Carey. "'June Recital': Virgie Rainey Saved." In Trouard, ed. *Eudora Welty: Eye of the Storyteller.* 14-31.

Waters, Frank. *Masked Gods. Navaho and Pueblo Ceremonialism.* New York: Ballantine Books, 1970.

Watkins, Floyd C. *The Flesh and the Word: Eliot, Hemingway, Faulkner.* Nashville: Vanderbilt UP, 1971.

Welty, Eudora. *The Collected Stories of Eudora Welty.* New York: Harcourt, Brace Jovanovich, 1980.

— . *The Eye of the Story: Selected Essays and Reviews.* New York: Vintage Books, 1979.

— . *One Writer's Beginnings.* Cambridge, Mass.: Harvard UP, 1984.

Weltz, Friedrich. *Vier Amerikanische Erzählungszyklen.* Diss Universität München, 1953.

Westling, Louise. *Eudora Welty.* London: Macmillan, 1984.

Wharton, Edith. *Old New York.* New York: Scribner, 1964.

White, Ray Lewis. Winesburg, Ohio: *An Exploration.* Boston: Twayne Publishers, 1990.

— , ed. *The Achievement of Sherwood Anderson: Essays and Criticism.* Chapel Hill: U of North Carolina P, 1966.

Wilson, John F. *Public Religion in American Culture.* Philadelphia: Temple UP, 1979.

Winchell, Mark Royden. "Fishing the Swamp: 'Big Two-Hearted River' and the Unity of *In Our Time.*" *South Carolina Review* 18:2 (Spring 1986): 18-29.

Winn, Harbour. "Hemingway's *In Our Time*: 'Pretty Good Unity'." *Hemingway Review* 9:2 (Spring 1990): 124-41.

— . "Short Story Cycles of Hemingway, Steinbeck, Faulkner, and O'Connor." Diss Univ of Oregon 1975. *DAI* 36:7: 4500A.

Wittgenstein, Ludwig. *Philosophical Investigations.* Oxford: Oxford UP, 1978.

Wood, Carl. "*In Our Time*: Hemingway's Fragmentary Novel." *Neuphilologische Mitteilungen* 74:4 (1973): 716-26.

Worringer, Wilhelm. *Abstraction and Empathy: A Contribution to the Psychology of Style*. New York: International Universities Press, 1953.

Yaeger, Patricia S. "'Because a Fire Was in My Head': Eudora Welty and the Dialogic Imagination." In Devlin. ed. *Welty: A Life in Literature*. 139-67.

Young, Philip. *Ernest Hemingway: A Reconsideration*. New York: Harcourt, Brace and World, 1966.

Zuckerman, Michael. "Identity in British America: Unease in Eden." In Nicholas Camry and Anthony Pagden, eds. *Colonial Identity in the Atlantic World 1500-1800*. Princeton: Princeton UP, 1987.

Index